Development and Work Ethic
in sub-Saharan Africa

For my father Hein van Eijk (1919-2006: Someren, Noord-Brabant, The Netherlands) and my father-in-law *Mzee* Yusuph Maimu (± 1897-2005: Fuka, Kilimanjaro, Tanzania):
Two examples of hard-working, sober farmers.

Let's drink to the hard-working people
Let's drink to the lowly of birth
Raise your glass to the good and the evil
Let's drink to the salt of the earth

Say a prayer for the common foot soldier
Spare a thought for his back-breaking work
Say a prayer for his wife and his children
Who burn the fires and who still till the earth

[…]

Raise your glass to the hard working people
Let's drink to the uncounted heads
Let's think of the wavering millions
Who need leaders but get gamblers instead

Spare a thought for the stay-at-home voter
His empty eyes gaze at strange beauty shows
And a parade of gray suited grafters
A choice of cancer or polio

The Rolling Stones, *Beggars Banquet, The Salt of the Earth*
(Jagger & Richards 1968)

Development and Work Ethic
in sub-Saharan Africa

The mismatch between modern development and
traditionalistic work ethic

Toon van Eijk

www.lulu.com

ISBN: 978-1-4092-8868-8

Contents

Introduction

Introduction

Frequently cited causes for the lagging economic development in Africa are: the heritage of colonialism and slave trade, the Cold-War period with its geo-political ramifications in African countries, uneven economic relations, dumping of heavily-subsidized Western agricultural products in Africa and tariff walls in the West, unreliable rainfall patterns in large parts of Africa, relatively infertile soils, unchecked population growth, ethnic conflicts, corrupt regimes, weak nation-states, civil wars, the material and cultural gulf between western development experts and local rural populations, the gap between rich local elites and poor rural populations, the lack of a middle class and (sometimes) development cooperation itself.

In (mostly informal) discussions about the effectiveness of development cooperation foreign aid staff sometimes also mentions cultural factors. Especially the 'other' (non-western) attitude towards work emerges then as a bottleneck to economic development. In the formal literature on the African development process, however, the work ethic is never mentioned as a constraint. Since I think that the work ethic plays an important role in the development process and that it is, erroneously, kept silent about in the literature on development cooperation, I want to focus in this book on the work ethic[1]. The prevailing work ethic in sub-Saharan Africa is studied with the aim to generate pointers which can initiate a process of change. Sometimes it is important to call a spade a spade. To simply ignore the crucial role of the work ethic in the development process is certainly of no help.

The work ethic has not received attention in literature because it is a (politically and culturally) sensitive topic. A discussion of the work ethic can easily degenerate into paternalistic and racist reflections on certain ethnic groups. Yet it must be possible to discuss this topic in a (more or less unprejudiced) social-scientific manner without lapsing into mere platitudes. I write 'more or less unprejudiced' because a completely 'objective' scientific approach is not possible, also not in the natural sciences[2].

I am trained as a natural scientist, but as a tropical agronomist with a wide-ranging interest in all aspects of rural development I have also studied social science subjects. The longer I worked in Africa, the more I came to the conclusion that the main bottlenecks to development are socio-cultural in nature. Agronomists *do* know how to achieve high yield levels in Africa, but the actual realization of such yield levels in the fields of millions of small-scale farmers is quite a different story. Social-economic factors block the realization of these potential yields: for example, limited access to - and high price of - external means of production, inadequate infrastructure and restricted marketing opportunities. Beyond these social-economic factors, however, more fundamental cultural factors, the work ethic being one of them, hamper modern development. In order to better understand how socio-cultural factors can hamper or promote economic development, the role of the work ethic is here studied.

This book is mainly grounded in my work experience in the rural areas of sub-Saharan Africa and in social science and philosophy-of-science literature. But also my daily life experiences during more than two decades in sub-Saharan Africa provided insights. The fact that persons from different cultures adopt different attitudes towards work and time gave me ample food for thought. These cultural differences influence both the domain of professional work and everyday life[3]. Ernst Schumacher (1989) says:

"Could it be that the relative failure of aid, or at least our disappointment with the effectiveness of aid, has something to do with our materialist philosophy which makes us liable to overlook the most important preconditions of success, which are generally invisible? Or if we do not entirely overlook them, we tend to treat them just as we treat material things - things that can be planned and scheduled and purchased with money according to some all-comprehensive development plan. In other words, we tend to think of development, not in terms of evolution, but in terms of creation (ib.:176) ... Among the causes of poverty, I am sure, the material factors are entirely secondary - such things as a lack of natural wealth, or a lack of capital, or an insufficiency of infrastructure. The primary causes of extreme poverty are immaterial, they lie in certain deficiencies in education, organisation, and discipline. Development does not start with goods; it starts with people and their education, organisation, and discipline. Without these three, all resources remain latent, untapped, potential.

There are prosperous societies with but the scantiest basis of natural wealth, and we have had plenty of opportunities to observe the primacy of the invisible factors after the war. Every country, no matter how devastated, which had a high level of education, organisation, and discipline, produced an 'economic miracle'. In fact, these were miracles only for people whose attention is focused on the tip of the iceberg. The tip had been smashed to pieces, but the base, which is education, organisation, and discipline, was still there.

Here, then, lies the central problem of development. If the primary causes of poverty are deficiencies in these three respects, then the alleviation of poverty depends primarily on the removal of these deficiencies. Here lies the reason why development cannot be an act of creation, why it cannot be ordered, bought, comprehensively planned: why it requires a process of evolution (ib.:178/9) ...

All three [invisible factors] must evolve step by step, and the foremost task of development policy must be to speed this evolution. All three must become the property not merely of a tiny minority, but of the whole society (ib.:179) ... It follows from this that development is not primarily a problem for economists, least of all for economists whose expertise is founded on a crudely material philosophy ... Why care for people? Because people are the primary and ultimate source of any wealth whatsoever" (ib.:180).

Schumacher's emphasis on development as a process of long-term evolution and on the centrality of people is well reflected in this book on development and work ethic. Goran Hyden (1983:2) defines 'development' as "changes in behavioural and institutional patterns that sustain growth". Since institutions are always established and maintained by (collections of) individuals, 'development' is thus first of all about 'changes in individual behaviour' and secondly about 'changes in collective behaviour'. The work ethic is one of the most crucial components underlying human behaviour.

From the literature used in this book I want to single out five books that have been particularly important to me: H. Achterhuis (1984): *Work-a Peculiar Medicine*; H.-J. Chang (2008): *Bad Samaritans*; J. Diamond (1998): *Guns, Germs and Steel*; D.S. Landes (1999): *The Wealth and Poverty of Nations*; and R. van der Veen (2004): *What Went Wrong With Africa?*

1   Development Cooperation in Wider Perspective

About 300 million Africans have to survive on one dollar per day. This amounts to some 4100 Africans for each word in this book.

An important dimension of development is the ability to incorporate the lessons of the past in such a way as to increase the ability to stand on one's own feet (Goran Hyden 1980:253*)*.

1.1   Marginalization of Africa and free-market rhetoric

Some facts about sub-Saharan Africa:

- The combined Gross National Product (GNP) of the more than 40 countries in sub-Saharan Africa was in 2004 only 84 percent of the GNP of The Netherlands[4].

- Between 1981 and 2001 the international donor community provided 300 billion dollars in foreign aid to sub-Saharan Africa. Yet the number of Africans who have to survive on one dollar per day has almost doubled in the same period[5].

- The average life expectancy in Africa is 47 years (in the rich countries 78 years).

- According to the United Nations Development Programme cows in the European Union got in 2003 about 913 dollars in subsidy per head, while the EU in the same year provided some 8 dollars foreign aid per African.

Around 1990 Africa contained about 10 per cent of the world's population but produced only some 1 per cent of its goods and services. "An average African country with a population of around ten million produced no more goods and services than the average Dutch municipality" (Van der Veen

2004:208). In the 1990s world trade with Africa accounted for about 2 per cent of overall global trade and the share of non-primary products was virtually nil (raw materials and agricultural products are the primary products). Since South Africa accounted for almost half of this figure, the other forty-plus countries in sub-Saharan Africa were left with just 1.2 per cent (ib.:214). This figure illustrates the marginalisation of Africa in the world economy.

Although the West now propagates free-market mechanisms, some experts maintain that Western economic dominance is grounded in a sustained period of protectionism and state-oriented economic growth. Grint (1998:310) says:

"Not only have Japan, Singapore and Malaysia trodden this path but, ironically, this is how first Britain and then the USA achieved pre-eminence. Organized capitalism, not a free-for-all, has been the trademark of successful economies, and it is only when domination has been achieved that countries suddenly 'discover' the wonders of *laissez-faire* and the free market".

In chapter 17 we will seen that Chang (2008) holds the same opinion. Grint (1998:301) also said in 1998 that the global financial system hinges on "a socially constructed and extraordinarily fragile creature" called 'confidence', which became evident during the financial crisis in 2008. Completely free markets could be very dangerous. According to Ismael Serageldin, former vice-chairman of the World Bank, we must delete the concept 'free market' from our vocabulary[6]. Trade has to comply with numerous rules, thus 'free trade' simply does not exist. The contradiction between market and state is artificial. Effective markets, on the contrary, demand strong states.

Van der Veen (2004:227) remarks that the subsidies which rich countries paid their farmers at the end of the twentieth century were, on an annual basis, equal to Africa's total agricultural production. Especially the EU's Common Agricultural Policy is notorious for its inconsistency with European development policy. Nevertheless, the potential income that Africa is losing as a result of western trade barriers needs to be put in proper perspective. "Even the many products on which no import duties at all were levied were exported in limited quantities, and exports of some products even declined over the years" (ib.).

The lowering of western import tariffs is sometimes nullified by new product requirements with regard to food security, packaging and hygiene. Otto Genee, director of the Coherence Unit in the Dutch Ministry of Foreign Affairs - a unit which must prevent conflicts between general government policy and development cooperation efforts - gives the example of the aflatoxine-norm in the EU[7]. Aflatoxine is a fungus on, for example, groundnuts which can be poisonous to people, but only when you consume huge quantities of these nuts daily. In order to reduce the (statistically hardly measurable) risk to one death person per one billion people per year, the import norms were extremely tightened. The resulting loss in export earnings will cause many more victims in groundnut producing countries. Such incoherent policy restricts the export opportunities of developing countries. Food products from these countries are in the EU sometimes treated as if they were nuclear waste, says Genee. Everybody knows that a policy of zero-tolerance in security risks is impossible, but nonetheless ever higher, non-tariff trade restrictions are imposed.

In practice most trade is regional. Seventy percent of the Dutch export, for example, is to neighbouring countries (Germany, England and France). Free trade among African countries themselves would be most helpful. Liberalization of European agricultural markets will not, or hardly, favour small-scale farmers in sub-Saharan Africa. Agricultural products from Australia, New Zealand, the USA, Asia and Latin America will fill the new market space. With regard to industrial products and services, sub-Saharan Africa has little or nothing to offer for the time being.

Niek Koning at Wageningen University in The Netherlands is opposed to the present policy of liberalization. In his view the reform in 2003 of the European agricultural policy is not a real liberalization, because the re-placement of price-support with direct income-support to European farmers does not end the oft-criticized practice of dumping. It remains a disguised form of dumping, because also income-support promotes export. Moreover, liberalization hampers the protection of markets in developing countries against dumping from rich countries. Developing countries are disarmed in the domain of trade policy, while income-support as rich peo-ple's instrument for disguised dumping is being allowed[8].

The following example shows how large the technological gap between rich and poor countries is: on African markets Dutch onions are cheaper than locally produced onions, even without a penny agricultural subsidy from the EU. This is due to a very efficient system of production, packag-ing and transport of onions from The Netherlands to West Africa, based on advanced technology. Also in a free market system EU-countries might produce cheaper than poor countries. Niek Koning says that developing countries should get the right to protect their agricultural markets against dumping. These countries cannot compete with the technological innova-tion in the West. Although labour and land are much cheaper in developing countries, their productivity is very low compared to the West[9]. According to Koning agriculture has been the start of economic develop-ment in western countries. Only after self-sufficiency was secured, farm-households slowly got accustomed to trade with others, first locally and then on larger regional and national scales. Then services and industry gradually developed, but without the preceding history of protection of agriculture this would have been impossible.

Anne van den Ban (2002a), emeritus professor extension science at Wageningen University, says that in developing countries labour productivity in agriculture is less than 1% of that in the western countries with the highest labour productivity. Labour productivity differences between countries and differences in the rate of change of this productivity are very large (see Table 1). Table 1 not only shows that agricultural labour productivity in sub-Saharan Africa is very low (only 0.7% of the one in The Netherlands), but also that in a period of ten years this productivity only increased with 3%. This makes it practically impossible for small-scale farmers in sub-Saharan Africa to compete with farmers in rich countries - with or without European agricultural subsidies. There is no level playing field, neither in the political-economic nor in the technological domain.

Table 1:   Agricultural value added per worker per year (in 1995 dollars) and the change in this value between 1987-1989 and 1997-1999

Country/region	Labour productivity in agriculture: 1997-1999	Increase in labour productivity in agriculture: 1987-1989 to 1997-1999
Australia	31.423 USD	37 %
Brazil	4.030	47
China	316	42
India	395	22
South Korea	12.252	123
France	50.171	73
The Netherlands	51.594	65
sub-Saharan Africa	**380**	**3**

(Source: World Bank 2001)

Increasing agricultural productivity results in fewer employment opportunities in agriculture. Therefore the problem of large scale (rural) poverty can only be solved by creating more non-agricultural employment. The diabolical dilemma in sub-Saharan Africa is that even with an increase in agricultural labour productivity (for example, through more use of appropriate intermediate technology), the problem of insufficient non-agricultural employment remains. Van den Ban (2002b) says that the creation of employment opportunities for the millions of farmers who will be pushed out of agriculture is a huge problem, which has not been solved yet.

1.2   Make poverty history: but how?

Geraldine Bedell wrote during the *Live 8* concerts in 2005 the pamphlet 'Make Poverty History. How You Can Help Defeat World Poverty in Seven Easy Steps'. According to Rosan Holak the tone in this pamphlet can best be described as 'cheerful cynicism'[10]. The pamphlet is exemplary for the double character of Western attempts to reduce poverty. Says Holak:

"Yes, we must remain cheerful because we cannot give up hope. And yes, every question we ask and every answer we look for, anticipates an actual cynicism, because we tried already so much to reduce poverty and yet cannot find a structural solution ... Is it useful to demonstrate against poverty and debate it, without oneself adopting a fundamentally different lifestyle? And, if you are prepared to do that, how do you go about it?"

Also the Dutch historian Chris van der Heijden says that the proponents of the continuation of development cooperation exhibit an attitude of 'negative optimism', which stems from awareness that an opposite attitude cannot be ethically justified nor emotionally coped with[11]. The conclusion from three studies by the International Monetary Fund (IMF) in 2005 was that no robust positive relationship exists between foreign aid and economic growth[12]. Foreign aid is a 'political minefield' and economic research on this topic rarely is value-free. Now that aid to Africa is fashionable, says the IMF-economist Rajan, the tendency to attribute past failures simply to a lack of means or a lack of good intentions is common.

Piet Emmer, extraordinary professor of the history of European expansion at the University of Leiden in The Netherlands, does not see what good foreign aid can do. In his view economic growth does not occur from without but from within. He thinks that many African countries will remain poor for a long time to come. 'What England could do in 1750, Mali cannot yet do in 2050'[13]. Emmer maintains that foreign aid does help in very special circumstances, such as the American aid at the re-industrialisation of a devastated Western Europe after 1945. This Marshall Plan, however, could only *then* and only in certain parts of Western Europe promote economic growth. The concept 'Marshall Plan' should not be improperly used. But recently Thabo Mbeki as well as Tony Blair spoke about a Marshall plan for Africa (in connection with the New Partnership for African Development - NEPAD - and the Commission for Africa, respectively). But in Western Europe after 1945 a *re-*industrialisation took place, not a newly emerging process of industrialisation. At the same time the quality of education, infrastructure, government, et cetera was incomparable with today's situation in sub-Saharan Africa. Moreover the work ethic in Western Europe in 1945 was different from the one in sub-Saharan Africa today.

The World Bank-economist François Bourguignon says that many poor African countries face political or ethnic conflicts. A sound climate for investment demands long-term stability, which is hampered by a lack of development. This is a vicious circle and ready-made solutions for the complex problem of development do not exist. It is difficult to manage an economy and the notion of one universal model - one size fits all - needs to be relinquished. According to Bourguignon, policymakers in foreign aid have the tendency to embrace simple recommendations which is danger-ous[14]. The Marshall plans for Africa seem to be based on the assumption of a uniform continent: the enormous variation in ecological, social-economic, political and cultural factors in the 53 African countries is not recognized. The underlying idea is that one uniform approach - more money through foreign aid and debt cancellation, and removal of trade barriers - will lift all countries in Africa out of poverty.

The vicious circle of underdevelopment and political/ethnic instability is backed up by the 2003 World Bank report titled *Breaking the Conflict Trap*. This report studies data from 52 civil wars between 1960 and 1999 and concludes that civil war implies a failure of development policy. The usually presumed causes of civil war are ethnic and religious hatred, lack of democracy, economic inequality and colonialism. However, none of these causes matches with the data from the civil wars studied. Significant factors are height of income, growth of this income and availability of natural resources such as oil, diamonds and timber. Statistical analysis indicates that doubling the per capita income halves the risk of conflicts. The most common source of income for rebel factions is smuggling of oil, diamonds, timber and cocaine. Often such natural resources turn out to be a curse for developing countries.

1.3   The Millennium Goals

The American professor Jeffrey Sachs, economic advisor to previous UN Secretary-General Kofi Annan, is the ideologist behind the Millennium Villages Project which aims to demonstrate that the in 2000 formulated millennium goals are attainable. An 'all-embracing approach' in various model-villages must show that sustainable rural development is possible. The harvest in the Kenyan model-village Sauri has already doubled and the expectation is that within five years the village will escape the poverty trap[15]. The all-embracing approach entails environmental awareness, clean drinking water, a health clinic (one quarter of the population is HIV-positive), new agricultural practices including free fertilizer, establishment of crop markets, free mosquito nets, installation of electricity by the government, installation of internet connection by a private company, environment-friendly stoves, five cows donated to the school, free milk for the pupils, tree planting for firewood and for restoration of soil fertility, and, finally, the villagers get a car donated to transport their maize to the market 'that is when they establish a special management committee for the car'. Some villagers immediately sold the free mosquito nets and fertilizer to get money for food.

Primary education in Kenya is free since 2003 (but an annual levy of 18 kilos of maize per student for school porridge exists): this is one of the millennium goals. Unfortunately, free education often results in lower quality education, because many new students arrive but no additional teachers. In Sauri the average number of pupils per class grew to sixty, sometimes eighty, resulting in 'half-baked pupils' at the end of the educational period. The Millennium Villages Project cannot provide extra teachers to Sauri because that would create problems at the national level. "We must restrain ourselves to not play Santa Claus", says the head teacher of Sauri[16].

This last sentence, in my view, adequately summarizes the potential danger of this kind of project. The question is whether we learnt something from similar initiatives in the past? The results of 'community development projects', 'integrated rural development projects' and the Sasakawa Global 2000 programme in the last half of the previous century do not provide much reason for optimism.

Demonstration plots of improved agricultural practices in farmers' fields have been used for decades in the field of agricultural extension - and are sometimes still used - but impact has been minimal. The demonstration of packages of improved agricultural practices (for example, a combination of new varieties, fertilizers and herbicides) - which jointly can result in high yield levels due to positive interactions - did not convince neighbouring farmers to adopt these packages. Small-scale, resource-poor farmers tend to adopt (and adapt) step by step only those elements from the package that fit in their specific ecological and socio-economic circumstances. The packages demonstrated were - and still are - too costly for most smallholders (the farmers who participated in demonstrations got external inputs and agricultural advice mostly for free).

The all-embracing policy of the Millennium Villages Project seems to be a similar attempt to demonstrate a holistic approach, with free supply of the necessary external inputs. The likelihood that surrounding villages, without intensive guidance and without free inputs, will follow the example seems small. Professional guidance and free input supply for all villages in sub-Saharan Africa are not feasible, simply because insufficient trained staff is available and costs will be too high[17]. The guidance of such projects is complex and the number of competent facilitators limited. Sustainable development requires that dependency on outsiders is avoided.

The 'playing Santa Claus' in the model villages is well under way and is not reproducible at large scale. Although a holistic approach in the fight against poverty is necessary and the synergistic interactions between agriculture, health, education and environment must be fully exploited, the actual putting into practice of this approach is easier said than done (we come back to this issue later on). The (in 2005 agreed upon) doubling of foreign aid to Africa, the debt cancellation and the Millennium Villages Project constitute the umpteenth Marshall plan for Africa. However, the experiences of earlier attempts are not fully analyzed and one generally fails to indicate why the more recent approaches would be more successful.

At the African Green Revolution Conference in 2007 in Oslo, Pedro Sanchez, the director of the Millennium Villages Project, mentioned the following differences between the earlier 'integrated rural development projects' and today's MVP:

- In the 'integrated rural development projects' only 5-10 USD per capita was invested, while the MVP invests 110 USD per capita, a substantial difference.
- The MVP provides five years continuous support, which was not the case in earlier projects.
- Today more technology is available, including information and communication technology.
- The earlier projects lacked participatory approaches.
- With the ever increasing population pressure, people today are more motivated to accept change.

Whether these differences suffice to create sustainable impact remains to be seen. The all-important multiplier effect remains problematic.

The UNDP's Human Development Report 2005 mentions that rich countries get richer but not more generous and that inequality in the world increases. In the period 1990-2003 the average income per capita in the rich countries increased with 6.070 dollars, while in the same period foreign aid per capita decreased with one dollar. In 1990 the average American was 38 times as rich as the average Tanzanian; in 2005 it was 61 times. The 500 richest people of the world (according to the magazine Forbes) have the same annual income as the 416 million poorest people.

With regard to the millennium goals the same UNDP report notices that in sub-Saharan Africa the target to reduce child-mortality by two thirds between 1990 and 2015 will not be achieved in 2015 but only in 2115 - one century later - with the current pace. The consequence is that an additional 41 million children will die in the period 2005-2015; 41 million more than was 'planned' and 'promised'. Thus, also the targets of this Marshall Plan for Africa most likely will not be achieved. Per Pinstrup-Andersen, the director of the International Food Policy Research Institute, remarked in 2001 that in the previous twenty-five years 23 important international conferences on hunger and food took place, in which numerous targets were agreed upon. These targets were never achieved. The gap between reality and the targets of conferences was even increasing[18].

1.4 Trade, aid and debt cancellation

Despite foreign aid, the income gap between Western countries and sub-Saharan Africa keeps on growing. Around 1820 the GNP per capita all over the world was very small, even in Western-Europe and the USA it was just about 1.000 dollars. In 1998 it had become 18.000 dollars in Western-Europe, in the USA more than 25.000 dollars and in Africa (53 countries) the average was about 1.000 dollars (index 1990)[19]. Thus, the average GNP per capita in Africa *in 1998* was about equal to the GNP of Western-Europe and the USA *in 1820*. African GNP per capita in 1998 equalled thus the GNP of the West 180 years earlier. The often too optimistic estimates of (Western and African) development experts, who think that sub-Saharan Africa is just a few decades behind the West, need to be downsized.

Richard Dowden, director of the Royal African Society in England, thinks that the fashionable talk about the trio 'trade, aid and debt cancellation' will mean little for sub-Saharan Africa, because this region also now already can export products to rich countries - largely without trade restrictions[20]. According to Dowden internal African politics is the main stumbling block to development. He mentions as an example Nigeria where since 1966 about 260 billion dollars has been stolen by the governing elites, elites who until today call the shots and never have been prosecuted for corruption. Only in 2005, for the first time, stolen money has been transferred from a foreign bank account to an African government. The late military dictator General Sani Abacha looted oil-rich

Nigeria of more than $2.2 billion in the five years that he was in power. The Swiss government returned $290 million of this money to Nigeria in 2005[21]. Also the former top man of the World Trade Organization, Supachai Panitchpakdi, says that development largely is determined by appropriate domestic policies. He refers to Nigeria as one of the world's main oil producers. "Oil is a product that is traded in a completely free market. Yet Nigeria is very poor"[22].

Noreena Hertz argues that the so-called 'significant' debt cancellation, agreed upon in 2005, amounts to only 0.6 per cent of the annual agricultural subsidies provided by rich countries[23]. Referring to the Western high import tariffs on agricultural products and textile from poor countries, she says that free trade simply does not exist. "Free trade only exists when it suits rich countries"[24]. The World Commission on the Social Dimension of Globalisation of the UN says in a 2004 report: "Equal rules for unequal players result in unequal outcomes" (see also Chang in chapter 17.2).

The USA spent in 2004 and 2005 about 200 billion dollar per year on the war in Iraq. That is four times the annual worldwide budget for foreign aid. The global budget for poverty reduction is only about 5 per cent of the global annual expenses on arms. According to Jeffrey Sachs the annual American aid to Africa is about 3 billion dollars, "a sum that the Pentagon spends in about two days"[25]. About 1 billion dollar of this amount is spent on emergency food aid (half of which is for transport), about 1.5 billon is for technical assistance (for the most part salaries of American advisors) and the remaining 500 million (less than one dollar per African per year) is for education, health, agriculture and infrastructure together.

The Western idea that food production in Africa can easily be doubled or tripled is rather unfounded. Increasing food production is much more complicated than, for example, fighting diseases through relatively simple measures such as distributing treated mosquito nets against malaria. The belief that one can double or triple food production at large scale in the next ten years is a sign of limited historical understanding. The history of agricultural growth in developing countries since the early sixties indicates that average yield levels per unit of area - over long periods of time and over large groups of farmers - only increase with 1-2 per cent per year (Van Eijk 1998:78). The yield expectations of many (foreign and local) planners and economists simply are not realistic.

Louise Fresco, former Assistant Director-General of the FAO, remarks that insidious disasters such as malnourishment and underdevelopment are not very mediagenic and thus receive little attention. "But one should not forget that hunger in two weeks time claims as many victims as the [2004] tsunami"[26].

1.5   Vicious circle of low salary and low labour productivity

Above pages indicate that the contribution of foreign aid to the economic development of sub-Saharan Africa has been disappointing. Of course emergency aid has resulted in humanitarian gain, but sustainable economic development has not been achieved. Although some specific projects have been successful, for example in the field of healthcare, on the whole im-pact has been limited.

The content of this book does not come out of the blue. The past 30 years I have asked myself many times why the process of development in sub-Saharan Africa moves so slowly. I want to remark here that the con-clusions in this book mainly refer to Eastern and Southern Africa, since I worked only in that region - although for more than 20 years. Nevertheless the content may also be useful to other parts of Africa and perhaps even developing countries elsewhere. When I speak about Africa in this book, I refer to sub-Saharan Africa and more specifically Eastern and Southern Africa. But I expect that the main conclusions and recommendations also apply to the rest of sub-Saharan Africa. Although sub-Saharan Africa comprises many countries (each with its own peculiarities) and generalizations can be tricky, I think that the general thread of this book applies to the whole of sub-Saharan Africa.

With regard to my own field of expertise - agricultural research, extension and education - I must conclude that foreign aid in the end delivered little in terms of higher agricultural production. Obviously many factors play a role in this process, factors which frequently are beyond the reach of agriculturalists. Yet even those factors within our reach are insufficiently exploited. For example, African agricultural researchers are supposed to do research that is relevant and useful to the large group of resource-poor smallholders in sub-Saharan Africa. These farmers have little or no access to external means of production, such as fertilizer. However, quite some current research work is irrelevant to smallholders, because high levels of external inputs are used in the experiments. This specific problem and many others are discussed in my Ph D thesis on Farming Systems Research (FSR) in sub-Saharan Africa (Van Eijk 1998).

FSR, above all, is an attitude towards agricultural research. A competent FSR-practitioner does research which is relevant to the target group, even if it implies that (s)he has to leave the beaten path of conventional research. Many FSR projects were hindered by the low salaries of African researchers. According to Collinson (1988) the low morale and weak motivation of many local researchers were factors which (at least partly) explained the slow progress in FSR. Nevertheless, donors in the formulation phase of FSR projects continued to see the lack of incentives as a minor detail. After the start of FSR projects low salaries were subsequently disposed of as 'unfortunate external effects' which alas hampered the efficient implementation of the FSR methodology (Heinemann & Biggs 1985). Also Farrington & Bebbington (1993) argued that the lack of performance-related incentives needed to be tackled in order to make FSR more successful.

The heyday of FSR is over, but until now the low remuneration of agricultural researchers and extensionists in sub-Saharan Africa has not been dealt with. Of course one of the reasons is that other professional groups would make similar claims.

"Government agencies normally argue that the country cannot afford to increase the salaries of its civil servants, whereas donor agencies usually feel that various national regulations do not allow them to top up the salaries of staff working on projects funded by them. In many countries these attitudes have led to a serious vicious circle: No Pay > No Work > No Output > No Development > No Income > No Money to pay higher salaries" (Beets 1990:66).

Donor-funded topping up of salaries of local experts - always linked to regular performance evaluation - could enhance the quantity and quality of work implemented (Van Eijk 1998:114). But as we will see later on, higher salaries alone are not sufficient. The work ethic, just as FSR, is an *attitude* towards work and attitudes do not change very easily. Higher salaries are necessary but not sufficient to build high quality FSR work (and sustainable development). The vicious circle of low salaries and low labour productivity is hard to break. Employers say that they only can pay higher salaries when labour productivity increases. Employees, on the other hand, say that they only will work harder when salaries go up. The solution of this stalemate between employers and employees, above all, demands mutual trust.

Tanzania developed a National Development Vision for the year 2025. At the end of a speech on the implementation of this vision, the Minister of the State President's Office said: "Lastly, we have to reorient ourselves to be a nation of hardworking and disciplined people"[27]. Another African who highlights the importance of work ethic is the writer and journalist Venance Konan from Ivory Coast. He says:

"We want the same standard of living as Europeans, but nobody gives it a moment's thought what you all have to do to achieve it. Yes, you have to work for it. But that we don't want. We prefer to get aid. We don't assume our responsibility. If there is a problem, we go to a faith healer. If I get an accident, it is caused by witchcraft. If there is war, we blame France for it. We don't want to look in the mirror"[28].

Although Konan's depiction undoubtedly is too simplistic, he does raise an important point.

1.6   The importance of social-scientific analyses

A thorough analysis of the development process in sub-Saharan Africa ultimately runs up against social-scientific and/or philosophical problems. The study of these fundamental problems can generate a better understanding of the process of development and, more importantly, also contribute to solutions. Aid workers will claim to have no time for reflection and, to a certain extent, the argument is valid because their work demands much time and energy. I hope, however, that the reflection and analysis presented in this book will convince aid workers and (Western and African) policy-makers and -implementers that the social science literature cited here is relevant to them.

Perhaps most academics are not supposed to generate practical solutions, but tropical agronomists often do work at the interface of science and practice. I will attempt to show that thorough theoretical analyses and practical recommendations can go together. Reflection and analysis are needed if one does not want to be swayed by the issues of the day, which are increasingly pushed by media and politics. Building on the work of others, I hope to be able to produce a refreshing analysis of development. In the end, however, there is nothing new under the sun. At most, I have brought together a number of different issues - in a hopefully meaningful and perhaps unexpected way.

2 Paradoxical Situations in Development Cooperation

In this chapter some problematic issues in development cooperation are discussed, issues which often are not explicated and thus lower the effectiveness of aid.

2.1 Repression and charity

In his book titled *Work: a Peculiar Medicine* the Dutch philosopher Hans Achterhuis presents an interesting analysis of welfare work in The Netherlands. In his view welfare work is a mixture of repression and charity, of coercion and temptation (Achterhuis 1984:180). Basically a relationship of dependence exists between welfare workers and their clients (for example the unemployed and elderly), a relation based on exercise of power. According to those modern theories of change which deal with adult education, change agents have to go about behavioural change shrewdly and indirectly. Their strategies must encompass aspects of temptation *and* enforcement. Welfare workers must incorporate the themes from their clients' resistance in control strategies. Potential struggle has been already encapsulated before it can erupt. Any resistance to government policy has been incorporated in the planning process right from the beginning. In the Dutch 'polder model' welfare work neutralizes or renders impotent any resistance. "The fact that in modern society political and social action are increasingly made impossible is concealed precisely by the suggestion that via democratic procedures and participation joint action becomes possible" (ib.:272).

By analogy with the welfare worker one can argue that also many development workers combine repression and charity in their activities. The current approach of the World Bank, IMF and other multi- and bi-lateral

donors, which emphasizes participation and giving voice, can be characterized as pseudo-acting - as Achterhuis labels it. Much foreign aid is
conditional aid, not only in the sense that the money must be spent in the
country of the donor, but also in the sense that local participation is more
or less 'enforced'. At the same time the capacity to participate meaningfully is limited in many countries in sub-Saharan Africa. The presence of
foreign advisors, the relationship of dependence and the unequal financial
relations make it impossible, from the very start, to achieve the official
goals of development cooperation. The participatory approach by no
means guarantees that goals such as 'ownership' or 'recipient in the driver
seat' are realized. Development cooperation finds itself in a paradoxical
double-bind situation: de facto dependence and desired independence co-
exist simultaneously. This fact lies at the heart of the (mostly subdued,
unarticulated) tensions between donors and recipients of aid (be it African
governments or NGOs).

In social-cultural work in The Netherlands the initiative to undertake
action often lies with welfare workers. Likewise NGOs in developing
countries often are the initiators of action - the justification given is that
the target groups have not yet discovered their latent need for the work of
NGOs. At the beginning the initiative thus has to be with the NGOs themselves in order to engage the people in their own process of emancipation.
The paradox is that the liberation of colonial suppression and the ensuing
development cooperation often resulted in a process of 'disciplining and
normalizing' by Western development organizations. A disciplining enforced by Western financial power, but nevertheless 'for their own
benefit'.

Most African NGOs, which popped up in thousands during the 1990s,
have no well-defined political or societal goal, no real foundation in society and little or no funds of their own. These NGOs are in fact often
established to get access to foreign sources of money. They adapt their

image or programme to the wishes of their Western sponsors (Van der Veen 2004:295). Many NGO representatives are former public officials or others with close links to government. In this way the role of the true civil society in the process of development is undercut. NGOs often claim to represent poor target groups, but in reality the poor in sub-Saharan Africa are not organized. The 'countervailing power' of the millions of small scale farmers in sub-Saharan Africa is virtually nil, precisely because they are not organized. This constitutes one of the biggest obstacles to the economic development of sub-Saharan Africa and this political problem cannot be solved by development cooperation or liberalization of world trade.

2.2 Aided-self-help

The implicit starting point of foreign aid has been - and still is - that lack of progress can be alleviated by more and better progress. The solution is 'more of the same'. When the American administration under President Kennedy established the Peace Corps the leading motto was self-help, but the paradoxical character of this foreign aid immediately became clear in the term 'aided-self-help' projects. Self-help was only deemed possible through intervention by outside aid workers (Achterhuis 1984:307). The concept 'self-help' is taken from Kropotkin's book *Mutual Aid* in which the importance of mutual aid for the survival of human communities is emphasized. However, the anarchistic bottom-up movement, as epitomized by Kropotkin, was the opposite of the top-down self-help strategies designed by the top to discipline the people (ib.:304).

The Tanzanian and Mozambican experiments with *ujamaa* villages and *aldeias comunais* (communal villages) were such top-down designed and enforced self-help strategies. It is a fact that communal villages facilitate the development of social-economic infrastructure (schools, hospitals, market places, roads). Access to such infrastructure in thinly populated areas is difficult to organize and costly to provide without concentration of the population. Moreover, the (political) control of the population in communal villages is easier. Neither in Tanzania nor Mozambique, however, these villages have been successful, at least not in terms of self-help to economic development.

The two most important reasons are the overrating of the *ujamaa*-concept and the then common top-down approach. With regard to the last issue we can say that Tanzanian and Mozambican policy in the 1970s and 1980s was rather authoritarian. Although the presidents Julius Nyerere and Samora Machel initiated a (formally) socialist and democratic policy, the actual implementation of the plan to concentrate the population in communal villages was top-down enforced and coercion (and sometimes physical violence) was not always absent. Although today participation of target groups in the planning and implementation of developmental activities is fashionable, it often remains rhetoric - due to the inherent contradiction in aided-self-help.

With regard to the *ujamaa*-concept (familyhood), both Nyerere and Machel had inflated expectations of the range of solidarity in African communities. The African extended family comprises more people than the modern Western nuclear family and in general people take care of each other within these larger family units. It is a misconception, however, that social and economic solidarity extends far beyond direct family members and in-laws. Mutual aid and the inclination to collaborate in economic development (for example in cooperatives) are less encompassing than outsiders often assume (Van Cranenburgh 1990:96).

Development experts say that good aid leaves recipients free, but because gifts always endow donors with prestige it is paradoxical to tell recipients to go their own way. Aided-self-help leads to dependence and imitation of the aid worker. The power of mimesis (imitation) is such that the hidden message of the model is often more important than the overt, verbal one (Achterhuis 1988:336). Donors argue that a paternalistic attitude must be avoided, they emphasize that it is the own choice of recipients, but in reality dependence cannot be circumvented. The African proverb 'The hand that receives is always under the hand that gives' cannot be evaded.

2.3   Dependence and debt cancellation

In spite of (or perhaps due to) the rhetoric about 'participation' and 'ownership' developing countries remain dependent on rich countries. For example, the programme NEPAD emphasizes African ownership of the developmental process, but at the same time demands considerable funding from donors. Keeping in mind this continuing relationship of dependence, the old name 'foreign aid' perhaps is more correct than the more recent 'development cooperation'. Development cooperation is a masking name as long as most activities are initiated, guided and paid by donors. At the end of the day, the financial power of the World Bank and IMF, and in their wake the bilateral donors, is decisive.

In sub-Saharan Africa up to 40-50 per cent of the national budgets can be donor-provided. Whether donor assistance is provided as grants or (soft) loans is hardly affecting the degree of dependence, since recipients expect future debt cancellations. Moreover, long-term loans must be paid back by future generations and in the cultures of sub-Saharan Africa, characterized by short-term orientations in which long-term planning is unusual, repayment of loans is not a high priority. And the institutionalized corruption also does not favour repayment.

The considerable debts of Africa with their associated outflow of capital (for repayments and interest) are macro-economically problematic, but at the same time the loans and debts of African governments exist only on paper for most Africans (Van der Veen 2004:281). The average debt burden in the 1990s of about 500 USD per person suggests a burden that individual citizens did not actually experience. The connections between citizens and their governments, who negotiated the loans, are simply too weak. Mainly the national elites have profited from the loans in the past and, under similar conditions, this will remain the same in the future. Debt cancellation, therefore, is contestable. Most African citizens gained little from these loans and pay little or no tax, thus repayment of loans is largely irrelevant to them. Debt cancellation is only meaningful to the majority of the population when the funds that no longer have to be spent on repayment and interest actually benefit the poor. But *that* has exactly been the problem in the past. The question is thus whether today the relationship between elites and the common man has fundamentally changed?

The implicit tension between foreign control and national ownership also shows up in the so-called 'donor-democracy' - a democratization not enforced by the local population but emerging as an imposed condition for foreign aid. Such democratization can result into political crises when opposition parties start to threat the long-term dominance of the ruling party and subsequently repression of opposition increases. When donors refuse to increase pressure on ruling elites, they only pay lip service to democratization. A complex intermingling of conditionality for foreign aid (for example democratization and good governance), factual dependence on donor funding and lack of true ownership is the result.

2.4   Free markets and strong states

As argued in chapter 1.1 free trade is not the solution for sub-Saharan Africa. Also Ferdinand van Dam, who worked at the World Bank in Washington and at OECD in Paris, holds that African countries initially have to develop their own agriculture and industry through protectionist policies. "Why don't we allow the Africans to replicate the model that the Asians [and the Europeans and Americans] have used?"[29] Only between equals free trade is an option. Wouter van Dieren, member of the Club of Rome, argues that free markets are an illusion. "They don't exist, have never existed and will never exist"[30]. The world economy is regulated all over, through millions of rules and by legislature and supervision. Van Dieren is a proponent of the Rhineland model, a mix of state and market which emphasizes regulation and solidarity.

John Gray (2003) speaks of the so-called economic 'science'. The positivist doctrine that economic efficiency can be measured in terms of productivity lends free market thinking the authority of a science, he says. But in free market thinking societal goals and policies are replaced by means; the means of free market processes. Quality of life at the countryside, for example, is no longer central but the market. Various pro-globalization books have been written, which all emphasize that globalization and free trade have been beneficial to developing countries[31]. According to pro-globalization economists statistics show that in the long term everybody gains in a free trade system. Anti-globalization economists have less confidence (or faith) in the trickle-down effect and point out that both the gap between rich and poor countries and the gap between rich and poor within countries increase. Probably one cannot generalize: it is better to review the situation per country.

Moreover, it is impossible to pinpoint one factor - the free market system - as the main determinant of development. The multi-dimensional process of development cannot be captured in such simplistic terms. Most likely free markets require strong (and preferably democratic) states.

2.5   No time for reflection

Fundamental reflection on foreign aid rarely occurs, because aid workers are too busy to reach (and frequently adjust) goals and 'money is there to be spent'. In the World Bank 'disbursement' is a holy word. The development industry counts more doers than thinkers. The inability or unwillingness to spend time on a fundamental reflection on foreign aid is rather shocking since perhaps only ten percent of all projects are successful. Today the concept 'development' not only entails economic growth, but also poverty reduction, environmental issues, gender, good governance, etcetera. Each new failure of the concept results into its extension. 'Development' has become an amoeba-like word. As an amoeba it can assume dozens of forms, always parasitizing on the good intentions of the users of the word. Of course it is easy to criticize foreign aid, but it is much more difficult to provide workable alternatives. According to Achterhuis the generally accepted principle that after each failure of the concept *immediately* an alternative must be produced, has resulted into lack of reflection[32]. A temporary halt in development activities to create space and time for reflection on foreign aid is deemed unacceptable. The rhetoric of development cooperation and the underlying (undoubtedly) good intentions preclude fundamental questioning. Donors and recipients alike prefer to move on.

Causal links between aid and development cannot be easily established. Other factors also need to be taken into account (Van der Veen 2004:289). From the 1990s onward, criteria such as good policy and governance were attached to aid in order to foster a positive link between aid and development. A major drawback of this policy was that few countries in sub-Saharan Africa actually met such criteria. "So amidst mounting political and public pressure to give more aid to Africa, the opportunities to spend that aid in an effective way remained limited" (ib.:290). The policy of selective, conditional aid was undermined by the large aid budget for Africa and by the self-imposed donor need to spend it quickly. Also the original criteria for debt relief under the Highly Indebted Poor Countries (HIPCs) initiative got diluted "by pressure from the international public and from donors eager to use up their budgets". This disbursement craze allows no time for reflection. In recent years China and India started investing in Africa with the main goal to secure access to energy and minerals and without bothering the recipient governments with conditions on investments and aid. This will further accelerate the disbursement craze.

3   The Disciplining to Labour in North-Western Europe

In this chapter we discuss how the work ethic in North-Western Europe developed. This history of the process of 'disciplining to labour' could generate useful insights for sub-Saharan Africa.

3.1   The traditionalistic work ethic

Achterhuis (1984:273) speaks of the 'nearly intangible' phenomenon of the work ethic in order to indicate that the development of the work ethic in North-Western Europe was a complicated process[33]. In the beginning of the nineteenth century the work ethic was still quite different from today's attitude towards work. The Dutch workman was at the start of the nineteenth century still considered apathetic, lazy, unruly and full of vice, but at the end of that century he was transformed into a diligent and respectable labourer (ib.:164). This does not imply, however, that at the beginning of the twentieth century the normalization (adaptation) and disciplining of labourers was fully completed. Too many remnants of a 'traditionalistic' work ethic remained.

The modern North-West European attitude towards labour is not God-given. Max Weber (1864-1920) describes in his book *The Protestant Ethic and the Spirit of Capitalism*, published in 1905, the rise of the ideology that we call now work ethic. He emphasizes that the feelings of the European population initially were at odds with the new spirit of glorification of labour. Weber speaks of the 'traditionalistic' work ethic when he describes the way people viewed labour before the rise of capitalism. The 'traditionalistic' labourer does not ask: 'How much can I earn per day when I work as much as possible?' - as the capitalist labourer does - but he asks: 'How much must I work to earn enough to satisfy my (traditional) needs?' Modern capitalist economy demands an attitude towards labour as if work is a goal in itself, a true 'vocation' in the sense of 'mission', not just an 'occupation'. This attitude or mentality is not God-given and it cannot be directly shaped by high wages. The modern work ethic is the result of a long-term educational process (Achterhuis 1984:75-77).

In the past recruitment of labourers was problematic. The traditionalistic work ethic survived until into the twentieth century. Initially, wage increases to promote a modern work ethic were counterproductive: labourers simply reduced their working hours because they were able to earn sufficient income to satisfy their needs with less hours of work. In the capitalist economy, however, methodical and regular labour is central: labour in permanent positions or regular salaried employment. The Christian God not only demands hard work, but rationally organized work. In the process of economic development the irregular work of the day labourer is an unavoidable, but nevertheless undesired, intermediate position. The life of persons without permanent employment simply lacks systematic-methodical focus. In the capitalist economy labour is unlinked from being self-supporting, as is the case in traditional societies. When in early modern society labour became a goal in itself, the money earned was not to be used for increasing consumption, but for re-investment in order to accumulate ever more wealth by enhanced input of labour (ib.).

Weber emphasized the slow process of habituation in the adoption of the new work ethic and its ideological inculcation through religion, up-bringing and education. Also Erich Fromm pointed out gradual changes in the social character of man and he considered the new work ethic the most important psychological change in western man since the end of the Middle Ages. In modern society man was driven to work by inner urge rather than outer coercion, an inner urge that 'forced' him to work as only a very stern master in other societies could have achieved, and this was something new (Fromm 1972). Modern man became a prisoner of work, he voluntarily submitted to the yoke of 'the religion of labour' (Achterhuis 1984:106). Fromm, however, underestimated the important role of violence, from the middle Ages until today, in the enforcement of the new work ethic, while Karl Marx did emphasize this violent role. Michel Foucault (1975), in his history of the disciplining of the European masses, came to a synthesis of the more psychological (Weber and Fromm) and more power-based (Marx and followers) approaches (Achterhuis 1984:80).

With regard to the (presupposed) lack of diligence and responsibility with unskilled labourers, Haveman (1952:138) remarks in his dissertation on unskilled labourers in The Netherlands in the period immediately after the Second World War that the social norms of these labourers developed in circumstances 'of which the middle-class has no understanding'. He refers to Davis (1946:86) who writes:

"Just as the members of the higher, skilled working class and of management act in response to their culture, to their system of social and economic rewards, so do the underprivileged workers act in accord with their culture. The habits of 'shift-lessness', 'irresponsibility', 'lack of ambition', 'absenteeism' and of 'quitting the job', which management usually regards as a result of 'innate' perversity of underprivileged workers, are in fact normal responses that the worker has learned from his physical and social environment. These habits constitute a system of behaviour and attitudes which are realistic and rational in that environment, in which the individual of the slums has lived and in which he has been trained".

The process of disciplining to labour in North-Western Europe took at least one century. How long will this process, which is necessary for fast economic growth, take in sub-Saharan Africa? Many sub-Saharan Africans argue that the current traditionalistic work ethic will transform more or less automatically into its modern, capitalistic variant when salaries increase (or, in other words, one will start working harder when salaries go up). However, higher salaries alone cannot generate a different attitude towards labour, as this book will show. Much more issues play a role in this gradual process.

3.2   The Weber thesis

Since the pioneering work of Weber the common understanding is that protestant theology fundamentally changed the position of labour. According to Achterhuis, however, protestant theology is a mere accidental framework in which an emerging ideology of labour was veiled after the Middle Ages. The same ideology could also be veiled in Catholic or humanistic language (Achterhuis 1984:66). Landes (1999:171,175) disagrees and refers to the big difference in economic development between for example Catholic Spain and Protestant England at the time of the Industrial Revolution. In his view especially Calvinist Protestantism turned into a secular code of behaviour (characterized by hard work, honesty, seriousness and thrifty use of money and time), which produced a new kind of businessman.

Weber stressed that good Calvinists did not aim at riches; riches were at best a by-product of a certain way of living and working. A good Calvinist would say that Spain's gold and silver (from its colonies in the New World) was easy riches, unearned wealth. Although most historians today consider the Weber thesis implausible and unacceptable, Landes supports it. He points to the fact that in England at the end of the sixteenth century the Calvinists (Dissenters) were disproportionately active and influential in the factories of the nascent Industrial Revolution. He also mentions the following important characteristics of Protestants: the role of group pressure in the strict observance of the new virtues, emphasis on schooling for both boys and girls (independent Bible reading was considered crucial) and the importance of time discipline (most clockmakers were Protestant and the diffusion of clocks and watches in rural areas in Britain and Holland was exceptionally high).

Although Weber's 'ideal type' of the capitalist is not strictly confined to Calvinists, he shows that the religion of the 16th to 18th centuries in Northern Europe facilitated the appearance of a personality type that until then had been exceptional and accidental. And this Weberian entrepreneur with his specific way of life, self-respect and inclination towards continuity created a new mode of production which culminated in industrial capitalism (Landes 1999:175-8).

The shift in economic power and wealth from Southern to Northern Europe in the 16th and 17th century was not only caused by the emergence of a new business breed in the North, but also by a shift in (scientific) knowledge. "[The Protestant Reformation] gave a big boost to literacy, spawned dissents and heresies, and promoted the scepticism and refusal of authority that is at the heart of the scientific endeavour" (ib.:179). The late industrial development of Mediterranean Europe, in particular of Italy, Spain and Portugal, is partly caused by the religious and intellectual intolerance at the time of the reactionary Catholic Counter-Reformation. The Counter-Reformation had effects on economic development that stretched until in the 20th century. Around 1900 only 3 percent of the population of Great Britain was illiterate, while Italy, Spain and Portugal had illiteracy rates of 48, 56 and 78 percent respectively (ib.:250).

The modern work ethic was a cultural change in which labour became a means to display divineness. The Calvinist doctrine of predestination, manifest in the acquisition of a state of 'grace' by the chosen few, implied that Calvinists believed that their predestined future offered no room for knowing or changing their final destiny. This basic uncertainty made Calvinists search for signs of 'election' by God. They assumed that worldly success could be seen as a manifestation of 'grace', but obviously not as a means to achieve 'grace' (Grint 1998:105-6). Their radically new work ethic, ascetic lifestyle and reinvestment of almost all their profits made the Calvinists evermore successful capitalists. The development of rational capitalism had not been their intention. "They intended to serve God but ending up serving mammon" (ib.:106). The very material success of capitalism gradually undermined Calvinism, and eventually Christianity, which was 'associated' with its birth.

The word 'association' rather than 'cause' is used here because "it is not clear whether Weber's argument suggests that the cultural changes inspired by Calvinism were causally associated with the rise of capitalism" or that these cultural changes and capitalism were just correlated through a 'possible affinity' between the two phenomena (ib.). Also the French scholar Olivier Roy maintains that the relationship between capitalism and Protestantism is a correlation, not causality[34].

3.3   The inner urge to work

According to Fromm (1972:73) success in business indeed became a sign of divine grace for Calvinists, but the Calvinist beliefs of human powerlessness and uncertainty were not in contradiction with the urge to work incessantly. Compulsive labour was rather a psychological consequence of these beliefs. At first sight, incessant diligence seems in flagrant contradiction with a doctrine which claims that human endeavour is of no significance to salvation. A fatalistic attitude, which means that one refrains from any (beforehand futile) attempt to act, would be a more appropriate answer. Fear and feelings of powerlessness, insignificance and uncertainty create an unbearable mental condition. Feverish activity, attempts to do at least *something*, are a possible way out. Such activity, however, is markedly compulsive: man must work continuously in order to escape his feelings of uncertainty and powerlessness. This activity, however, is not the result of inner strength and self-confidence - at the contrary, it is a desperate escape from fear (ib.:72).

Work became irrational in this way. It did not aim at altering a predestined fate, predetermined by a God who was blind to all efforts of man, but only served to be able to predict a predestined (but hidden) fate. At the same time the feverish work made bearable an otherwise unbearable feeling of powerlessness. The inner compulsion to work came into being; an urge developed which made man his own slave driver. This inner urge was one of the essential production factors in the development of the capitalist industrial system, it was as important as steam power and electricity (ib.:73-5).

Today many western (often secularized) people suffer from a vague feeling of uncertainty and restlessness when they are not engaged in activity. In fact, for many modern people 'doing nothing' is an impossible assignment. One takes refuge in continual, obsessed activity. Work thus remains 'a peculiar medicine'. A few centuries ago it was prescribed as a medicine, at a massive scale and violently, but now it has led to symptoms of addiction (Achterhuis 1984:290). Modern society is characterized by a paradoxical tension between work and unemployment. Work can be unhealthy, it can make people sick, but at the same time people crave for it, as if it were a medicine.

Norbert Elias (1939:II,312) speaks of the 'societal compulsion to self-compulsion'. Man gets unwittingly subservient to his own collective actions, to unforeseen and uncontrollable consequences of his own initiatives. The 'societal compulsion to self-compulsion' plays also a role in the work ethic. People internalize a work ethic which ultimately leads to self-compulsion, but this internalization is enforced by the societal order. Societal compulsion and self-compulsion go hand in hand.

We can conclude that Christianity (especially, but not exclusively, Protestantism) has accompanied, facilitated and stimulated the development of the North-West European work ethic. This occurred partly directly (for example, through sermons in churches) and partly indirectly (via the influence of churches on education and upbringing). The gradual process of disciplining to labour was a combination of psychological and structural approaches, sometimes violently enforced. Both individual actors and societal structures were involved.

The disciplining to labour was not always easy and successful, as also the European colonization of other continents shows. Some people proved impossibly to discipline (in the short term), not even with brute force. The population of Sri Lanka in the last quarter of the 19th century, for example, massively refused to work on the British tea plantations. The British colonizers had to import almost one million Tamil-coolies from South India for this work. These Tamils were Hindus from the lowest class, whose religiously determined place in society made them docile and obedient enough to work on tea plantations (Achterhuis 1984:51). The North-American Indians are another example: they were seen unfit as labourers and the 'solution' was to import African slaves (ib.).

4 Is the Current Work Ethic in sub-Saharan Africa Problematic?

4.1 Farming as a way of life

In sub-Saharan Africa the division of labour is still small. The majority of the population is independent, self-supporting farmer. These small-scale farmers own the production factors land and labour, which enable them to live their own life - relatively independent from national and lower-level authorities. According to Goran Hyden (1980) this 'uncaptured peasantry' constitutes a big problem to government, which has little control and power over these farmers. Most farmers are only partially integrated in the national and world economy and pay little or no tax.

Hyden maintains that economic development will be slow as long as government cannot come to grips with these farmers and force them to integrate in the market economy. This would imply that fast economic development cannot be easily realized with a population of largely small farmers. In Tanzania in 2000/2001 about 80 percent of the population was still working in traditional agriculture (Government of Tanzania 2002:13). By way of comparison, at the beginning of the nineteenth century a bit more than one third of the population of England was working in agriculture. In 1871 this percentage had reduced to just 15 percent of the working population of England and Wales, and in 1911 it was 7.6 percent (Grint 1998:61).

In addition to the fact that governments in sub-Saharan Africa have little control over the majority of the population, it is also relevant that these countries are states but not yet nations. Eicher (1989) says that the African continent has many *national states* but few *nation states*. Many African countries are generations, and a few even several centuries, behind Asian and Latin America countries with regard to their level of human capability and institutional and political development (ib.:26). Eicher refers to the Africanist Colin Legum (1985:24) who says that the level of development of Africa's nation-state at the time of independence was roughly equivalent to that of Europe and China in the 14th and 15th centuries - latest the 17th century. The stage of institutional and political maturity of African countries determines whether foreign aid can be absorbed with integrity (Eicher 1989:2). Lack of national coherence makes the public interest often subservient to more specific (regional and/or ethnic) interests. The frequently praised African community spirit mainly lies with the extended family or ethnic group, not the nation. Social capital is big at the level of the extended family, but little at the level of the nation-state. The formal national state is weak in the sense that it has little authority over farmers and cannot easily influence the behaviour of its citizens (including their work ethic).

Modernization of the agricultural system and division of labour has not yet taken place in sub-Saharan Africa. The large group of small farmers is not just producer of agricultural goods; for them farming is still a way of life. This 'farming as a way of life' is not conducive to the development of a modern economy. The modernization of African agriculture, accompanied by more division of labour and specialisation, demands a modern work ethic.

4.2   Shadow-work

Illich (1981) introduced the term 'shadow-work' for the work that women, as mothers and housewives, do in their families. He uses the image of an iceberg to represent the capitalist economy. Only the upper part or tip of the iceberg is visible. The front side of the visible part is the formal economy as it is described in officially published figures and statistics. The hidden back side is the 'black market' or the informal economy, whose size can be estimated to some extent. The iceberg, however, floats due to its biggest part which remains under water - or in the shade. Similarly, the capitalist economy remains 'afloat' due to shadow-work, mainly done by women. The water in which the iceberg floats, and from which it developed, represents the subsistence-economy. For Illich the crystallization out of the water of the subsistence-economy represents the fact that the three modern forms of labour - registered wage work, black work and shadow-work - are something new. They do not occur, or to a much lesser extent, in subsistence-oriented economies (Illich as quoted in Achterhuis 1984:140-1).

Although shadow-work is unpaid labour, it is a necessary condition for the production of paid goods and services in industrial societies. Thus shadow-work is not accidental but the true shade of wage work (Achterhuis 1984:161). Empirical studies suggest that women consistently work more hours than men, whether they are employed outside the home or not. A full-time employed woman in the industrialised west works on average over 70 hours, with 33 hours spent on housework (Grint 1998:32). "The phrase 'a woman's work is never done' says more about women's domestic responsibilities than most books on the subject" (ib.). Paid labour could not continue in its present form without the unpaid domestic labour. The total costs of remunerating housework would be staggering. The British Office for National Statistics calculated in 1997 that domestic work represented 122 percent of the value of the economy - if it would be remunerated at the average hourly pay rate. Although the propaganda value of such claims is high, it nevertheless confirms the (female) inability to coerce or persuade men to undertake their share of domestic work (ib.:32-3). Gender relations play a role here, in the rich and less developed world. In sub-Saharan Africa women tend to spoil their sons to such extent that persuading men to do domestic work has a long way to go. In this sense women are part of the problem.

The crystallization of the formal and informal economy out of the sub-sistence-economy is far from completed in the African countryside. There rules the 'economy of affection' (Hyden 1980). This is an economy based on kinship over which government has little control (see also chapter 9). The (largely city-based) formal and informal economies as well as the more rural 'economy of affection' are, to a large extent, driven by female shadow-work. Part of the female shadow-work in western countries was - and still is - to instil a modern work ethic and time discipline in their children to make them fit for industrial labour and services-oriented jobs. In my view the importance of this process of internalization, based on com-pliance and identification, cannot be easily overrated. Successful economic development requires a modern work ethic. At this moment salaried jobs hardly exist in the African countryside and are low in number in cities. Nevertheless, African women will have to discipline their children, since the internalization of a modern work ethic is crucial for future develop-ment efforts and the process takes time. Today some disciplining takes place by sending children to school - if this occurs regularly and timely. Unfortunately, children in the countryside often start schooling at rela-tively old age, which implies that also this process of disciplining starts late.

Registered wage workers (in government offices and private compa-nies), black-workers (in the urban informal economy) and shadow-workers (housewives and house girls) are important groups in the bigger cities. Nevertheless, the group of small farmers is - and for the time being will remain - the biggest private sector in African economies. Thus it is incom-prehensible that donors and African governments have paid little attention to the agricultural sector, especially in the past decade. The reliability of the production figures of small farmers, as given in official statistics, is often low because acreages and yield levels of especially food crops are not measured but estimated (in often unspecified ways). This makes that in official statistics the significance of small farmers is erroneously represented. The economy of affection is systematically undervalued, economically as well as socially. The fact of life is that most African farmers in most years can feed and sustain their families. Although relatively little production of small farmers appears on markets, their total production is a significant component of the national economy.

In the informal sector the citizens are beyond the reach of the predatory state and do not pay tax (Van der Veen 2004:220). Yet the informal sector cannot develop fully without support from the state. The formal state must provide the facilities and services necessary for a flourishing modern economy, such as law enforcement and infrastructure. The nation-state and economy need to develop side by side and "bolster rather than stifle one another". The informal economy must gradually turn into a formal economy by establishing ties with the state. Ultimately all citizens with a (formal and informal) income must pay taxes. Democratic systems depend on material ties between states and their citizens "for people who do not make a financial contribution to the state will never have a lasting say in how it is run. Africa's economic development cannot be seen in isolation from political, social and cultural change" (ib.:368).

Also the transformation of the traditionalistic into a modern work ethic involves economic, political, social and cultural changes. Female shadow-work, gender relations and the economy of affection play a role in this transformation process, as will become clear in the following chapters.

4.3   Homo economicus

Man becomes *homo economicus* when individuals meet as economic subjects mainly. Other aspects of man are neglected because they cannot be expressed in money. The limited rationality of *homo economicus* is reflected in the acceptance of certain paradoxes and absurdities (Achterhuis

1984:35). The GNP, for example, increases when more traffic accidents and hospital admissions occur or when the use of medicine goes up. The fact that a child knocked down by a car enhances economic growth is revealing for the limited logic of the *homo economicus* (ib.:36). Another example is that cultivating vegetables in your own garden, instead of buying them, is bad for GNP because economic growth only takes place when production and consumption are separated, as is the case with wage labour. Modern consumer society with its focus on GNP - the holy cow of economic growth - results in irrationalities. Many goods in Western consumer society have only short-lived psychological value; they temporarily uphold the consumer's sense of personal identity. The production of truly sustainable goods, which are durable, can be easily repaired and recycled and are not subject to fluctuating fashions, is a distant ideal.

In the economy of affection in the African countryside farming is still a way of life. Production and consumption are not separated yet and people are largely self-sufficient in food. However, when modernization starts, individualization and predominance of the economic aspect of life will follow. In sub-Saharan Africa the GNP has already become an important indicator of economic development, despite the continuing existence of a large rural economy of affection and urban informal sector; and despite the notorious unreliability of economic data. The (probably unstoppable) advent of *homo economicus* in sub-Saharan Africa is linked to the transformation of the current traditionalistic work ethic.

The processes of individualization and disciplining to labour, and the emergence of wage labour and (female) shadow-work, are interrelated. Only as individuals, people can be held accountable for their own welfare, be motivated to work and develop a modern work ethic (Achterhuis 1984:164-5). People are formed, through the centuries, by many internal and external processes, including individualization, rationalization, self-alienation, disciplining and normalization, and Westernization. A complex

mix of structural and psychological factors is at work and it is impossible
to gain a comprehensive view of all processes involved, let alone to steer
them. Rationalizing with hindsight is easy, steering prospectively is difficult. It is hard to be fully aware of the many underlying processes, which
occur simultaneously and are interconnected.

At the same time, many people have the feeling that these underlying
processes occur, to some extent, automatically or autonomously. In my
view such parallel processes are 'steered' or 'guided' by a collective consciousness. This 'collective consciousness' is formed by - and a reflection
of - the levels of consciousness of the many individuals who live at a certain place in a certain period of time. The collective consciousness has its
own dynamics (it is more than the sum of its parts) which could explain
the apparently autonomous nature of underlying societal processes. More
on the collective consciousness will follow in chapter 14.

4.4   The modernization process

Can sub-Saharan Africa avoid following the Western modernization process? Does an alternative exist? Must sub-Saharan African agriculture be
modernized, for example? Should the millions of smallholders be exposed
to a process of rationalization, mechanization and automation? The implicit starting point of development cooperation is that lack of progress can
be alleviated by more and better progress: the solution is 'more of the
same' (chapter 2.2). Lack of modernization and scientization causes stagnation in African agriculture. If, however, African agriculture follows the
Western pattern of modernization, unprecedented social-economic chaos
will result. The creation of alternative employment opportunities for the
millions of farmers who will be pushed out of agriculture constitutes a
huge problem, for which no easy solutions are available (chapter 1.1).

When Western farmers were expelled from agriculture, sufficient jobs in the industrial and service sector were on hand.

It is difficult to see which alternative employment opportunities could be created in the nearby future in sub-Saharan Africa. Which African goods could be competitive in the world market of industrial and service products? One has to keep in mind that the gap in education, infrastructure, and political and institutional maturity between Africa and the other continents is very big. Moreover, the new economic activities should be labour-intensive in order to be able to create sufficient jobs for millions of ex-farmers. The continual trend of automation, robotization and computerization, however, leads to labour-extensive (but capital and knowledge-intensive) production; and exactly capital and sophisticated knowledge are scarce in sub-Saharan Africa.

Agricultural labour productivity in the industrialized world is much higher than in sub-Saharan Africa and thus agricultural production costs lower. It is evident that free markets are advantageous to farmers with the lowest production costs, to farmers who are front runners. Development, however, is not a running contest in which all participants, ultimately, arrive. It rather resembles professional soccer in which a rich soccer team can buy the best players, earns more, etcetera[35]. In the front-runner model early innovators (farmers who first adopt new technologies) make big profits, while farmers who adopt later are forced to adapt to the new technological system or quit farming. This process can push millions of smallholders in sub-Saharan Africa out of agriculture.

Developing countries will have to pay dearly for the import of new technologies (for example, genetically modified crops), but will never be front-runners simply because these technologies are developed in the industrialized world. Current emphasis in agricultural policy is on market liberalisation, global competition and diminishing public investments in the agricultural sector (although very recently agriculture attracts more attention again). This is thought to be the best policy to ensure worldwide food security and develop a sustainable agriculture. Yet it makes the position of smallholders in sub-Saharan Africa insupportable. They are not able to compete with the products from the industrialized world, which after decades of investments in agricultural education, extension and research and in land consolidation and subsidies have acquired a nearly unassailable position.

The front-runner model, which seems to work more or less autonomously, is disastrous for small farmers in sub-Saharan Africa. The underlying assumption is that free markets create equal opportunities for everybody, but with the existing large gap between developing countries and the industrialized world this is clearly wishful thinking. The introduction of new technologies in the Western world (such as genetically modified crops) makes the playing field even more uneven. The introduction of information and communication technology (ICT) most likely will not close the gap, as many seem to think today. Robust and cheap ICT, which does not depend on a highly evolved infrastructure of electricity and phone lines, undoubtedly is helpful. But even then, one needs well trained people who have the knowledge, capabilities and motivation to search for - and exploit - possible niches in the world market.

The gap in technological development between sub-Saharan Africa and the Western world is continuously increasing instead of becoming smaller. The contrast between super-fast ICT development in rich countries and nearly stagnating technological and economic development in rural sub-Saharan Africa is enormous (the use of mobile phones perhaps being the exception to the rule). One needs to keep in mind that technological development in the West has been preceded and accompanied by certain social-cultural changes, such as the development of a modern work ethic. The development and introduction of modern technology is only one side of the story.

Can sub-Saharan Africa become materially prosperous without the internalization of the concomitant work ethic? Desiring fast economic development without accepting the price tag of hard work is a common human characteristic, as the history of the process of disciplining to labour in North-Western Europe shows. The modern attitude towards work is by no means a product of nature. Max Weber says:

"Labour must ... be performed as if it were an absolute end in itself, a calling ... [Such an attitude] cannot be evoked by low wages or high ones alone, but can only be the product of a long and arduous process of education. Today, capitalism once in the saddle, can recruit its labouring force in all industrial countries with comparative ease. In the past this was in every case an extremely difficult problem"[36].

Also many African leaders realize that economic development cannot be obtained without much hard work. In sub-Saharan Africa work is not an end in itself yet and according to Hyden (1980:222) it is no coincidence that African political leaders continuously underline the importance and virtue of work. The necessary transformation of the work ethic cannot be achieved by political education alone. Even the managers and supervisors themselves have not always internalized a modern work ethic; they have not developed self-discipline yet. Thus they are unable to set personal examples to the workers and impose authority and discipline (ib.). President Nyerere in Tanzania emphasized since 1974 that discipline in work was essential for (socialist) development: laziness among workers had to be stamped out. The target of the political education of both managers and workers became *uzembe* - laziness - which, according to Nyerere, characterized most work-places in Tanzania (Hyden 1980:167). The leading motto was *uhuru ni kazi*: freedom is work. The civil employees and factory workers, however, maintained their traditional ties with production on the land.

"... not only are the peasants in Tanzania capable of ignoring state demands but so are the state's own employees. By virtue of having an alternative livelihood and by being involved in the economy of affection, most public sector employees can remain indifferent to demands for devoted service to the nation" (ib.:170).

Another example is President Chiluba from Zambia who appeared on Zambian television at 27th July 1994. Early in the morning he brought a surprise visit to some government offices and complained bitterly about the dirty walls and many public servants who came late to work. He said that work discipline was absent in Zambia and that developing a flourishing economy was impossible with the prevailing attitude towards work. These are only two examples of the many African leaders who I, during my 20 year stay in sub-Saharan Africa, have heard complain about the inadequate work ethic in their countries.

Does sub-Saharan Africa still have the choice to reject modernization (and the implicit Westernization)? The richness of Western people and African urban elites is known everywhere now through the ever increasing availability of television in the countryside. The Western economic-technological complex is so tempting that fighting it is virtually impossible. The attraction on especially the youth in developing countries is enormous. One of the most frequently used arguments in Tanzania with regard to the alleged 'trickle-down' effect of macro-economic growth is that one can buy Coca Cola now in every village in the countryside. But this Coca Cola does not come alone. Attempts to protect local cultures from modernization are mainly rearguard actions. Probably some blending will occur, as is the case now with African and Western music.

Another question is whether sub-Saharan Africa can build up material prosperity without its usual adverse side-effects, such as environmental pollution and physical and mental burn-outs caused by an overdone work ethic. Does a tested alternative to the Western path of economic development really exist? In theory sub-Saharan Africa can learn from Western mistakes, but it hardly happens. All attention and energy are directed towards fast economic development, without time for reflection. Leisure time of African men, but also women, undoubtedly will decline in the modernization process. Rural women in sub-Saharan Africa now work about 10-13 hours per day (including domestic and agricultural work). Their labour input cannot increase much further.

4.5   Underutilization of labour

Although in The Netherlands quite some houses have a tile on the kitchen wall with the wise text 'work to live', the actual situation in Dutch society is better characterized by 'live to work'. In the countryside in sub-Saharan Africa, though, 'work to live' still applies: especially to the male part of the population. Men are more or less politically autonomous, because they are economically independent. Their own labour and that of their wives and children makes them largely self-sufficient. The position of many women can be described as 'serf' or sometimes even 'slave'. Men, literally and figuratively, make women *animal laborans*. The prevalent gender balance enables them to discipline women to labour. The transport of large quantities of water, firewood and crops on the head of women (and women alone) makes them literally beasts of burden. Collinson (1972:23) remarks that this continent-wide tradition enabled men in the past to keep their hands free and thus use their weapons against would-be-thieves or predators.

According to Hyden (1980:18) the leading motto in the economy of affection is 'work to live' while in the modern capitalist economy the motto is 'live to work'. However, gender differences do exist. Hyden (ib.:85) quotes Routh who makes the following remark about a farm-household in Tanzania in the late sixties of the previous century:

"He [the head of the peasant household] is a man of considerable authority for whom the eternal economic problem has been satisfactorily solved. He eats well, he has a bed to sleep in, a chair to sit on. For recreation, he has his evenings of conservation round the *pombe* [beer] pot. There is no character in the economic textbooks who is more misinterpreted than he is. He is conservative because he has a good deal to conserve and much more to loose than his chains. To suggest that he is 'underemployed' and imagines that one is bestowing a favour on him by providing more work, is ludicrous. It is his *aim* to be as under-employed as possible and to allow himself to be disturbed from his aim only by the need to meet his austere objectives".

In this situation, Hyden says, women and children are *dependants* in the most literal sense of the word. Collinson (1972) says in his book *Farm Management in Peasant Agriculture* the following about the African smallholder:

"Where the opportunities do arise, peasant farmers are rapid to respond. But in the absence of organized markets and cash crop opportunities, farmers act rationally in producing foods for their families ... The frustration of government-directed, market-oriented development efforts by the dominance of non-market priorities has generated views of peasant irrationality and has brought disillusion with small farm improvements as an instrument for development ...

Views of irrationality have been reinforced from time to time by the attention of social scientists to the apparent paradox of excessive leisure preferences in a situation of dire poverty. In Africa the leisure-preference dilemma has centred on underemployment of labour resources. Studies repeatedly demonstrate a low proportion of total available labour used in farming but ignore three crucial aspects: seasonality, the extent of non-farm tasks, and nutritional adequacy. [Collinson then discusses these three aspects briefly] in the hope of removing further barriers to the use of existing agriculture as a vehicle for development [I focus here only on the last aspect] ... (ib.:33).

The effects of poor nutrition have often been ignored in assessing labour avail-ability. Where the food intake is low in calories, people will not have the same capacity for prolonged physical effort. Important in compounding the effects of a low protein diet is the hunger gap before the new harvest. In some areas this will clash with the period of most demanding physical effort (ib.:35) ... Brought to-gether, seasonality, a multiplicity of off-farm chores, and nutritional adequacy explain an apparent distaste for field work ... [and have contributed to] misinter-pretation of the smallholder character" (ib.:37).

Thus, most small farmers in sub-Saharan Africa are not conservative, lazy or stupid, but act rationally under prevalent conditions. The male head of the farm-household, mentioned by Routh, also acts rationally under the given circumstances, which happen to be favourable to him. In addition to the three aspects mentioned above, the endemic disease malaria also con-sumes much energy. Moreover, today the aids epidemic makes things worse. The availability of young, energetic workers has been reduced dras-tically in some areas.

With regard to the alleged 'underutilization' of labour in pre-colonial Tanzania, Koponen (1988) remarks the following:

"It is sometimes suggested that economies like those of pre-colonial Tanzania suffer from 'underutilization' of labour power and concomitant 'underproduction'. Indeed, there is much evidence to indicate that labour input in the main branches of Tanzanian pre-colonial economies was rather modest, both in quantitative terms (working hours) and qualitative terms (intensity of technology) ... Yet I find the suggestion of 'underproduction' problematic. Even when no definition of 'full' use of labour power and production exists, the criteria utilized carry an obvious bias towards the European historical experience. This hardly helps us to understand the African situation. What matters in a given historical situation is the actual relation between labour input and material output and not their hypothetical potentialities.

In my view it is more fruitful to conceive the ratio between labour input and material output in Tanzanian pre-colonial economies not in terms of 'underutilization of labour' but in terms of indicating a relatively high degree of labour productivity ... Most of [the early European travellers] were amazed at the small amount of work with which Africans, especially men, apparently contrived to live (ib.:292) ... [The crucial role of women in agriculture was often overlooked] ... It can be hypothesized that Africans did not actually *need* to have more sophisticated cultivation technology or do more manual work in order to achieve a sufficient output; i.e. that the productivity of their work as traditionally organized was high enough for the satisfaction of their needs (ib.:293).

[With reference to Allan (1965) Koponen continues:] One can approach the question of the heavy consumption of *pombe* [a food as well as a drink] from an angle very different from that of the early observers and suggest that far from being a sign of extravagance and short-sightedness of the people it can be interpreted as a concrete indication of the capacity of the African agricultural systems to produce a continuous 'normal' grain surplus (ib.:297) ...

Yet I do not wish to resurrect the 'myth of the lazy native' and imply that precolonial societies in the Tanzanian area are to be imagined as an African Arcadia for whose inhabitants 'with little effort almost everything [grew] ready for eating' [as a German colonizer wrote in 1925]. It is not to be thought that there never was need to work hard, nor that the people were incapable of hard work when necessary (ib.:302) ... The great industry of people engaged in banana-based cultivation such as the Chagga and the Nyakusa was often noted. Chagga had to work hard, 'much harder than a European would be able to do in this country' [as another German observed] (ib.:303) ...

[In the pre-colonial societies] there was no point in hoarding. That is, as long as there was no way to convert surpluses which were produced in the form of food or drink into something more durable, there were obvious limits to the use of them, and no possibility for private accumulation (ib.:388) ... [This could have changed after the introduction of cattle and trade goods that were prestige assets which could be accumulated]. But the point is that neither cattle nor trade goods were 'economic' wealth amenable to productive accumulation. Rather, it can be argued that they were a 'social' wealth amenable to reproductive accumulation. They could be used to create new social relations like marriages and client relations" (ib.:389).

Koponen's observations on pre-colonial Tanzanian society certainly bear relevance to other countries in sub-Saharan Africa. What he describes has impact on the functioning of today's societies and is still (partly) applicable. The remarks of Hyden, Collinson and Koponen illustrate that the traditionalistic work ethic cannot be simply equated with laziness.

4.6　The process of enculturation

Fully objective perception of reality is impossible. Nobody perceives the world 'with pristine eyes' (Benedict 1960:18). Herskovits (1967) speaks of the process of 'enculturation': each individual is subjected to 'enculturative conditioning'. Man always observes through an 'enculturative screen' which determines how the physical and social worlds are perceived and which subsequently determines behaviour. Perception and behaviour are mediated by one's culture. Ethnocentrism is the primary mechanism that directs the evaluation of cultures. "Ethnocentrism is the point of view that one's own way of life is to be preferred to all others" (ib.:68). The process of early enculturation makes that most people feel this way, whether they verbalize it or not.

Ethnocentrism - the universal inclination of groups to take their own way of life as a standard for humanity as a whole - encompasses the work ethic. The present Western glorification of labour not only colours the view of our own past, but it also results in a highly coloured version of the (assumed) mentality in developing countries, as described by many development economists (Achterhuis 1984:77). A specific work ethic is internalized in a process of early enculturation and cannot be changed overnight. Obviously, also my view on the work ethic is affected by my Dutch background. Complete objectivity in the description of a work ethic is fictitious. One can attempt to describe a work ethic as objectively as possible, but one's own enculturation cannot be fully eliminated. Precisely because I am aware of the potential dangers of the nearly automatic process of ethnocentrism, I do not only use in this book my experiences in sub-Saharan Africa, but also the history of the North-West European work ethic. This hopefully provides better insight in the importance of the work ethic for economic development.

Most people in North-Western Europe feel guilty when they do nothing or are not engaged in wage work. This internal feeling of guilt, without any external enforcement, indicates that the work ethic has been deeply internalized in a process of early enculturation. In sub-Saharan Africa the process of enculturation hitherto does not include the internalization of such a modern work ethic. Especially some men in sub-Saharan Africa are experts in doing nothing during a considerable part of the day, without feeling guilty - this 'doing nothing' might include chatting and drinking.

4.7   Work ethic: more than a mentality

The preceding subchapters showed that the work ethic is inextricably bound up with a multitude of other phenomena, such as the economy of affection, shadow-work, individualization, rationalization, modernization and enculturation. Advocating simply a change in work ethic, therefore, will not do the trick; that is too superficial (Achterhuis 1984:46). Transformation of the prevalent work ethic in sub-Saharan Africa demands changes in many other mentalities, practices and institutions. This implies that the process is complicated since many issues simultaneously must be taken into account and they must be mutually attuned.

The modern work ethic - the religion of labour - is not just a mentality. The work ethic is not an ideology that can be altered by education and change of mentality alone. It is grounded in a material system of production and consumption on which people depend for their survival (ib.:278). The modern work ethic is rooted in the material reality of the capitalist economy. Part of this economy is modern technology. The philosopher Lewis Mumford says that modern technology is the result of a process of modernization which spans centuries. Science and technology are societally constructed processes which are culturally embedded (Achterhuis 1992:176). Changes in mentality and culture precede technological change. The cultural and societal embedding of modern technology encompasses the modern work ethic. Since the modern work ethic preceded and accompanied modern technology and both work ethic and technology evolved gradually, realistic expectations about the pace of technological and economic development in sub-Saharan Africa are due. It is always possible that small islands of high-tech economic development emerge quickly, but for the majority of the population the pace of development most likely will be modest to slow. The conditions in sub-Saharan Africa today are different from those at the time of the emergence of the modern work ethic in North-Western Europe. A simple copying of the Western path of development is therefore no option. Nevertheless, the history of the development of the North-West European work ethic can provide useful lessons for sub-Saharan Africa.

For example: the fact that the modern work ethic preceded modern technology has consequences for the mechanization of African agriculture. Can modern technology function adequately without the concomitant work ethic? Effective and efficient operation of modern technology demands a certain attitude towards machinery. A tractor, for example, requires adequate and regular maintenance and some planning of the availability of spare parts and fuel. Sustainable use of tractors cannot do without persons who feel internally responsible for correct use and timely maintenance of machinery. The internalization of a modern work ethic and this internal feeling are related (internal feeling means here: in the absence of continuous external supervision). The numerous graveyards of discarded machinery all over sub-Saharan Africa are the silent witnesses of the mismatch between modern technology and the current African mindset towards technology.

Achterhuis (1984:65) is of the opinion that the distinction between outer material changes (for example, in societal structures) and inner mental changes (in human mentalities and attitudes) is artificial. This distinction is only made for clarification purposes. Outer and inner changes are inextricably bound up and a discussion on primacy is meaningless (ib.). I agree with Achterhuis that the distinction between outer changes (in structures) and inner changes (in actors) is artificial. Both aspects of the change process are inseparable and affect one another. I disagree, however, with his proposition that a discussion on primacy is meaningless.

The actor-structure debate plays an important role in the sociology of rural development. This debate focuses on the dualism between actors and structures, between individual human behaviour at micro-level and the impact of societal structures at macro-level, between individual voluntary behaviour (which is always coupled to a certain space for manoeuvre) and more or less complete determination by structures. It is the dynamic interaction between actors and structures which makes that both aspects can be distinguished for analytical purposes, but not separated in their effects. Nonetheless, I am of the opinion that primacy rests with actors rather than structures.

We face here a chicken-and-egg problem, a vicious (or virtuous) circle, in which individual actors influence societal structures and these structures have impact on actors, etcetera. However, since structures are formed by individuals - are collections of individual actors - changes in structures ultimately are engineered by individuals. Although structures sometimes seem to lead a life of their own, this apparently 'autonomous' behaviour of structures in the end is tolerated by the group of actors who constitute these structures. In this sense primacy rests with actors. Similarly the 'autonomous' development of technology ultimately is created by man.

Experience teaches that structures are difficult to change. The same applies to the personal behaviour of individual actors. The earlier mentioned concept 'collective consciousness' provides possibilities to break vicious circles, as we will see later on. Changes in individual and collective behaviour (including behaviour related to work) are to some extent always possible, but acceleration of behavioural change demands new, unconventional methods. Transformation of the prevalent traditionalistic work ethic in sub-Saharan Africa is necessary for economic development. The question is whether societies can speed up the normal process of learning by experience. Can we break with the 'business as usual' mentality?

5 Work Ethic and Gender

Investing in women and girls makes sound economic and social sense
(*State of World Population 2005*, UN Population Fund)

In this chapter various aspects of the relationship between work ethic and gender are discussed.

5.1 Categories of social stratification

In most societies in sub-Saharan Africa inequality and hierarchy are still matter-of-course phenomena and societal roles are more or less 'voluntary' adhered to. This applies especially to the position of youth and women. In Tanzania, for example, a strong '*shikamoo mzee* culture' persists. The Ki-Swahili word *mzee* refers to an older person and *shikamoo* is the salutation used to greet older persons. *Shikamoo* literally means 'I hold your feet'[37]. This does not imply that younger persons literally have to kneel to older persons, but in Tanzanian society young people do occupy a subjugated position. For example, high positions often are allocated on the basis of age (seniority), not capability (merit).

Age-based inequality and hierarchy are not conducive to fast economic development. Economic development demands respect due to merit, not respect due to age (and/or gender). Respect must be earned. Young women find themselves in a doubly unfavourable position. Most women in sub-Saharan Africa still play their subjugated role 'voluntarily' because local tradition and culture require so. The idea of equality between men and women certainly has set foot ashore, but largely through external pressure. Gender has been promoted mainly by Western donors and many African men consider it enforced Western interference in local affairs. The internalization of the idea of equality is only partial.

With regard to aids, for example, it is amazing what African women have to accept in marriage, even highly educated women who studied abroad. Some women play a kind of Russian roulette, because quite some men have extra-marital affairs and do not use condoms, and women are not in a position to refuse intercourse without condom within marriage. Although divorce in theory is an option, the informal-cultural and formal-legal conditions are not favourable to women. Equality of men and women is laid down in, for example, the Tanzanian constitution, but it is equality on paper only, because compliance with the law and control of its enforcement often leave much to be desired. The police and judicial system are often corrupted. Women, who divorce, are at risk to lose their house and sometimes also their children; and economically they might go back to square one.

According to Grint (1998:4) the three most important categories of social stratification in modern capitalist society are class, gender, and race and ethnicity. Individuals are composite and heterogeneous embodiments of these three categories. Men and women experience work through these three categories simultaneously. There is however a distinction between the composite as a whole and the sum of its parts. A 'black-female-worker', for example, is a heterogeneous composite of ethnicity, gender and class (ib.:200). For heuristic purposes it can be important to identify and separately investigate these three different categories of stratification, but the actual life experiences of this specific individual are only fully expressed in the composite whole. A comprehensive analysis must be based on the fact that racism, patriarchy and capitalism are not parallel mechanisms of oppression, but "a contingent and discordant whole riddled with internal tensions and contradictions" (ib.).

A useful analogy to differentiate dualist models from (holistic) composites is the distinction between interleaved metals and an alloy: bronze has properties which are distinct from the copper, tin and zinc or lead metals on which it is based (ib.:200-1). In dualist models, on the other hand, different categories are separated and the whole is just the sum of its parts. Class, gender and ethnicity are not only the three most important categories of social stratification in contemporary capitalist societies, but they are also constraints *and* facilitators. In this context the concept 'agency' is relevant. Agency refers to the relationship between the freedom of individuals to choose their own future and the socially constructed constraints and facilitators which they encounter (Grint 1998:227). We will come back to the concept agency in chapter 15.

One can argue that 'African rural women' are in a threefold unfavourable position, based on their race, class and gender. The realization of the universal rights of man in sub-Saharan Africa demands major adjustments in society. More equality between men and women, and between the elderly and youth, requires adaptation of the *shikamoo mzee* culture. Without the emancipation of the countryside and the farmers sustainable economic development seems impossible. Adequate agency is what African rural women need most.

5.2 Confinement to housekeeping

In pre-modern, traditional subsistence-economies women are subjugated to men, but at the same time they have their own unassailable domain. They are by no means helpless or fully dependent on men (Illich 1984; Achterhuis 1984:118). In non-industrial societies the sexes have their own domain, which is not open to the other sex. Not equality, but diversity between men and women is central. Complementarity between the sexes prevails, although it is often asymmetric. In the rural societies of sub-Saharan Africa agriculture is a domain accessible to both sexes, although some specific crops might be cultivated by women only. Men, however, do not do domestic work; that remains a fully female domain (sometimes men are not even allowed to enter the kitchen). Because women often occupy subjugated positions, asymmetric complementarity is the rule.

Rural women in sub-Saharan Africa still have their own domain, precisely because the Western ideal of equality has not yet been fully internalized. At first sight this statement appears paradoxical, because Westerners generally see African women as dependent and dominated. African women, however, are not confined to housekeeping yet, as Western women were just one or two generations ago. In this sense they are more independent than many of their Western colleagues, since they still work in agriculture and are more or less self-sufficient. Many women cultivate their own food crops (the so-called 'women crops') without any help from men, so that they are fully independent in the use and (partial) sale of these crops. In this way women, in most years, can sustain themselves and their children without much support from men. In the countryside many female-headed households can be found and although these households in general are economically less prosperous than male-headed households, they do survive. The high percentage of single women with children is due to the (temporary) migration of men to cities and the aids epidemic.

In Europe the confinement of women to housekeeping was coupled to an industrial revolution, which resulted in many new jobs outside agriculture. The female shadow-work of domestic duties included the inculcation of a modern work ethic and time discipline in children. The current situation in sub-Saharan Africa is fundamentally different: hardly any employment opportunities outside agriculture exist. Moreover, the prospect for new jobs, linked to export possibilities, is not bright. The internalization of a modern work ethic, directed towards disciplined execution of wage work, is thus not yet very urgent in rural sub-Saharan Africa - for the time being. Yet the development of a modern work ethic is indispensable, *if* sub-Saharan Africa wants to join the global economy sooner or later - whatever the sector is in which it wants to compete effectively. Efficient (thus relatively cheap) production of goods and services of constant high quality requires a modern work ethic and the process of instilling a modern work ethic takes time: one better starts as soon as possible. The current performance of salaried government staff and wage workers in the urban industrial sector and in the services sector (amongst others, tourism) would immediately improve with a modern work ethic.

True emancipation of rural women in sub-Saharan Africa would entail more social-cultural equality (including the field of sexuality), while retaining their present economic independence and while achieving a more balanced input of labour between the sexes.

5.3 Modernization of agriculture

At present the working day of rural women in sub-Saharan Africa is (too) long: the combination of domestic and agricultural work is heavy. A (partial) modernization of agriculture could alleviate this problem. A reduction in the labour input of women, however, should not result in less say over allocation of household income and thus loss of economic independence.

Modernization of agriculture often implies introduction of cash crops which tend to be labour-intensive. The cultivation and sale of cash crops becomes, more or less automatically, an activity dominated by men. Women are expected to contribute (much) labour, but without concomitant say over the allocation of future cash income. The cultivation of cash crops can diminish the area under food crops and upset the household food supply (unless women are allowed to buy food with the money earned with cash crops). Female labour is often the most limiting production factor - in the sense that under the current gender balance women work much more hours than men. Changes in farming systems can have great impact on women.

Another example of modernization is the introduction of tractors to plough fields. The resulting extension of crop acreages implies that larger areas must be weeded. Weeding is rarely mechanized and to a large extent done by women. Extension of crop acreage thus implies more work for women. Moreover, weeding must be done early in the season in a relatively short time span, since late weeding results in significant yield reductions. Given the fact that in many farming systems in sub-Saharan Africa labour is the most limiting production factor and not land, ploughing with tractors is an attractive option to men. The negative consequences of this men-dominated mechanization, however, are shifted on to women.

Precisely because - under the current gender balance - female labour is the most limiting production factor, phenomena such as the prevailing work ethic and gender balance are related. Lack of labour emerges especially in the busy periods of the agricultural season: at the time of land cultivation, weeding and harvesting. The current balance of power between the sexes limits the potential annual labour input. An altered gender balance, resulting in a larger male labour input, would considerably alleviate the task of women. Rural women work so hard because men enforce this. But in the quiet periods of the year with less or no agricultural activities, women have less work to do. A modern work ethic, which drives people to be continually active, is not common, also not with rural women. As said before, at this moment in time a modern work ethic would not (yet) be relevant. And at a later stage in the development process a modern work ethic must be accompanied by sound enabling conditions (e.g., good infrastructure and attractive farm-gate prices) in order to result into higher labour productivity and higher agricultural production.

At the time of the Industrial Revolution people in Europe rebelled against the introduction of labour-saving technology. In sub-Saharan Africa neither large-scale industrialization nor significant mechanization of agriculture took place. A few rich farmers plough with tractors, but other labour-saving technology has not been adopted in neither agricultural nor domestic work. Taking into account the total availability of manpower, the necessity for such technology is disputable, since only women hitherto are fully occupied in the busiest periods of the agricultural season. Drudgery or monotonous-stultifying work, however, could be reduced by labour-saving technology.

The introduction of intermediate technology for agricultural and domestic tasks has not been very successful. 'Intermediate technology' has been a buzzword for some time in development circles, but large investments in research and development of such technology never occurred. As a result, little intermediate technology is in fact available. A useful form of intermediate technology is animal traction. Part of agricultural and domestic work can be alleviated by animal traction. Ox-ploughs and -weeders, and donkey- and oxcarts for transport of water, firewood, agricultural inputs and harvested crops, are very helpful. Although animal traction is here and there used in sub-Saharan Africa, it has not been adopted at large scale.

One of the reasons is that politicians and also many agricultural experts in sub-Saharan Africa consider animal traction old-fashioned or outmoded. One believes that African farmers can easily jump from hoe to tractor and skip the intermediate stage of animal traction altogether. This modernization-syndrome hinders proper assessment of the value of animal traction. Animal traction would constitute a true technological revolution in rural Africa. Drudgery would decrease considerably (for example, the back-breaking, heavy, monotonous work with hoes during land preparation). Moreover, labour productivity would increase, but the lack of alternative employment opportunities remains problematic. A larger assortment of (improved) tools would also be a big step forward (for example, weeders with a long handle in order to be able to weed in upright position). More use of bicycles would also be a smart form of intermediate technology.

The little interest of men in intermediate technology is linked to the gender issue, since women do most of the heavy work.

Unfortunately the production factor labour is not a straightforward issue. On the one hand, labour is deficient in the busy periods of the agricultural season and women work much more hours than men. On the other hand, unemployment is widespread, especially in the cities, and men are underutilized. Moreover, a large part of the youth is not interested in agriculture, precisely because of the manual work in this sector. Especially young males move to the cities, enticed by a modern way of life in which manual labour gives little prestige. In general a white-collar mentality prevails: getting dirty hands and feet is avoided as much as possible. Unfortunately, this also applies to some of my African counterparts: agricultural researchers and extensionists lack field experience, partly because of this white-collar mentality. The result is unrealistic views on development opportunities and constraints in rural Africa. In conjunction with an often Western academic training and its concomitant modernization-syndrome, the white-collar mentality results into irrelevant agricultural research and extension.

In an increasingly Westernized world the white-collar mentality is understandable, but for some African farming systems it is detrimental since they rely on manual labour. An example is the beautiful farming system at the lower slopes of Mount Kilimanjaro in Tanzania, the homeland of the Chagga. The farming system comprises shadow trees, bananas, coffee, vegetables, fruit trees and some dairy cows which are permanently stabled (zero-grazing system). This varied and ingenious farming system on steep slopes is sustainable: erosion is absent and external inputs are hardly used. However, it demands a lot of manual labour and that is where today the shoe pinches. Most young people prefer city life and only few show agricultural ambitions. Undoubtedly this is partly caused by the low cash income derived from coffee cultivation, but the attraction of city life also plays a big role - as does the growing distaste for manual labour.

In this context the introduction of labour-saving technology to alleviate drudgery would be appropriate, but in the farming system on the steep slopes of Mount Kilimanjaro, unfortunately, little or nothing can be mechanized. It will always rely on much hard manual labour. Perhaps only a higher (farm gate) price for coffee and a work ethic which sings the praise of manual labour, can save the Chagga farming system. The (earlier mentioned) industrious nature of the previous generation of Chagga was, at least partly, based on an unequal gender balance and a hierarchical relationship between parents and children. Since free labour from women and children becomes increasingly difficult to extract, an inner urge to work needs to be developed soon. Outer enforcement by older males becomes ever more obsolete.

5.4   Organization of women

The fact that African women work considerably more hours than men is by no means unique. Also in modern Western society shadow-work of women is significant. Emancipation of women in sub-Saharan Africa might not only result in a more balanced division of work between the sexes, but also in more material prosperity, less drudgery, enhanced say over family income and own body, and a better legal position of women. However, the legal equality of men and women often exists on paper only, because of the informal economy of affection (based on strong relations of kinship) and the weak formal state which cannot enforce compliance with laws.

Within the economy of affection social control is strong and thus individual autonomy weak. Individual autonomy is laudable (also for women, at least in Western eyes) and promotes economic development. The collective autonomy of the economy of affection vis-à-vis the formal state rests to a large extent on the (enforced and unpaid) labour of women. Ultimately, men control the production factors land and labour. Emancipation of women requires that the economy of affection is pushed back. A strong, democratic state, which enforces the formal equality of men and women, would be the natural ally of women. The present weak state, however, is an affair dominated by mainly men. At the end of the day, only strong organizations of women can improve their lot. Women have to create 'countervailing power' in the form of political and economic clout.

With regard to the introduction of animal traction, for example, only strong organizations of women in their specific communities can enforce this innovation. Adoption of such innovations is not in men's interest, thus women need to enforce it. When only one woman starts refusing to transport heavy loads of firewood on her head, her husband will (more or less violently) discipline her. When, on the other hand, all women in the village simultaneously 'go on strike' men have no other option than to accept the innovation (or men themselves can transport the firewood).

A study in Africa found that, over the course of a year, women carried more than 80 tonnes of fuel, water and farm produce for a distance of 1 km. Men carried only one-eighth as much, an average of 10 tonnes for 1 km each year[38].

Joint action by women is also required in the fight against aids, for example with regard to the slow adoption of condom use by men. 'Women' are however not one homogeneous group in which all individuals face the same opportunities and problems. A utopian image of natural sisterhood is unrealistic (Grint 1998:208). Different (but somehow internally homogeneous) groups of women jointly need to create countervailing power.

A strong formal state would also be the ally of women in the fight against aids, because hitherto women have little say in sexual relations.

Women's right to choose (for only safe sex, planned pregnancy, abortion and etcetera) is still a far dream. A strong formal state, which sincerely enforces human rights, would also protect the rights of homosexuals. Some African presidents, including Mugabe from Zimbabwe and Njoma from Namibia, say that homosexuality is European import: originally it was absent in Africa.

Van der Veen (2004:277) argues that higher levels of education for women can instil a better understanding of development processes, economic trends and historical contexts. These insights will encourage women's emancipation. Today almost universal agreement exists that development funds yield greater returns if given to women (ib.). "Development progressed fastest if girls were sent to school. More educated girls tended to have children later in life, when they were better able to provide for them" (ib.:278). The United Nations Population Fund emphasizes that the Millennium Goals can only be achieved with equal rights for women and adequate reproductive healthcare. Investments in education, healthcare and in economic opportunities for women are catalysts for development. Mutually reinforcing factors - such as equal educational opportunities for boys and girls, widespread access to family planning, possibilities to postpone marriage and pregnancy, and more employment opportunities for women - diminish hunger and poverty.

6 Work Ethic, Clock and Christianity

In this chapter the disciplining and regulation of daily life in Europe are discussed. This disciplining and regulation became especially possible via the large-scale introduction of the mechanical clock and the influence of Christianity. Also European colonization of other continents was partly based on this disciplining.

6.1 Arms and discipline

According to Michael Adas (1989) European technology initially lagged considerably behind Asian technology in many fields. With regard to European colonization Achterhuis (1992:221) remarks that European power largely was based on highly developed technology in only one area: the field of warfare. But Europeans were superior not only materially (rifles and canons), also socially (organization and discipline) they were ahead of other continents. Mumford (1934) argues that all important modern instruments were already available in other cultures: the clock, printing press, water mill, magnetic compass and loom as well as gunpowder, paper, mathematics, chemistry and mechanics. The Chinese, Arabs and Greeks had these instruments and knowledge long before the North-Europeans.

Only in North-Western Europe, however, people were prepared to adapt their entire way of life to the speed and requirements of machines. Why was this so? Mumford says that technology could only dominate European society because this society, from the very start, had given in to technology - culturally and societally (in: Achterhuis 1992:223). Cultural preparations for the arrival of the machine, says Mumford, can be found in Christianity, which ended the animation (enchantment) of the world, in the monetary economy of capitalism and in the emerging disciplining and regulation of daily life. Mine workers, engineers and especially soldiers were the actors who actively propagated the mechanical worldview. Prince Maurits of The Netherlands, with his well drilled troops, serves as a model for the order and discipline, which - out of the army - started to influence society. The military uniform, the for each soldier identical clothes, lead to the first standardized mass production, soon also applied to other army necessities (Achterhuis 1992:226).

In mining machines such as pumps, steam engines, lifts, steam trains and underground transport systems were used and labour was organized in shifts. With regard to the European colonization also Wesseling (2003:55) emphasizes the social-cultural aspect of the strength of European armies. The European armies had discipline and training, they knew how to maintain their weapons, had high morale and strong *esprit de corps*. They constituted an instrument ready for use.

6.2   The clock

One of the most important forces underlying the drive to mechanization is the clock. The clock is not only an instrument to measure time, but it also facilitates the accurate synchronization of human behaviour (Achterhuis 1992:223). The advent of the mechanical clock in European cities started from the fourteenth century onwards. Since then time could be measured everywhere, independent of natural conditions; water clocks were affected by frost in winter time and sundials became ineffective under cloudy conditions. Soon, however, the clocks which were invented to serve people, started to dominate their entire lives.

Mumford (1934:14) says that the clock is the key instrument to understand the modern technological era, not the steam engine. The impact of the mechanical clock on European culture was so overwhelming that only one century after its introduction, the first European explorers were truly amazed at the lack of (instrument regulated) time discipline which foreign people exhibited. The Indians and Chinese did have complex instruments to measure time, but they never developed mechanical clocks which were available at large scale and which made it possible for everybody to share a common time (Adas 1989:61). With the advent of capitalism chronological time also became valuable: 'time is money' was the new slogan. It became a bourgeois ideal to live as regular as a clock. The adoption of chronological time resulted into undreamed-of gain in mechanical efficiency, because human behaviour could be coordinated - today even worldwide - and operations accurately planned and divided. Without the clock industrial society would simply collapse (Achterhuis 1992:226).

In the economy of affection in sub-Saharan Africa the clock and chronological time are much less important than in the Western industrialized world. The adage 'time is money' is closely connected to the modern work ethic and the division of labour. In spite of the European colonization of Africa, one did not succeed in instilling the western work ethic and time discipline in the local population.

The mechanical clock was invented in the last quarter of the thirteenth century: it was "the greatest achievement of medieval mechanical ingenuity" (Landes 1999:49). Public and private clocks brought order and control, both collective and personal. The very notion of productivity is a by-product of the mechanical clock, since this device made it possible to relate performance to uniform time units (ib.).

"One moves from the task-oriented time consciousness of the peasant (one job after another, as time and light permit) and the time-filling busyness of the domestic servant (always something to do) to an effort to maximize product per unit of time (time is money). The invention of the mechanical clock anticipates in its effects the economic analysis of Adam Smith: increase in the wealth of nations derives directly from improvement of the productive powers of labour" (ib.:50).

Increases in labour productivity resulted in more prosperity. But the mechanical clock remained a European (Western) monopoly for some three hundred years; "in its higher forms, right into the twentieth century" (ib.).

The Islamic world and China were falling behind Europe in economic development even before the opening of the world started (by the European voyages of discovery from the fifteenth century onwards) (Landes 1999:54). From about 750 to 1100 the level of Islamic science and technology far surpassed that of Europe: the Islamic world was Europe's teacher. From then on, however, things changed when Islamic science was denounced as heresy by religious zealots. Religious and secular issues were not separated. Similarly, Chinese industry long anticipated European. For example: the Chinese had a water-driven machine for spinning hemp in the twelfth century, some five hundred years before England's Industrial Revolution. But China's industrial history offers examples of technological oblivion and regression instead of a cumulative build-up of knowledge and know-how (ib.:55).

Some partial explanations of the Chinese technological stagnation are: the absence of a free market and institutionalized property rights; the larger values of society, including gender relations which made that women did not work outside the home; and the totalitarian government control and stifling state-intervention which made any innovation suspect (ib.:56-7). Possible reasons of the peculiarly European cultivation of invention - the invention of invention - are related to religious values: the Judeo-Christian respect for manual labour, the Judeo-Christian subordination of nature to man and the Judeo-Christian sense of linear time. In the last analysis, however, the market and free entrepreneurship were decisive (ib.:58-9). Europeans were, most of all, doers.

Europe's great virtue was that it was a learner, unlike China, and used earlier Chinese inventions and discoveries, while China (after all, China was the 'Celestial Empire') rejected or belittled Western science and technology (ib.:348, 337). The scientific revolution of the seventeenth and eighteenth centuries was predominantly a European affair. Today, however, Asian countries are using Western science and technology to boost their economies.

6.3   Colonialism and slave trade

"It has to be acknowledged that in a project where people of developing and European countries collaborate, both partners undergo an influence of the colonial past. Colleagues of the developing countries may be sensitive to any trace of neo-colonial attitude, whereas we may not be sufficiently aware of this or too much aware in the sense that we are too prudent and cautious"[39]

After the abolition of slavery in the European colonies, naked violence was no longer an option to obtain free labour. The introduction of a money-economy had to solve the problem. Hut taxes were introduced, which forced Africans to accept wage work at plantations or to cultivate cash crops on their own land in order to earn money. This disrupted the (ecological and economic) balance in local communities, authentic food systems collapsed, and food became for the first time something which was traded and bought for money (Achterhuis 1988:321).

According to Wesseling (2003:75) the purpose of the head taxes in colonial eyes was threefold. Firstly, income for the colonial budget was raised which otherwise would have to come from taxpayers in the mother country. Secondly, the indigenous population was forced to engage in wage work in order to be able to pay the taxes. In this way they would acquire a taste for regular labour without the necessity of forced labour. Thirdly, the monetarization of the economy was enhanced and thus also the modernization of the colonies.

The slave trade was a matter of demand and supply (ib.:124). The demand came from Europeans, the supply from Africans. In Africa, from way back, an internal slave trade existed since the relative underpopulation of the continent resulted into a permanent shortage of voluntary labour supply and slaves had to fill this gap. The European slave trade joined in with this tradition, but gave it a new and radical turn. The large European demand changed the character of the slave trade: the Atlantic slave trade from Africa to North- and South-America started (ib.). From 1450 to 1900 about twelve million people were transported. The Arab slave trade comprised fourteen to fifteen million persons, but this trade started earlier, in the seventh century, and continued longer, till the end of the nineteenth century. The Europeans transported more than six million people in the eighteenth century alone, as much as the Arab slave trade did in six centuries (ib.:125-6).

Also Landes (1999:9, 69) points to the abundant testimony to the existence of slavery in Africa long before the arrival of the Europeans and to the active slave trade by Arabs. In his view the Industrial Revolution also would have taken place without the triangular trade between Europe, Africa and the New World - with the slave trade as vital part. The pioneering developments in energy (coal and the steam engine) and metallurgy (coke-smelted iron) were largely independent of the Atlantic system. The same applies to the initial attempt to mechanize wool spinning (ib.:121). Without the slave trade, however, the British economy and its North American colonies would have developed slower.

The wide diversity in development outcomes in the Third World (spectacular successes in East-Asia, mixed results in Latin-America and outright regression in much of Africa) shows that "colonization in itself, even enslavement, does not dictate failure" (ib.:433). Although imperialism, practically without exception, has brought material and psychological suffering for the conquered people, at the same time imperialism has not prevented a few colonies from developing as autonomous, industrial-economic centres (for example the British colonies in North America and

Finland as part of the Russian empire) (ib.:434,436). In a review of some recent books on the history of European colonialism, Paul Scheffer says that the balance sheet of profit and loss due to colonial enterprise is difficult to calculate, in an economic and moral sense. He adds that cultural relativism and the ensuing multicultural tolerance in today's Western societies are nurtured by a guilty conscience about colonial history.[40]

In the following long quote Koponen (1995) speaks about the central role of the 'labour question' in German colonial policy in Tanzania. It describes how difficult it is to instil a modern work ethic in an as yet 'uncaptured peasantry' which still enjoys the advantages of a (strongly gender-biased) 'economy of affection'.

"Although colonialism was basically an exploitative system, much of what we nowadays call development began in Mainland Tanzania during the early phase of German colonialism. Indeed, only 'development' made colonial exploitation possible (ib.:*i*) ... Colonial exploitation required economic development; economic development required the exploitation of African labour ... A formidable problem was how to extract the necessary labour from those who possessed it, and how to make it available to the colonialists ...

But Tanzanian Africans were not immediately ready to provide the colonialists with surplus labour in required amounts, and the 'labour question' became the field where the most vital interests of the colonizers and the colonized confronted one another and where the great struggle between intruding Europeans and resisting and accommodating Africans was daily re-enacted in a myriad silent everyday forms (ib.:321) ... But the issue was not work as such. What the colonial power needed was work specifically adapted to its purposes and form of organization, i.e. either systematic plantation work, 'regulated strictly in terms of hours, weeks or months', or alternatively peasant surplus labour allocated to crops favoured by colonialism.

For this kind of work Africans showed little inclination even if they quite obviously did not spend the whole of their time on their fields. The Africans, remarked a colonial agricultural expert, 'are very unwilling to let activity degenerate into work'. It was only half a joke. In fact, the concept of 'work' (*Arbeit*) acquired a very specific meaning in the language of colonialism: it came to denote sustained physical toil for production geared to satisfy non-local, external needs. The lack was not of people 'available for work', but of those 'with a will to work' in this very particular sense. It was not, remarked a colonial official-turned-planter with cynical honesty, that 'the negro needs work for his own welfare, but it is we who use the negro's work in our own interest' (ib.:322) ...

If Africans did not wish or know how to work, most colonialists concluded that they must be 'educated' for work. Just as the 'labour question' became the most important practical problem of German colonialism, so 'education for work' (*Erziehung zur Arbeit*) became the key concept of German colonial ideology (ib.:324) ... [Colonialists] who believed that the main problem was an inborn laziness and indolence demanded measures of compulsion which only the state could produce. Their proposal was that a state-directed system of forced labour should be instituted ...

But those who attached more importance to the 'lack of want' and to the fact that Africans were not economically obliged to seek employment from whites, were unwilling to resort - exclusively or even primarily - to measures of coercion; in the long term, they believed, Africans must be led to realize the need for work themselves. This aim must include not only 'provision of an inducement to perform work, but also...a reshaping of mental attitudes for creation of an urge to work for the sake of work itself' [as a German colonial officer remarked in 1902]. This would be achieved mainly by 'habituating Africans to higher needs', by 'educating them in consumption and in needs', which in turn meant 'raising the level' of existing needs and creating quite new ones among Africans (ib.:325) ...

There were also colonialists who perceptively recognized the structural root cause of the problem. The Africans were under no economic compulsion to work for Europeans. They had labour and access to land and could thus provide for their own livelihood (ib.:326) ... An important feature of the discussion was that it was aimed specifically at the utilization of *male* labour ... Inadequate use of underutilized male labour was explicitly understood to be the core of the labour question ... Most [colonial] writers who complained of African 'laziness' made it clear that they were speaking exclusively of African men, and showed an awareness that domestic and field work was done by women ... 'Women look after the household and often the fields too, while men make their life as free and pleasurable as they possibly can', wrote Professor Wohltmann in a discussion of labour conducted in *Deutsche Kolonialzeitung* in 1902-03 ... Lieutenant Hermann reported [in 1892] from Ugogo that 'men spend most of the day in a state of *dolce far niente*, sitting in groups in the shade, smoking or taking snuff and gossiping' (ib.:327) ...

There were always, however, a number of colonialists who did not accept the primary assumption of basic African laziness in any form. In their view Africans, far from being indolent and phlegmatic, were industrious and enterprising people with an economic sense who readily responded to market impulses by allocating their labour power where the best return was promised ... If plantations wished to obtain workers they simply had to make wages and working conditions competitive [a colonial official remarked in 1907] ... It remained a minority view but it always had influential protagonists (ib.:328) ... [But] even those who regarded Africans as industrious and diligent shared the assumption that male labour was underutilized ... (ib.:329) ...

Also missions played a most important part in education for work ... *Ora et labora*, pray and work, was a motto they often repeated. 'Religious and moral instruction is a precondition in educating the negro for work', said an inspector of the Bremen Missionary Society [in 1902] (ib.:355) ...

Creation of a labour force meant not only obtaining labour but also subjecting it to discipline. Africans had followed the rhythm of sun and the rains. They had to be adapted to hours, weeks and months, to working days and rest days. They had listened to the spirits of ancestors speaking in the rituals of sowing and harvesting. They had to be taught to follow the commands of plantation overseers. They had to be taught what it meant to be 'contracted' to the European employer and what followed from a 'breach' of the contract ...

To discipline a workforce demanded still more force and coercion than to assemble it, and if a 'rational core' behind the seemingly excessive violence of German colonialism is sought it can perhaps be found here (ib.:359) ... The instrument in busiest use and the most telling symbol of German power was the *kiboko*, a long whip of hippopotamus hide (ib.:360) ... [25 strokes] which the law officially allowed was the norm in practice. The expression *hamsa [wa] ishirini*, meaning 'twenty-five', became a refrain which was still current at the end of the 1960s among Africans who had experienced German rule. [In a footnote Koponen says:] Cameroon, another German colony, was known among the English-speaking neighbours as 'The twenty-five country' " (ib.:366).

6.4   Impact of Christianity

Although Christianity was introduced in Africa already before the colonization, it could not bring about the internalization of a modern work ethic. The number of missionaries in Africa was always small, as were the groups of Africans who had intensive contact with these clergymen. Large-scale and systematic disciplining to labour by religious organizations never took place. Yet some Christian groups did have impact on the local work ethic at smaller scale. These groups have an economic ethic which brings about 'revolutionary' change in prevailing relationships and realises an important economic take-off, also because hard work and sober living are strongly emphasized. In such religious groups the customary skimming off of each other's economic surpluses is confined to the group (NAR 1989:47). The rural sociologist Norman Long (1970) has analysed such behaviour in a group of Jehovah's Witnesses in Zambia. In these cases entrepreneurship emerges which is effective, creative and even aggressive and it results into economic development - based on a specific economy of affection (NAR 1989:47).

The conversion to Christianity can also entail that the earlier attitudes towards magic and witchcraft change. People assume more responsibility for their own life and actively take steps to enhance their economic position. The Jehovah's Witnesses in Zambia simply no longer believed that those who adopted certain innovations - and thus 'stepped out of line' - would become victims of sorcery (Seur 1992:425). A Christian philosophy of life can also lead to less alcohol consumption and more savings. Thus a true change in style of living can be realized.

Koponen (1995) writes the following about the missionaries in Tanzania at the time of the German colonization:

"They propagated a doctrine which stressed individual responsibility: they taught reading and writing, a technique which favoured individuality; they treated the sick by the 'biotechnical' methods of western medicine, not the 'social' or 'collective' ones of popular healing; and they acted in economic matters like private entrepreneurs (ib.:582) … [In 1913 a German missionary expounded] the utilitarian value of Christianity to the colonial power, to assure that only conversion to Christianity would guarantee that 'internal colonization' of the African mind without which the colonial enterprise was doomed to abort" (ib.:583).

Christianity, the money-economy, modern technology and the modern work ethic have been important (interrelated) factors in the development of Europe. The fact that these four factors have only partially permeated African societies, can explain a large part of their lack of development. Van der Veen (2004:235-6) observes that against a background of global cultural homogenisation - in practice Westernisation - Africa remains on the fringes of the 'global village'. Globalisation resulted in Africa in cultural confusion. Socialism, nationalism and even 'development' were no longer realistic ideologies in Africa after the end of the Cold War.

"Together with the collapse of secular ideologies, Africans' sense of social and often also personal insecurity led to a spectacular growth in religion … The simultaneous rise in the popularity of Christianity and Islam in Africa around the turn of the millennium supports the hypothesis that religions may to a large extent shape the twenty-first century" (ib.:236).

Whether in Africa in the coming decades the enhanced interest in Christianity will contribute to a modern work ethic, remains to be seen. The complex process of 'disciplining to labour' is hard to plan. Moreover, the process of modernisation is always ambivalent. On the one hand, the dominant Western culture is adopted, at least partially. On the other hand, resistance to the dominant culture occurs, usually accompanied by a romanticisation of one's own culture (ib.:237). This ambivalent attitude of adoption *and* rejection is reinforced by the worldwide presence of television. Also with regard to the modern work ethic both adoption and rejection might play a role.

6.5   Case study: Jehovah's Witnesses in Zambia

Norman Long (1977:47-8) says that the precise relationships between social, cultural and economic factors in the process of development must be investigated empirically case by case. The assumption of a one-to-one relationship between traditionalistic or conservative value systems and lack of economic entrepreneurship cannot be made just like that. In this context Long refers to a study of the Hutterites of Canada, who combine a conservative religious ideology - exhibited in a highly traditionalistic family organization and strong moral sanctions against conspicuous consumption - with commercial wheat farming, which is characterized by modern economic rationality and efficient production techniques (ib.:48)[41].

The assignment of causal priority to cultural factors, which might curb or stimulate economic development, cannot be *a priori* justified. The total complex of both internal and external factors - technical, economic, structural, social, cultural and ideological - must be considered (ib.:50). The interplay of all these factors determines socio-economic change processes. Max Weber emphasized in *The Protestant Ethic and the Spirit of Capital-*

ism and in his comparative studies on religion the role of ideology in social development (see chapter 3).

"Like that of other founding fathers, Weber's work is surrounded by a massive body of exegetical writings aimed at elucidating his central ideas and presuppositions. However, some of this literature has oversimplified or misconstrued his arguments. This is most noticeably the case with the Protestant Ethic essay. Several writers, for example, have attributed to the Protestant sects a central causative role in the rise of western capitalism rather than see Weber's analysis in terms of the 'correlations between forms of religious belief and practical ethics' which, indirectly, influence socio-economic behaviour" (Long 1977:195).

Following Weber's attempt to trace the origins of Western economic rationality to the religious asceticism and rationality of certain puritan Protestant sects, several studies have been conducted in non-Western countries to check whether similar incentives, derived from religious beliefs, could be identified there.

In both Hinduism and Islam ascetic religious sects exist which play an important role in economic development (ib.:61). The Sikhs, Parsis and Jains in India stress the values of hard work and an austere style of living and they inculcate in their children a puritanical attitude over wasting of time and money (time is money). Also here, however, it is not necessary to assume an exclusive causality between religiosity and economic practice. The fact that these two components of lifestyle are linked stands however beyond any question. "This linkage appears to have developed in a spiral of mutual reinforcement over time"[42]. Although India generally is described as conservative in religious beliefs, with a caste system that inhibits social mobility, these few examples of ascetic religious sects nevertheless show that small groups of religiously motivated entrepreneurs do exist. And that they practise ethics similar to that of Protestant Christian groups in Europe (ib.:64).

The study of Long (1968) of the group of Jehovah's Witnesses in rural Zambia emphasizes that membership of a religious congregation should not be seen merely in terms of the ideological dimension, but also in terms of organizational and interpersonal networks. The Witnesses developed church-based social networks, both within and without their home area, that were mobilized to solve problems of shortages of labour, capital and knowledge in their farms. Long's study also illustrates:

"How a religious ethic is used situationally, when appropriate, to legitimize new patterns of socio-economic behaviour or to repudiate traditional ones ... Clearly a wide range of socio-cultural factors, including religious disposition, may facilitate development in specific contexts, but one should not preempt analysis by assuming that certain value orientations constitute necessary preconditions ... We should guard against converting historical facts (e.g. the role of Calvinism) into the status of logical prerequisites since this implies the untenable notion of historical necessity" (Long 1977:66).

Catholicism, for example, often characterized as a conservative social force, did not impede the high rate of growth in certain Latin American countries (but, Landes would say, it did delay economic growth very much). "Nor does an analysis of religious beliefs throw any light on why overseas Indians and Chinese have been so much more entrepreneurial and productive outside their home societies than within" (ib.:67). Landes would argue that within their home countries the governments or local rulers did not allow entrepreneurial activity; it was suffocated by bureaucratic control.

Entrepreneurship and economic growth are partly determined by the interaction between socio-cultural factors and the resources available to members of a (religious) group, but also their life-experiences play a role. Another dimension adding to the complexity is the degree of flexibility in the interpretation of the religious doctrine - how much flexibility do the religious authorities tolerate - since this affects the adaptability of the religious ethic in the face of changing external circumstances (ib.:69). Ascetic forms of religion often become obsessed with the minutiae of everyday life and can be rather dogmatic in nature. Moreover, religious groups tend to be closed and incapsulated. All this can lead to decreasing competitiveness in the long term. An ideology which in the initial phases of the process of economic development actively encourages capital accumulation and investment in profitable enterprises can later on get in the way of necessary re-organizations of businesses. A search for persistent value systems (which remain constant over time) is thus difficult to justify (ib.).

Taking into account the numerous facilitating factors it is extremely difficult to specify the necessary preconditions for rapid economic growth. Moreover, when one has selected a particular set of factors one will always encounter contrary cases which refute this interpretation. According to Long (ib.:70) the problem of selection of prerequisites is difficult to solve as long as one aims at broad generalizations, for exceptions to the rule will always surface.

"The fundamental errors involved in this type of approach remain those of positioning a linear, Western-biased model of development and of abstracting specific factors from a complex socio-historical process and assuming them to be crucial" (ib.).

Han Seur (1992) did field research in the same area in Zambia as Norman Long, but twenty years later. The sub-title of his dissertation *Sowing the good seed* reads: *The interweaving of agricultural change, gender relations and religion in Serenje District, Zambia*. This sub-title points out that the various processes of change are interwoven "such as to make it impossible to identify a prime mover that could be said to have caused change in the area" (Seur 1992:439).

The processes of agricultural, social, political and economic change cannot be understood without considering the role played by the Jehovah's Witnesses, but at the same time these processes had, in turn, profound effects upon their religious ethic (ib.). External and internal factors interact. Changing external circumstances can influence the interpretation of certain aspects of religious doctrine and the resulting changed religious ethic can, in turn, affect the management of farming enterprises. Today many Witnesses no longer consider labour a sacred calling or an absolute end in itself, but they rather stress the importance of a balance in life (ib.:412). They search for a balance between material, social and spiritual needs.

The Jehovah's Witnesses in the study area play an active role in the gradual dismantling of the traditional matrilineal system of kinship and inheritance. They use their religious ethic to shirk traditional obligations towards relatives and to promote individual ownership of property and land (ib.:391). In this sense they undermine the traditional economy of affection. Besides religious ideology, a wide variety of other factors have affected change in the study area: factors and processes such as population growth, ecological change, formal education, migration to towns, urban employment, availability of investment and consumer goods, growing importance of the market economy, structural conflicts between matrikin, government interventions (e.g. the introduction of ploughs, hybrid maize, subsidies on agricultural inputs, etc.) and the ideology of the dominant political party.

"Since a multiplicity of factors and change processes and responses to these factors and processes by different individuals and groups stand at the basis of other change processes (which in turn may affect the very processes that caused them), I find it impossible to define accurately the contribution of the Witnesses and their religious ideology in bringing about or giving direction to these processes ... In other words, it is impossible to discern a particular prime mover, and it seems that the changes … should be treated as specific historical events with multiple and cumulative causes" (ib.:391-2).

Weber says that in modern Europe the initial role of religion in the transformation of the traditionalistic work ethic into its modern variant is no longer necessary. The post-Protestant society relies on a secularized value system in which work is no longer a sacred calling. Religious devotion as a motivating force was replaced by a preoccupation with "quantitative bigness and a desire for the power and recognition that the mere fact of wealth brings" (Seur 1992:425; referring to Weber 1989:71). In my view this last remark points to the 'rat race' in modern Western society or to the endless competition between individuals, which is fuelled by the mimetic desire (the wish or longing to imitate others). We will come back to this issue in chapter 11.

6.6   Planning and work ethic

The disciplining and regulation of daily life in Europe was prepared by actors such as monks, mine workers and especially soldiers (chapter 6.1). The military uniform reflects order and discipline. Uniforms result into uniformization, standardization and normalization (with the higher ranks setting the norms). Standardized uniforms, as worn by monks and soldiers, are symbols of subjugation to the group and its leaders. Also the uniform of modern western man - the suit with tie - has this function. Although the literal and figurative uniformization in the army facilitates the disciplining to labour, ultimately too rigid discipline can be the result - in which the expression 'over my dead body' not only figuratively but also literally applies.

The discipline and order in European life, the modern work ethic, the synchronization of human behaviour and the ensuing gain in efficiency

would not have been possible without the invention and large-scale introduction of the clock. The mechanical clock, as key instrument of the
modern era, resulted in the Western adage 'time is money'. The best
known proverb in Ki-Swahili by contrast is *haraka haraka, haina baraka*
corresponding to the English saying 'haste makes waste'. Although too
much haste indeed can make waste, the proverb is often used in sub-
Saharan Africa to mask or validate flagrant inefficiency (both Africans and
expatriates do this).

Although I lived for more than twenty years in sub-Saharan Africa, it
remains difficult to become accustomed to a foreign concept of time and a
different work ethic. In one's youth these matters apparently are so deeply
internalized in a process of enculturation that other attitudes afterwards are
hard to accept. The adoption of a modern work ethic by Africans will have
to commence at early age. *If* sub-Saharan Africa wants to participate in the
global economy, it has little choice but to adapt to the concept of time and
the work ethic that prevail in today's dominant economies. This may
sound Eurocentric, paternalistic and imperialistic, but if one wants to
achieve a high level of material welfare (something almost everybody
wants, also in Africa), then internalization of the concomitant concept of
time and work ethic seems inevitable.

In sub-Saharan Africa the formulation of goals and plans consumes a
lot of time, but the subsequent implementation usually leaves much to be
desired. Attending meetings, workshops and conferences, and writing and
reading reports, is a full-time job for many local and expatriate development experts. The Poverty Reduction Strategy Papers (PRSPs) and
Millennium Development Goals (MDGs) are examples of such time-
demanding exercises without much impact. What sub-Saharan Africa
needs most of all are deeds, not words, i.e. *walk the talk*. Development
simply does not come about without much hard work. Hyden (1980:230)
says:

"[Development planning in Africa is mainly part of the art of government, in which planning goals are used as] carrots rather than as realistic predictions ... To expect planning to be an important *economic* development tool in the context of the African economies is illusory".

Development simply cannot be stage-managed. Development planning in Africa is more an instrument of political strategy than social or economic policy (NAR 1989:19). Also the MDGs suggest that socio-economic change can be effected by governments and donors, as if they can 'manage' change in an effective and efficient way.

7 Work Ethic and Industrial Revolution

In this chapter first the British Industrial Revolution will be discussed. Next the importance of (culturally determined) human capital for the Industrial Revolution will be emphasized. A crucial component of this human capital is the work ethic. The subchapters 7.1 and 7.2 rest heavily on David Landes' book *The Wealth and Poverty of Nations*. Subsequently basic technological differences between Eurasia and Africa will be discussed.

7.1   The British Industrial Revolution: ca 1770 to 1870

The Industrial Revolution started in England in the eighteenth century and emulated around the world. "Some countries made an industrial revolution and became rich; and others did not and stayed poor. This process of selection actually began much earlier, during the [European] age of discovery" (Landes 1999:168-9). Ironically, the countries that had started the exploration of the world, Spain and Portugal, ended up losers. Particularly Spain became rich in the New World, but chose to spend on luxury and war. Unexpected and undeserved wealth is easily squandered (ib.:171). Other countries, such as England and Holland, saved money, invested in technological development and built their economies on hard work rather than on depletable minerals (ib.:174).

In the eighteenth century the British cotton manufacture was transformed by a series of inventions, which ultimately gave birth to a new mode of production: the factory system (ib.:186). The extraordinary technological advances were not achieved overnight. In all, steam engine development took two hundred years (ib.:189). In the Industrial Revolution precision gauging and fixed settings (standard sizes, interchangeable parts) were very important. Here the clock- and watchmakers gave the lead. "It is no accident that cotton manufacturers, when looking for skilled craftsmen to build and maintain machines, advertised for clockmakers" (ib.:191). Mass production is based on interchangeable parts. The merging stream of innovations in the last decades of the eighteenth century was not just a lucky harvest. "Innovation was catching because the principles that underlay a given technique could take many forms, find many uses" (ib.). Mechanization and the factory system was the core of the process. Mechanization was a general phenomenon subject to wide application and it gave rise to the disciplined organization of work under supervision in factories (ib.:192).

It is not easy to put dates to the Industrial Revolution, because of "the decades of experiment that precede a given innovation and the long run of improvement that follows" (ib.). The British Industrial Revolution ran about a century, from 1770 to 1870 (ib.:193). "Large changes and economic revolutions do not come out of the blue. They are invariably well and long prepared. But continuity does not exclude change, even drastic change" (ib.:194). The consequence of the technological and economic advances was a growing gap between modern industrial countries and laggards, in Europe to begin with. "In 1750, the difference between Western Europe (excluding Britain) and Eastern in income per head was perhaps 15 percent; in 1800, little more than 20. By 1860 it was up to 64 percent; by the 1900s, almost 80 percent" (ib.). The polarization between Europe and the Third World was even much sharper.

An important (twofold) question is why the Industrial Revolution took place only in the eighteenth century and why in Britain? After all, examples of mechanization and use of inanimate power are known which did not result into an industrial revolution. "One thinks of Sung China (hemp spinning, iron making), medieval Europe (water- and windmill technologies), of early modern Italy (silk throwing, shipbuilding), of the Holland of the 'Golden Age'" (ib.:200). With regard to the timing of the Industrial

Revolution, Landes (ib.) stresses two factors: "*build-up* - the accumulation of knowledge and know-how; and *breakthrough* - reaching and passing thresholds". As already noted, the Islamic and Chinese intellectual and technological advance was not only interrupted, but the stoppage was also institutionalized. In Europe, however, a continuing accumulation of science and technology did take place. Landes (ib.:201) mentions three critical, distinctively European sources of success:

"(1) the growing *autonomy* of intellectual inquiry; (2) the development of unity in disunity in the form of a common, implicitly adversarial *method*, that is, the creation of a language of proof recognized, used, and understood across national and cultural boundaries; and (3) the invention of invention, that is, the *routinization* of research and its diffusion".

The intellectual autonomy in Europe was promoted by political fragmentation and the resultant competing pretensions of secular authorities, but also by religious dissent. "These heresies may not have been enlightened in matters intellectual and scientific, but they undermined the uniqueness of dogma [of the Roman Church] and, so doing, implicitly promoted novelty" (ib). The widening of personal experience via the voyages of discovery was also shattering of authority.

The scientific method with its powerful combination of perception and measurement was the key to knowledge and made replication and verification possible. "Nothing so effectively undermined authority" (ib.:202). However, almost four centuries elapsed before the research strategies and instruments of observation and measurement were of such quality that the scientific method bore fruit in the spectacular advances of the seventeenth century. The routinization of research, the third *institutional* pillar of Western science, was mentioned before in chapter 6.2.

The large interest in mechanization of the textile industry in England in the eighteenth century was primarily caused by the fact that the growth of this industry was beginning to outstrip labour supply.

"England had jumped ahead on the strength of rural manufacture (putting-out), but the dispersion of activity across hill and dale was driving up costs of distribution and collection. Meanwhile, trying to meet demand, employers raised wages, that is, they increased the price they paid for finished work. To their dismay, however, the higher income simply permitted workers more time for leisure, and the supply of work actually diminished. Merchant-manufacturers found themselves on a treadmill. In defiance of all their natural instincts, they came to wish for higher food prices. Perhaps a rise in the cost of living would compel spinners and weavers to their task.

The workers, however, did respond to market incentives. They were contractors as well as wage labourers, and this dual status gave them opportunity for self-enrichment at the expense of the putter-out. Spinners and weavers would take materials from one merchant and then sell the finished article to a competitor ... They also learned to set some of the raw material aside for their own use ... (ib.:208).

Little wonder, then, that frustrated manufacturers turned their thoughts to large workshops where spinners and weavers would have to turn up on time and work the full day under supervision. That was no small matter. Cottage industry, after all, had great advantages for the merchant-manufacturer, in particular, low cost of entry and low overhead. In this mode, it was the worker who supplied plant and equipment, and if business slowed, the putter-out could simply turn off the orders. Large shops or plants, on the other hand, called for a substantial capital investment: land and buildings to start with, plus machines.

Putting-out, moreover, was popular with everybody. The workers liked the freedom from discipline, the privilege of stopping and going as they pleased. Work rhythms reflected this independence. Weavers typically rested and played long, well into the week, then worked hard toward the end in order to make delivery and collect pay on Saturday. On Fridays they might work through the night.

Saturday night was for drinking, and Sunday brought more beer and ale. Monday (Saint Monday) was equally holy, and Tuesday was needed to recover from so much holiness (ib.:209) ...

But manufacturers found that they had to pay to persuade people out of cottages and into mills ... In spite of higher wages, the mills still seemed a prison to the old-timers. Where, then, did the early mill owners find their labour force? Where else but among those who could not say no? In England that meant children, often conscripted (bought) from the poorhouses, and women, especially the young unmarrieds (ib.:209-10) ...

Employers dislike being dependent on their workers, and the substitution of capital for labour - thus the original mechanization of cotton spinning and the imposition of the factory - was often motivated by considerations of power as well as of money" (ib.:281).

The above quotation reflects the traditionalistic work ethic (chapter 3.1) quite well. This attitude towards work in eighteenth century England is still largely prevalent in today's sub-Saharan Africa. The urban informal and formal sectors are plagued by 'freedom from discipline' and heavy drinking after pay is not uncommon. Farmers engaged in contract-farming get inputs from one company, but may sell their produce after harvest to another. Building workers set aside some construction material for their own use or sell it. In sweatshops in some Asian countries (more or less forced) child labour and young unmarried women dominate. Foreign companies prefer to invest in capital- rather than labour-intensive activities in sub-Saharan Africa. Unfortunately, the transformation of the traditionalistic work ethic into a modern one is a complex process that takes time.

According to Landes the Industrial Revolution started in England and not in some other European country, because by the early eighteenth century England was well ahead:

"in cottage manufacture (putting-out), seedbed of growth; in recourse to fossil fuel; in the technology of those crucial branches that would make the core of the Industrial Revolution: textiles, iron, energy and power. To these should be added the efficiency of British commercial agriculture and transport (ib.:213) ... One can hardly exaggerate the contribution of agricultural improvement to Britain's industrialization" (ib.:214).

Agricultural productivity started already to rise in the Middle Ages. Market gardening (fruits and vegetables) around London spread in the sixteenth century as did mixed farming (grain and grain-fed livestock). "This development made for richer and more varied diets, with an exceptionally high proportion of animal protein" (ib.). Here the important contribution of agricultural advance to industrial development is stressed as well as the centrality of rich and varied nutrition in economic progress: two issues that deserve more attention in today's attempts to enhance welfare in sub-Saharan Africa. Also transport infrastructure (roads and canals) was crucial to Britain's development, as it is to sub-Saharan Africa today.

"This advance *cum* transformation, this revolution, was not a matter of chance, of 'things simply coming together'. One can find reasons, and reasons behind the reasons. (In big things, history abhors accident). The early technological superiority of Britain in these key branches was itself an achievement - not God-given, not happenstance, but the result of work, ingenuity, imagination, and enterprise ... To understand this, consider not only material advantages (other societies were also favourably endowed for industry but took ages to follow the British initiative), but also the nonmaterial values (culture) and institutions ... Such terms as 'values' and 'culture' are not popular with economists, who prefer to deal with quantifiable (more precisely definable) factors. Still, life being what it is, one must talk about these things ... These values and institutions are so familiar to us (that is why we call them modern) that we take them for granted. They represent, however, a big departure from older norms and have been accepted and adopted, over time and in different places, only in the face of tenacious resistance" (ib.:215-7).

An example of such a nonmaterial value is the work ethic. The transformation of the traditionalistic work ethic in Britain and North-Western Europe not only took time, but also faced tenacious resistance. It was not an automatic or accidental process. Deliberate efforts were needed. A crucial *institutional* issue was England's social precocity: it was a true 'nation'. In chapter 4.1 we have seen that the African continent has many national states but few nation states. According to Landes (ib.:219) it was not a coincidence that the first industrial nation, Britain, came closest earliest to this new kind of social and political order.

"To begin with, Britain had the early advantage of being a *nation*. [It was not] simply a state or political entity, but a self-conscious, self-aware unit characterized by common identity and loyalty and by equality of civil status. Nations can reconcile social purpose with individual aspirations and initiatives and enhance performance by their collective synergy. The whole is more than the sum of the parts" (ib.).

Later on we will see that collective synergy and holistic performance, above all, are grounded in societal trust, which, in turn, is grounded in collective consciousness. In addition to Britain's societal precocity, the importance it gave to time and to saving time was also crucial.

"Two pieces of 'unobtrusive' evidence: (1) the passionate interest in knowing the time; and (2) the emphasis on speed of transport. The British were in the eighteenth century the world's leading producers and consumers of timekeepers, in the country as in the city (very different here from other European societies) ... The coaching services reflected this temporal sensibility: schedules to the minute, widely advertised; closely calculated arrival times and transfers; drivers checked by sealed clocks; speed over comfort; lots of dead horses" (ib.:224).

As said before, the value of 'temporal sensibility' or time awareness is related to the work ethic.

7.2   Culturally determined human capital

According to Landes (1999:252-3) Europe's development gradient ran from west to east and north to south:

"from educated to illiterate populations, from representative to despotic institutions, from equality to hierarchy, and so on. It was not resources or money that made the difference; nor mistreatment by outsiders. It was what lay inside - culture, values, initiative".

The countries that were most ready for mechanization, the first follower countries of the British Industrial Revolution, lay in the northwest quadrant of the European continent: France, the Low Countries, the Rhineland, the Protestant cantons of Switzerland, and outliers in the northeast corner of Spain (Catalonia) and in Bohemia (ib.:237). "By the time Europe's first follower countries got going (post-1815), Britain had known two human generations of growth and industrial development" (ib.:257). But it took these follower countries something more than a century to catch up (ib.:231).

"Institutions and culture first; money next; but from the beginning and increasingly, the payoff was to knowledge" (ib.:276). The divergent development stories of, for example, North America (ex-British) and Latin America (ex-Spanish and Portuguese) require multiple explanations. In addition to the difference in natural resources - the luck of the draw - culture and institutions are important (ib.:295-6). Another example of the importance of culture is the spectacular German 'economic miracle' after World War II. In addition to the substantial aid of the Marshall Plan, one should credit above all "the energy and work habits of the defeated Germans" (ib.:471). The Japanese recovery was even more spectacular. "The Japanese, like the Germans, built their recovery on work, education, determination" (ib.). Landes (ib.:383) speaks of a Japanese version of Weber's Protestant ethic. Also in the later Asian newcomers, Taiwan and Korea (former Japanese colonies) and the global city-states Singapore and Hong-Kong, the primary asset has been "a work ethic that yields high product for low wages" (ib.:475). As a last example Landes (ib.:477) mentions expatriate (overseas) Chinese.

"The Chinese, middleman minority par excellence, are the leaven and lubricant of Southeast Asian trade, and from there around the world. They cherish a work ethic that would make a Weberian Calvinist envious...".

Culturally determined human capital along with facilitating government initiatives makes so-called economic miracles possible (ib.:391). See also what Ernst Schumacher said in the Introduction of this book.

With regard to the disappointing performance of African countries, Landes (ib.:506) speaks of 'statistical misinference' as one of the games economists play: more or less comparable numbers from different countries are used to draw conclusions about past and future.

"The same World Bank report that deplores African performance in 1965-90 cites Asian figures for 1965 ('conditions similar to those in Africa in 1990') to envisage African growth over the next quarter century. Equal levels [for example in GDP per capita] at different times constitute for these experts similar conditions. Oh yes, the proportion of children in school was higher in Asia, but that is easily remedied. Otherwise, no problem. Of cultural and institutional differences, nothing (ib.) ... The continent's problems go much deeper than bad policies, and bad policies are not an accident. Good government is not to be had for the asking. It took Europe centuries to get it, so why should Africa do so in mere decades, especially after the distortions of colonialism?" (ib.:507).

At the end of his book Landes says:

"If we learn anything from the history of economic development, it is that culture makes all the difference. (Here Max Weber was right on). Witness the enterprise of expatriate minorities - the Chinese in East and Southeast Asia, Indians in East Africa, Lebanese in West Africa, Jews and Calvinists throughout much of Europe, and on and on. Yet culture, in the sense of the inner values and attitudes that guide a population, frightens scholars. It has a sulphuric odour of race and inheritance, an air of immutability. In thoughtful moments, economists and social scientists recognize that this is not true, and indeed salute examples of cultural change for the better while deploring changes for the worse. But applauding or deploring implies the passivity of the viewer - an inability to use knowledge to shape people and things. The technicians would rather do: change interest and exchange rates, free up trade, alter political institutions, manage. Besides, criticisms of culture cut close to the ego, injure identity and self-esteem. Coming from outsiders, such animadversions, however tactful and indirect, stink of condescension ...

Besides, if culture does so much, why does it not work consistently? Economists are not alone in asking why some people - the Chinese, say - have long been so unproductive at home and yet so enterprising away. If culture matters, why didn't it change China? (It is doing so, now) ... On the other hand, culture does not stand alone. Economic analysis cherishes the illusion that one good reason should be enough, but the determinants of complex processes are invariably plural and interrelated. Monocausal explanations will not work. The same values thwarted by 'bad government' at home can find opportunity elsewhere. Hence the special success of emigrant enterprise ... Meanwhile, because culture and economic performance are linked, changes in one will work back on the other" (ib.:516-7).

Inner values and attitudes guide our behaviour. Behaviour and inner values can change, but our ability to actively 'shape people' is limited. Moreover, our tendency to search for monocausal explanations makes our attempts at behavioural change unproductive. Yet, this tendency is understandable since the limited human intellect cannot oversee the multitude of interacting actors and factors at play in complex development processes. We will come back to this topic in the chapters 12 and 13.

With regard to the relation between rich and poor countries and the giving of foreign aid, Landes (ib.:523) remarks that we must be aware of "the inextricable tangle of conflicting motives and contradictory effects". Constant adjustment and correction is the only option. On the last page but one of his book, Landes (ib.) says:

"And what of the poor themselves? History tells us that the most successful cures for poverty come from within. Foreign aid can help, but like windfall wealth, can also hurt. It can discourage effort and plant a crippling sense of incapacity. As the African saying has it, 'The hand that receives is always under the one that gives'. No, what counts is work, thrift, honesty, patience, tenacity. To people haunted by misery and hunger, that may add up to selfish indifference. But at bottom, no empowerment is so effective as self-empowerment.

Some of this may sound like a collection of clichés ... Today, we condescend to such verities, dismiss them as platitudes. But why should wisdom be obsolete? To be sure, we are living in a dessert age. We want things to be sweet; too many of us work to live and live to be happy. Nothing wrong with that; it just does not promote high productivity. You want high productivity? Then you should live to work and get happiness as a by-product".

The African proverb mentioned by Landes was earlier quoted in chapter 2.2 on the phenomenon of 'aided-self-help'. The conclusion was that notwithstanding the rhetoric, dependence is unavoidable. Ultimately, the cure for poverty indeed has to come 'from within' via 'self-empowerment'.

And yes, this *is* a platitude, but only *as long as* self-empowerment is understood in its limited, superficial sense of political awareness, work ethic and so on; and *as long as* effective and efficient ways to realize self-empowerment and behavioural change are lacking. Although the superficial forms of self-empowerment are important and hitherto mostly absent in the discussion on foreign aid, a more in-depth or fundamental form of self-empowerment - consciousness development or spirituality - is needed. Only then (material, mental and spiritual) poverty reduction will come 'from within' and effectively be achieved. Philosophical and spiritual wisdom is never out of date, also not in the discussion on foreign aid and poverty reduction. We will come back to these issues.

According to me Landes' view that happiness is merely a by-product of 'live to work' - of an exaggerated, overblown work ethic - is not correct. The ultimate purpose of life *is* happiness. 'Work to live' and 'live to be happy', and high productivity, can go together. We need to find a balance between work to live and live to work.

7.3   Differences in technological base

In his book *Technology, Tradition and the State in Africa*, Goody (1971) indicates some of the economic and political implications of the basic technological differences between Eurasia and Africa. The analysis of political systems must be related to their economic possibilities, which, in turn, are dependent on technology (Goody 1971:73). The technological gap between Africa and pre-industrial, medieval Europe was between a shifting agriculture based on the hoe and an advanced agriculture based on the plough. "One of the implications of this difference between Africa and Eurasia (reinforced by the relatively poor soil and the sparseness of population) lay in land tenure, that is, in the ownership of the means of production" (ib.). African farmers owned the production factors land and labour. The concept 'feudal' of pre-industrial Europe is inappropriate to traditional African states. "The economic rights of the African rulers over land meant less than those of their European counterparts" (ib.). A social-political consequence of shifting cultivation was that "chief-ship tended to be over people rather than over land" (ib.:30). Economic control over serfs, as in medieval Europe, was less common. When the military power of the African rulers was destroyed by European conquerors in the latter part of the nineteenth century, "they had little to fall back upon except ritual status, ethnic loyalty and collaboration with the new dispensation" (ib.:73). Hyden's concept 'uncaptured peasantry' applies here, until today.

The age-old technological difference between Eurasia and Africa has important implications for the economic development of Africa. In development planning the base line or starting point must be taken into account. "Too many projections are less than realistic because they assume a general [equal] level of 'peasant agriculture' in Europe of 1850 and Africa of 1950" (ib.:74). That was certainly not the case. The small-scale technology of Eurasia was lacking in Africa and sometimes still is.

"But the corollary of these technological limitations is that a great deal can be achieved with much less. Where farming has been done with the hoe, the introduction of the [oxen-] plough can achieve a notable leap forward ... Where loads have been carried on the head, the wheel is a revolution" (ib.:75).

Goody refers, however, also to the fact that many African leaders, politicians and agricultural officers do not promote locally-made oxen-carts and ploughs, because they are not considered 'modern'. Although for example President Nyerere of Tanzania said already in 1967 that the African farmer is not ready for the tractor 'either financially or technically', animal traction never really took off.

Goody's emphasis on technological differences in means of production as well as means of destruction (weaponry) does not make him a materialistic determinist. His opinion is that technological changes are only one factor in the process of social change (ib.:76). "We must avoid not only historical particularism, but also ill-considered generalities" (ib.:16).

"[But] in the absence of wheel, plough, and all the concomitant aspects of the 'intermediate technology', Africa was unable to match the developments in productivity and skill, stratification and specialization, that marked the agrarian societies of early medieval Europe … [This absence of technology] is of critical importance in the developments of the present day" (ib.:76).

The absence of the wheel in sub-Saharan Africa not only meant that animal power could not be used, but also the power of wind and water remained untapped. It limited also the possibilities of water control for agricultural purposes (ib.:26-7). Without productivity increases in agriculture, an industrial revolution in Africa was impossible.

8 Work Ethic and Geography

In this chapter we will see that agricultural productivity in medieval Europe was probably equal to, or higher than, productivity in contemporary sub-Saharan Africa. Subsequently, Jared Diamond's book *Guns, Germs and Steel* will be briefly discussed. He emphasizes the influence of primary geographical factors on work ethic and technological development.

8.1 Crop yields in medieval Europe and present-day sub-Saharan Africa

The yield levels of wheat in some areas of Europe since the Middle Ages are presented in Table 2. As an indication of current yield levels in sub-Saharan Africa some data from Tanzania are given: the average yield level of the 3.2 million Tanzanian maize farmers in the season 1998/1999 was 850 kg/ha and the 700.000 farmers who cultivated rain-fed rice produced on average 750 kg/ha[43]. The average yield levels of grain crops in other countries in sub-Saharan Africa are today also still (far) below 1000 kg/ha. Of course, different crops and farming practices are used in Africa and Europe, and climate and soil differ. Nevertheless, it is clear that the yield levels of present-day sub-Saharan Africa were achieved already in the Middle Ages in North-Western Europe. This indicates how huge the gap in productivity level is: sub-Saharan Africa is not behind a few decades but rather many centuries. Naturally this fact does not imply that no large jumps in productivity can be made, but one has to keep in mind that significant and large scale technological change is dependent upon various other societal changes. Unfortunately, also in the field of political maturity some sub-Saharan African countries are behind centuries rather than decades.

Table 2: Average yield levels of wheat in Europe since the Middle Ages

Location	Year	Average Yield Level of Wheat in kg/ha
Winchester (England)	1200-1499	570
Merton College (England)	1333-1336	640
Grantchester (England)	1455-1465	810
Roquetoire (Northern-France)	1318-1327	860
Gosnay (Northen-France)*	1332-1343	1250
Harwell (England)*	1612-1620	1820
Klundert (Flanders)	1740-1780	1260
Dutch sea clay areas	1851-1860	1350
England	1895-1914	1970

(Source: Slicher van Bath 1977:195)

*These two yield levels are exceptionally high. Such yields became normal only at the end of the eighteenth or beginning of the nineteenth century.

8.2 Differences in geographical conditions

The systematic disciplining to labour in North-Western Europe was enforced in a complex of interdependent processes. The identification of a prime mover is impossible. Also in sub-Saharan Africa a complex of interdependent factors determines what kind of work ethic develops. These factors might include geographical circumstances, colonization and mission, degree of penetration of the money economy and ethnic-cultural factors. It is impossible to disentangle this complex in such a way that the most decisive factor can be identified. Geographical factors (for example, climate) undoubtedly play an important role. A cultural factor such as work ethic does not come up in Diamond's (otherwise very interesting) book. Probably he would label a discussion of differences in work ethic irrelevant and even racist. That is precisely why I discuss his work here. He says:

"Our present lack of ... ultimate explanations leaves a big intellectual gap, since the broadest pattern of history thus remains unexplained [broad refers here to large geographical and time scales]. Much more serious, though, is the moral gap left unfilled. It is perfectly obvious to everyone, whether an overt racist or not, that different peoples have fared differently in history ... The whole modern world has been shaped by lopsided outcomes [and Europeans and European immigrants have played a decisive role in this development]. Hence they must have inexorable explanations, ones more basic than mere details concerning who happened to win some battle or develop some invention on one occasion a few thousand years ago.

It *seems* logical to suppose that history's pattern reflects innate differences among people themselves. Of course, we're taught that it's not polite to say so in public ... We're told that [the glaring, persistent differences among people are] to be attributed not to any biological shortcomings but to social disadvantages and limited opportunities. Nevertheless, we have to wonder ... We're assured that the seemingly transparent biological explanation for the world's inequalities as of A.D. 1500 [at the start of the European voyages of discovery] is wrong, but we're not told what the correct explanation is. Until we have some convincing, detailed, agreed-upon explanation for the broad pattern of history, most people will continue to suspect that the racist biological explanation is correct after all. That seems to me the strongest argument for writing this book" (Diamond 1998:24-5).

The conclusion of Diamond's book, summarized in one sentence, is: "History followed different courses for different peoples because of differences among peoples' environments, not because of biological differences among peoples themselves" (ib.:25). He distinguishes between primary geographical factors (providing ultimate explanations) and secondary or proximate factors. The two most important geographical factors that underlie the broad pattern of history are in his view: the presence of wild plant and animal species suitable for domestication and the orientation of continental axes (predominantly west-east for Eurasia, predominantly north-south for the Americas and Africa). These continental axes affect the rate of spread of domesticated plants and animals. The most important secondary factors are: horses, guns, steel swords, the wheel, ploughs, clocks, ocean-going ships, political organization, writing, organized religion and epidemic diseases. The chains of causation lead up to proximate factors (such as guns, germs and steel), enabling some peoples to conquer other peoples, from primary geographical factors. "For example, diverse epidemic diseases of humans evolved in areas with many wild plant and animal species suitable for domestication, partly because the resulting crops and livestock helped feed dense societies in which epidemics could maintain themselves, and partly because the diseases evolved from germs of the domestic animals themselves" (ib.:86-7). According to Diamond food production was indirectly a prerequisite for the development of proximate factors. "Hence, geographic variation in whether, or when, the peoples of different continents became farmers and herders explains to a large extent their subsequent contrasting fates" (ib.:86).

According to Diamond (ib.:261) variations in three factors - time of onset of food production, extent of geographic and ecological barriers to diffusion of technology, and size of human population - led directly to the intercontinental differences in technological development. Eurasia is the world's largest landmass with the two centres where food production began the earliest (the Fertile Crescent and China). Moreover, "its east-west major axis permitted many inventions adopted in one part of Eurasia to spread relatively rapidly to societies at similar latitudes and climates elsewhere in Eurasia" (ib.:262). Eurasia, therefore, had a considerable initial advantage which "translated into a huge lead as of A.D. 1492 - for reasons of Eurasia's distinctive geography rather than of distinctive human intellect" (ib.:264).

With regard to Europe's colonization of Africa, Diamond (ib.:398) remarks that the Europeans enjoyed the triple advantage of technology (including guns), widespread literacy, and "the political organization necessary to sustain expensive programs of exploration and conquest". These three issues, however, are secondary factors and arose historically from the development of food production. Food production in sub-Saharan Africa was delayed (compared with Eurasia) by "Africa's paucity of domesticable native animal and plant species, its much smaller area suitable for indigenous food production, and its north-south axis, which retarded the spread of food production and inventions" (ib.).

"In short, Europe's colonization of Africa had nothing to do with differences between European and African peoples themselves, as white racists assume. Rather, it was due to accidents of geography and biogeography ... That is, the different historical trajectories of Africa and Europe stem ultimately from differences in real estate" (ib.:400-1).

On the last pages of his book Diamond briefly discusses the influence of cultural factors on the broad pattern of history. In his view cultural factors are history's wild cards that tend to make history unpredictable. Cultural and individual idiosyncrasies "throw wild cards into the course of history" (ib.:418-20). Cultural idiosyncrasies that initially are of little significance can evolve, however, into influential and long-lasting cultural features, whose significance constitutes an important unanswered question. "[This question] can best be approached by concentrating attention on historical patterns that remain puzzling after the effects of major environmental factors have been taken into account" (ib.:419). The unexplained residue could then be ascribed to cultural factors. They could explain differences on smaller spatial scales and over shorter times. Diamond argues that the long laundry list of independent factors behind technological innovation (a list that includes cultural factors) "actually makes it easier, not harder, to understand history's broad pattern" (ib.:251). These myriad factors convert societal variation in innovativeness into essentially a random variable. "That means that, over a large enough area (such as a whole continent) at any particular time, some proportion of societies is likely to be innovative" (ib.:254).

People tend to seek easy, single-factor explanations of historical developments. But, Diamond argues:

"Human societies [and biological systems] are extremely complex, being characterized by an enormous number of independent variables that feed back on each other. As a result, small changes at a lower level of organization can lead to emergent changes at a higher level ... Physicists and chemists can formulate universal deterministic laws at the macroscopic level, but biologists and historians can formulate only statistical trends ... [Historians are] plagued by the impossibility of performing replicated, controlled experimental interventions, the complexity arising from enormous numbers of variables, the resulting uniqueness of each system, the consequent impossibility of formulating universal laws, and the difficulties of predicting emergent properties and future behaviour.

Prediction in history ... is most feasible on large spatial scales and over long times, when the unique features of millions of small-scale brief events become averaged out. Just as I could predict the sex ratio of the next 1,000 newborns but not the sexes of my own two children, the historian can recognize [primary] factors that made inevitable the broad outcome of [history, but he cannot predict the outcome of individual events]" (ib.:422-4).

Development practitioners deal with human societies (and agricultural interventions under the umbrella of foreign aid also deal with biological systems). Their complexity and emergent properties can lead to unpredictable behaviour. Development practitioners are plagued by the same set of difficulties as historians. Realistic expectations for development interventions and modesty are thus due.

In the long run and over large areas geographical factors undoubtedly play a decisive role, as argued by Diamond. But in my view he tends to push the role of geographical factors too far at smaller spatial and time scales. At those scales cultural factors are crucial.

9 Work Ethic and Economy of Affection

The roots of Africa's underdevelopment are not found in the international system, but in the rural areas of that continent (Goran Hyden 1980:233).

According to Hyden (1983) the rural areas of sub-Saharan Africa are characterized by a *peasant mode of production*, which is linked to a peculiar type of economy: the *economy of affection*. This peasant mode of production is characterized by very little division of labour and virtually no product specialization, thus structural interdependence among farms is nonexistent (all are more or less self-sufficient) and the scope for surplus production is limited. Rural society is characterized by fragmentation: many independent farm-households operate with a high degree of autonomy (ib.:6). Because the farmers own the production factors land (or at least have the undisputed right to till it) and labour, their ability to escape state demands is large. From the point of view of individual farmers the state is superfluous. It has limited political, economic and social control over them.

"In this respect, African countries are societies without a state. The latter sits suspended in 'mid-air' over society and is not an integral mechanism of the day-to-day productive activities of society" (ib.:7).

The economy of affection throws important light on governance, policy-making and management in these societies. The economy of affection denotes "a network of support, communications and interaction among structurally defined groups connected by blood, kin, community or other affinities, for example, religion" (ib.:8). The functional purposes of this economy are basic survival, social maintenance and development. The economy of affection links together a variety of discrete farm-households which in other regards may be autonomous. "In spite of the cellular struc-ture of the production system, household units are co-operating for both productive and reproductive purposes" (ib.). This co-operation, however, tends to be *ad hoc* and informal. These co-operative ventures within the economy of affection are thus 'invisible organizations' which are readily forgotten in the development debate. Hyden's principal premise - "the peasant mode keeps alive opportunities for the rural producers to escape the demands of any given macro-economic system" - implies that the posi-tive and negative sides of the economy of affection, its opportunities and constraints, deserve more attention in the development debate (ib.:9). Ac-knowledgement that the principles of the economy of affection penetrate much of Africa's economic and social policies is required.

Since the process of proletarianization of the peasantry has not ad-vanced much in sub-Saharan Africa, the rural producers are left with "economic options outside the scope of the macro-economic system" (ib.:10). African farmers stand with one foot in the economy of affection and the other in the wider national economy. Their decisions are some-times "supportive of, at other times contrary to, macro-economic and national objectives" (ib.). The economy of affection prevails to some ex-tent over the 'rational peasant' or the western concept of 'economic man'. The invisibility and intractability of the economy of affection make it dif-ficult to measure its quantitative and qualitative impact on the national economy. Its positive side, for example, its function as a safety net for the poor, is important but the negative side of the economy of affection is un-derestimated, i.e.:

"its tendency to hold back development by delaying changes in behavioural and institutional patterns capable of sustaining economic growth at the national level. It must be accepted that the economy of affection imposes social obligations on individuals that limit their interest and capacity to support public concerns outside their community ... The potential benefits of the economy of affection are likely to be most easily discernible at the grass-roots level and in small voluntary organizations but hardly in large-scale, formal organizations based on western models of administration or management ... With political independence ... the natural tendency in most countries was to Africanize the state by taking political control of it, accelerating the appointment of Africans to senior positions, gaining control of key economic and financial institutions, and changing the rules of behaviour in public places ... The intensity of the feelings generated by the struggle [for political independence] has quite understandably guided political strategies after independence ... This inevitably meant taking a 'populist' view of things ... [resulting in] a dismantling of the colonial edifice ... What had been a [colonial] state with limited access was now turned open to a flood of popular demands ...

[The capacity of post-colonial politicians] to defend the need for organizational efficiency, strict supervision and work discipline was not very developed. The economy of affection tended to swamp the public realm ... [The post-colonial state] has created one of the most problematic paradoxes in contemporary Africa: the existence of a state with no structural roots in society which, as a balloon suspended in mid-air, is being punctured by excessive demands and unable to function without an indiscriminate and wasteful consumption of scarce societal resources. This paradox, which is clearly discernible throughout sub-Saharan Africa, tends to paralyse society ... How to resolve this paradox is perhaps the key problem facing African countries in the years to come ... There is no doubt that the public realm needs to be relieved of the strong pressures from the economy of affection. But can that be done?" (ib.:17-9).

According to Hyden (ib.:22) the post-independence rulers are left with the same challenge as their colonial predecessors: "how to capture a multitude of small producers, engulfed in the economy of affection, for the benefit of national, macro-economic objectives and concerns?". I think that the African politicians and international donors have no idea how to handle this uncaptured peasantry. More likely even, they have no idea that they are facing an uncaptured, more or less autonomous peasantry over which they have little say. They tend to focus on macro-economic issues, but the typical lack of 'trickle-down' makes that the welfare of farmers does not, or hardly, improve. Since the African state is suspended in mid-air, the macro-economic measures of its representatives (the local and international policy makers) fail to have much impact on the majority of the population, i.e., the farmers. Since the economy of affection delays "the development of a public morality that sustains effective state power" and since it promotes corruption, the development of strong nation-states and strong formal economies is hampered (ib.:29).

If the economy of affection holds back development by delaying changes in behavioural and institutional patterns, as Hyden claims, the swamping of the public realm by the economy of affection must be stopped. Remember that Hyden defined 'development' as 'changes in behavioural and institutional patterns that sustain growth' in the *Introduction* of this book. The weak formal state cannot enforce 'organizational efficiency, strict supervision and work discipline' neither in government offices nor in non-governmental workplaces. The development of a strong and effective public morality, including the work ethic, demands then new approaches to African policy and foreign aid.

Since in rural sub-Saharan Africa the economy of affection is still dominant and independent (male) farmers own the production factors land and labour, they themselves decide how much they want to work. The traditionalistic work ethic is thus a logical consequence of the economy of affection, which also functions as a safety net. Why worry about financial problems or why work hard when basic necessities are guaranteed by one's social group? A work ethic is always socially constructed.

Koponen (1995:662) says that access to land was, and is, the fundamental structural determinant of colonial and post-colonial development (or underdevelopment) in Tanzania.

"The continued access to land prevented the Africans from becoming proletarians under economic compulsion to take up wage work, and on many occasions they had to be brought to contribute their labour input in some other way ... Becoming a peasant engaged in cash crop production on one's own land, primarily with household labour, increasingly became an option ... A further option was the 'exit', perhaps more adequately called the strategy of minimum contact [with colonial agents] ... One could easily move between these three different positions - wage-labourer, peasant, and dodger - and do so either voluntarily or by being forced ... (ib.:662) ...

Both the Africans and the colonial state resisted the logic of proletarianization inherent in the process of commodification of labour power ... One matter dreaded by the great majority [of the colonialists] was proletarianization ... It was believed ... that a peasantry working the land produced 'better workers and more reliable subjects than a proletariat deprived of its property'. A peasantry was also assumed to be less prone to rebellion than a proletariat: 'A person must have owner's mood, in order not to burn and loot' [as a German colonial officer remarked in 1913] (ib.:660) ... In early colonial Africa ... the emergence of a proletariat deprived of its independent means of production was prevented by the continued access to land, and colonial land policies accepting this basic fact" (ib.:675).

If it is true that independent farmers are less inclined to rebellion than an impoverished proletariat, then this could be the reason that in sub-Saharan Africa few or no revolutions occurred. In spite of the poignant gap between the (often corrupt) rich urban elites and the poor rural population, the poor seem to have resigned themselves to their fate.

10 Work Ethic and the State

The informal economy of affection operates as a relatively powerful entity within the weak formal state. Weak formal states with many ethnic groups are continually exposed to the slumbering danger of ethnic conflicts. The fear of many African leaders for democracy (modelled on European examples) is not entirely ungrounded. Precisely because the development of nation-states in many African countries is far from completed and strong middle classes are absent, the formation of political parties along ethnic lines is natural. Hence the strong preference for one-party states in sub-Saharan Africa. It is obvious that the combination of a strong economy of affection and weak formal state easily results into corruption. A weak formal state also cannot enforce a more demanding work ethic, the main topic of this book. This has serious negative consequences for development. In this chapter the weak formal state is central.

10.1   One-party states

The weak formal state is the central topic in Van der Veen's (2004) book on the recent history of Africa. In his view the African elites, who came to power after independence, lacked a real power- and economic base within their own societies, unlike the elites in the West.

"A very few countries (Ivory Coast, Kenya and Botswana, for instance) had a black middle class, but in most African countries the elite carried on no economic activity of their own. They were entirely dependent on their control over the state apparatus bequeathed to them. For this reason, they had a supreme personal stake in safeguarding their position: their individual incomes (and, indeed, personal safety) depended on it. The elite had no choice but literally to appropriate the state. Within just a few years of independence, the two had become indistinguishable ... Politicians who lost elections forfeited their incomes ... [Via the mecha-nism of cooptation virtually all members of the elite] were united in a one-party political system which itself became fully identified with the state [resulting into one-party states].

In practice, the new elite regarded the independent state and its resources as their own property. Public revenue, part of it donated from abroad, was used not only to finance normal state expenditure ... but also to fund private consumption, co-opt rebellious compatriots and purchase and maintain a network of 'clients' ... It is true that this system of clientelism (also known as patronage) produced na-tional stability through informal networks of individuals, but it also damaged the political system. It encouraged corruption and was a major cause of the develop-ment of ever greater and less efficient bureaucracies" (Van der Veen 2004:26).

The aim in traditional African societies was economic and social security through redistribution mechanisms, not growth (ib.:77). This affected the post-colonial states. Elections in these states were "a zero-sum game where the winners took all and the losers were left empty-handed" (ib.:86). This 'winner takes all' mentality still prevails today. Most citizens do not believe that opposition parties will behave differently when they come to power. In a system of clientelism "organised mistrust in the form of a par-liament or a free press has no place": the opposition is regarded as the enemy (ib.:101). The Nigerian historian Claude Ake argues that poverty reduction and national development are by no means the main priorities of African governments. "Given their fragile political and economic power bases, they [have] what they [see] as higher priorities than development" (ib.:293).

In addition, the Western representatives of donors mainly deal with rep-resentatives of the local elites, and both inhabit "a world far removed from the everyday lives of ordinary Africans" (ib.:294). The local elites operate in a double web as a link between domestic African networks and interna-tional circles of donors; they are spiders in two webs. Since the beginning

of the new millennium the World Bank and IMF encourage African ownership.

"After all, development could only succeed if Africans themselves took the lead.
However, this theoretical argument entirely failed to take account of the political
conditions in African countries. The national elites, who were the main contacts
for the international financial institutions, were not in a position to make development their priority. That would have required a fundamental shift in Africa's
political culture (at the very least) ... [The necessary reforms would] inevitably
erode the power base of the ruling elites. This was one of the many fundamental
dilemmas facing African states; if they wanted to make social and economic progress, they had to make decisions that would ultimately undermine the authority
of the decision-makers. It is no wonder that African rulers preferred talk to action"
(ib.:303-4).

The problematic nature of African ownership is clearly exposed by Van
der Veen.

10.2   Four long-term features of pre-colonial African societies

The donors saw the progressive disintegration of state institutions in the
two to three decades after independence increasingly as the number one
African development problem (ib.:79). The introduction of modern states
in the colonial days and the following Africanisation of these states after
independence resulted into a fragile process of state formation. However,
we cannot fully comprehend this inadequate state formation if we look no
further than the colonial era and the subsequent decades. According to Van
der Veen (ib.:351) the erosion of the postcolonial states, their hollowing
out from within, is mainly due to "age-old African principles of political
culture, political economy and social relations. They date back to well before the days of European colonialism in Africa, although they were

sometimes profoundly influenced by it". He mentions four of those under-lying, long-term features.

The first one is the earlier mentioned patron-client relationship, which is difficult to reconcile with rule of law. "[Such relationships] undermine the work of government and people's trust in the state" (ib.:353). The cru-cial importance of societal trust for economic development has been indicated before. The pre-colonial, authoritarian attitude of African rulers towards their subjects was reinforced by colonialism. "In the preceding centuries, in most parts of the world rulers' power had gradually been re-duced by the separation of powers and systems of checks and balances, but in Africa the trend was just the opposite" (ib.).

The second traditional feature is the all-pervasiveness of power, also re-inforced by colonialism. The patron can exercise power in all areas of life; political, economic, social, etc. Separation between public and private spheres is non-existent. This is related to the collectivist nature of African cultures. The third crucial set of features could be labelled pre-modernism, which implies a static perspective on the world and society. The long-term aim is maintaining the status quo through redistribution, but nevertheless short-term events (the ripples of the broad pattern of history) might create a dynamic impression.

"In pre-modern systems, change was not valued, since economic growth was not an end in itself, as it is in modern societies. Instead, investment was seen in terms of redistributing existing resources ... The emphasis was on consumption rather than production. There was no general awareness of a link between consumption and modern industrial production, which requires a certain work ethic, organisa-tion and discipline" (ib.:352)[44].

The emphasis on status quo is related to the short-term orientation of Afri-can cultures. In the age of globalisation, competition is becoming more and more important and the lingering pre-industrial habits bring about relative decline in Africa (ib.). The fourth underlying feature is the tenacity of sub-national 'ethnic' feelings (ethnicity), having their origin in the pre-colonial period but also often reinforced and frozen in place by European colonial authorities. "In some African countries ethnic affiliations are so strong that they undercut national identity" (ib.:354).

These four features of the pre-colonial societies increasingly influenced after independence the modern state, a foreign body that was superimposed by Europeans. Although the four features are far from uniquely African and partly a colonial legacy, the problems of the colonial state (no separation of powers, power concentrated in the capital and interwovenness of political and economic interests) were certainly exacerbated by the new African rulers (ib.).

"Africa is so large and varied that not one of the features mentioned can fairly be said to be found in every African country or people ... Europeans have 'traditionally' been quick to call various African phenomena traditions ... [While this] indicates the need for the utmost caution when identifying 'African traditions', it does not rule out the existence of African ways of life that truly do predate colonialism" (ib.:354-5).

According to Van der Veen (ib.:355) the erosion of the inherited modern state followed "a fairly consistent pattern, which after about twenty-five years [after independence] culminated in general dysfunction, along with financial and moral bankruptcy". Zimbabwe became independent in 1980 only and the Africanisation of the state is now completed, as reflected in President Mugabe's authoritarian style of leadership and its financial bankruptcy (ib.:356).

Probably the Africanisation of the state is a necessary step in the modernisation process, but the question is now how to advance the further

emancipation of the state. The state must become emancipated from society, but if the colonial state and society at the time of independence were
not intertwined to start with, how can one be emancipated from the other?
It is precisely the Africanisation of the state since independence which has
"at least managed to bring the state and society together in a cultural
sense" (ib.:368). The further emancipation of the state will only succeed
"if the people of Africa are the driving force behind it. Democratisation
and economic improvement is still the key" (ib.).

10.3   Ownership and bottom-up institutional innovation

Words as democratisation, decentralisation (in actual practice often limited
to deconcentration), empowerment and good governance are central in the
contemporary debate on foreign aid; and all this under the umbrella of
'ownership'. However, the thorniest problem affecting development cooperation is the unequal status of donors and recipient countries. The
fundamental inequality between developing countries and international
donors touches "on both the politics and the psychology of the relationship
between rich and poor" (ib.:296). Although inadequate ownership by African countries is now considered the main reason for the ineffectiveness of
aid, the fundamental question remains to what extent donors can hand over
ownership to recipient countries (ib.:297).

"Ownership was surely something individuals had or took, rather than something
they were given. The term 'ownership' concealed a contradiction in terms ... The
term may have masked the fundamental imbalance of power but it did nothing to
correct it ... [Ownership] was clearly prompted less by enthusiasm for the freedom to set policy priorities than by the desire to persuade developing countries to
accept externally prescribed policies as their own ... The dialogue [between donors and recipients] was to continue to take the form of negotiations. Donors

could not dictate terms to the recipient country, nor could they simply give the recipients whatever they wanted ... Ownership may have been a necessary requirement for development, but it was by no means sufficient. Donors could not support poor policy decisions, no matter how firmly recipients stood behind them" (ib.:297-302).

In order to boost African ownership donors in recent years invested heavily in capacity-building. Poor oversight of authorities in many African countries posed a serious problem and good governance (including financial accountability) was difficult to achieve. "As a result, more ownership in the long term sometimes required more donor intervention in the short term. This illustrated the fluid nature of ownership" (ib.:303). Despite these investments in capacity-building, the question of ownership and sound economic strategies remains problematic.

"After all, a new economic policy could achieve little without sufficient attention to political and cultural factors, such as the way institutions worked (or failed to work). Moreover, these political and cultural factors could not be influenced by the international financial institutions; money was of little relevance. The World Bank and the IMF could not override the internal workings of African society, despite all their knowledge of what constituted good policy" (ib.).

This shows that foreign aid can do relatively little to improve the performance of weak formal states, despite the rhetoric on ownership by donors and African rulers. It also indicates that cultural factors are of overriding importance.

Also in The Netherlands the development of nation-state, civil society and economy was closely interwoven (van Zanden and van Riel 2000). Economic and social-political transformations intertwine in complex interactions between markets and institutions (ib.:20, 25). Moreover, these processes take much time. Since sub-Saharan Africa is far behind in economic and social-political development, the potential impact of foreign aid must be seen in its proper context. However, many Western (and African) policy-makers and development workers do not seem to recognize the complex nature of the development process and are not familiar with the long history of European development.

The state is the first layer in the institutional framework of an economy, while interest groups (pressure or lobby groups or civil society) constitute the second layer (ib.:22). In The Netherlands a phase of spontaneous, bottom-up institutional innovation, starting after 1870, laid the foundation of the corporative structures which would become so characteristic of the fast economic development in the twentieth century. These new corporative institutions included labour unions, farmers' organizations, employers' organizations, etc. The elites in sub-Saharan Africa do not face such countervailing power. The economy of affection with its patron-client relationships and the absence of an effective civil society make that elites more or less undisturbed can go their own way. Bottom-up institutional innovation has not got off the ground yet: effective interest groups (for instance farmers' unions) hardly exist in sub-Saharan Africa.

The rise of mechanized industry and modern economic growth changed the character of labour in The Netherlands (see also Chang in chapter 17). Labourers were gradually subjected to the discipline of factory work, but industrial entrepreneurs had to pay considerably higher wages to convince labourers to substitute factory work for home work (at farms or in the cottage industry): the so-called 'premium to discipline' (ib.:302). The gradual move from 'daily pay' to 'merit pay' implied that the reward of the subject (the labourer) with his specific needs to sustain a family was replaced with the reward of the object (the actually delivered labour). Day labourers had to get accustomed to performance-related pay: labour became a commodity - the commodification of labour (ib.:307). At the same time, however, this process increased labour productivity and real wages almost doubled between 1855 and 1880 - after centuries of systematic decline in real wages. For the first time in Dutch history the standard of living of the population substantially improved (ib.:308,316). This shows that within a few decades the standard of living can significantly improve (as Chang will argue in chapter 17), but only after certain conditions are met.

The improvement of the standard of living in The Netherlands, for example, was accompanied by a large number of factors: the process of disciplining to labour, high-quality primary school education, a relatively modern agricultural sector, gradual political emancipation of labourers and farmers, the emergence of a new civil society, etc. The complexity of this historical process makes fast improvements in the standard of living in sub-Saharan Africa not very likely. The political emancipation of the small farmers in sub-Saharan Africa, the majority of the population, has hardly begun. Formal suffrage exists, but the degree of organisation and the political and economic power of small farmers (their countervailing power) are minimal.

The liberal middle class in The Netherlands started a largely spontaneous 'civilization offensive' to 'educate' the poor and needy. The middle class attempted to impose on the poor requirements of order, neatness, laboriousness, thrift and devotion to duty. The middle class wanted to educate the poor to full citizens (ib.:319). The miserable living- and working conditions of the poor were considered largely a moral problem that could be solved by changes in morals, for instance via the cultivation of thrift and hygiene. This civilization offensive started in the last quarter of the eighteenth century and was, in the long run, effective. It led to a sharp decline in mortality rate, alcohol abuse and also in the number of illegitimate children (ib.:322). In sub-Saharan Africa only recently a small middle class emerged and a civilization offensive has not taken place yet. Although some religious groups and NGOs strive after an 'education' of the population, their impact hitherto has been limited. Excessive alcohol consumption, for example, is still quite common. Since the cultivation of neatness, laboriousness and thrift in The Netherlands (and other Western countries) has been a long-term process, it would be advisable to start this process in sub-Saharan Africa as soon as possible.

As indicated before, the process of institutional innovation in The Netherlands was bottom-up and spontaneous, without government interference. Farmers' unions in the Southern part of the country, for example, were initiated by the lower Catholic clergy, the priests in the countryside (ib.:322). The well-known dilemma in collective action is that large groups of people collectively have to decide to go for potentially risky attitudinal change (ib.:323). In such cases access to reliable informal information about the members of these groups is crucial, for example to judge the creditworthiness of farmers. Small groups of farmers and priests in the country had this kind of information. If, at all, farmers' unions and agricultural co-operatives were established in sub-Saharan Africa after independence, then they were initiated and controlled by government. Such top-down approaches were and are not effective. The recent proliferation of national and international NGOs in sub-Saharan Africa can only partially fill the void of civil society organizations, also because some NGOs do not truly represent the farmers' voice.

In 1896 the Dutch Farmers' Union was founded and in 1917 already more than 1.000 agricultural loan banks had been established (in just two decades). The new organizations in the country had economic as well as social-political functions (respectively co-operations and farmers' unions focussing on political lobbying) (ib.:415). A crucial issue in The Netherlands was the presence in the country of sufficient individuals who acted as initiators and facilitators, for example priests and schoolteachers who were both idealistic and pragmatic. The dire situation of small farmers in sub-Saharan Africa indicates that such focal points are not yet sufficiently at hand, the political opposition of the ruling elites is too strong and/or the degree of organization of farmers is too small.

At present micro-credit is a hot issue in development cooperation. Micro-credit is often allocated to small groups, not individual persons, so that the mechanism of social control can take care of repayment of loans: if one person does not pay back, the whole group is held accountable. In the view of the Indian banker Thallam Balaji micro-credit is not just credit, it is a method to teach people self-control.

"Discipline is the magic word and discipline irrevocably leads to self-respect. Poor people have only their character as collateral. No house, no land, nothing that the bank can sell to compensate for non-settled debts. Only the character of the debtor counts. The ability to forgo quick pleasures must be learned. That is the deeper meaning of micro-credit: people must learn to control themselves"[45].

Terms as 'civilization offensive' or changes in morals, discipline and self-control are not popular in the academic development debate, because of their moralistic or sermonizing undertone. As Landes remarked in chapter 7.2 these words sound like clichés or platitudes. Nevertheless, he says, such wisdom is not obsolete and self-empowerment is crucial. In my view the main question is whether effective and efficient methods to induce behavioural change are available.

10.4   The soft and hard state

Agriculture-based economic development in sub-Saharan Africa is not easy to realize, because of the very limited countervailing power of small farmers and the yawning gap (in economic, political and cultural sense) between these farmers and the urban elites. For example: during the last five years of the administration of President Benjamin Mkapa of Tanzania

(1995-2005) the average economic growth was 5.8 percent. But since 1995 Tanzania dropped to position 164 on the development list of the UNDP (total number of countries on the list is 177). The largest part of the population did not benefit from the economic growth. This is logical, according to Mkapa, because growth took place in mainly mining and tourism. Not in agriculture, the sector on which eighty percent of the population depends. Mkapa recommends his successor to make agriculture the absolute priority of government[46]. This is truly 'passing the buck' since even the first president of Tanzania, Julius Nyerere, declared already in 1968 that development should be based on agriculture. Nyerere also remarked that "through the hard work of people production of food and cash crops could be increased" (in: van Cranenburgh 1990:100). Here 'the father of the nation' stresses thus that development without hard work is no option.

The doctoral thesis of Oda van Cranenburgh (*The Widening Gyre. The Tanzanian One-Party State and Policy towards Rural Cooperatives*) concerns the problematic relation between farmers and the state.

"The apparent freedom of the government to change policies and their radical implementation we could call autonomy in policy-making or 'hardness' of the state. The state, thus, may appear 'strong' in its ambitious policy aims and rigorous - frequently authoritarian - style of policy implementation ... However, it would constitute a serious mistake to equate this type of state autonomy or 'hardness' with a state capacity actually to achieve its goals - i.e. with state strength ... Thus we should not infer from this type of autonomy of the government in policy-making an ability actually to steer societal developments in the direction envisaged ... Given the degree of autonomy farmers possessed *vis-à-vis* the state, they still retained a certain room for maneuver despite the policies implemented by the government ...

The same institutions which allowed the party-based policy-makers a great freedom to by-pass societal preferences (thus leading to authoritarian tendencies) did not allow inducements for farmers (and in some cases even local government officers) to comply, thus limiting the effect of government policies [the soft aspect of the state] ... Through the institutions of the one-party state, the distance between the Tanzanian farmers and the state has increased. Instead of linking the state with rural society, the party aided in increasing the distance between them ... Thus, the 'soft' and 'hard' aspects of the Tanzanian state are two sides of the same coin, both resulting from the lack of representation of the interests of common farmers in the policy process" (van Cranenburgh 1990:212-21).

According to van Cranenburgh the Tanzanian state was simultaneously hard and soft. This is still the case today. The hard aspect of authoritarian policy-formulation and implementation can only change when farmers succeed in enhancing their countervailing power. The soft aspect of limited actual impact of the state on the behaviour of farmers can change when via this countervailing power farmers' interests will be truly accommodated. They will then respond positively to the enabling environment created by the state. However, since the material and mental gap between the (as yet unorganised) farmers and the ruling elites is very large and elites normally do not give up their privileged positions voluntarily, it is not clear how this gap can be bridged peacefully. If the current political parties cannot bridge the gap between farmers and state, who can? The present stalemate in the relation between farmers and state remains thus troublesome.

The one-party state with its claimed intra-party democracy - the democracy within one party which supposedly is grounded in African traditional forms of consensus building - proved less democratic than expected. The net result was that the great majority of the population, the millions of unorganised farmers, were continuously neglected. The Tanzanian ideology of *ujamaa*-socialism, in which equality in the *ujamaa*-villages was central, did not improve the position of the masses (the masses, in fact, were many farmers and only a few labourers). Nyerere defined *ujamaa*-socialism as an 'attitude of mind' and emphasized that Tanzanians had to regain their former attitude of mind, their traditional African socialism (van Cranenburgh:96) (see also chapter 2.2).

"*Ujamaa* - 'familyhood' - meant that every individual found security in the community ... Nyerere used the concept of *Ujamaa* despite the fact that it traditionally only concerned the (extended) family unit. He implied that the principles of *Ujamaa* held throughout the tribe, which is disputed. He did argue for an extension of the concept of ujamaa [up to the level of the nation and even beyond]" (ib.:95-6).

Ujamaa-socialism, however, remained a vague utopia. Changing an attitude of mind is apparently not so easy. Hyden (1980:98) says about the *ujamaa*-ideology:

"Nyerere [tried] with his *ujamaa* ideology to develop the philosophical underpinnings of the economy of affection and formalize them into a nationwide strategy of development. He [was] trying to universalize the unwritten rules of living within rural households and apply them to larger social and economic forms of organization with modern objectives".

According to Hyden (1980,1983) the main cause of the weak state is the economy of affection, which results into an uncaptured peasantry with exit-options. The one-party state and its authoritarian style of politics represent in his view "desperate attempts by African elites to gain control in the face of their structural lack of power" (in: van Cranenburgh 1990:48). As a matter of fact, the formal state remains at the mercy of the farmers' informal economy of affection. At the same time the numerous and dispersed farmers in the country find it difficult to organize themselves and thus exercise influence over government policies (the earlier mentioned dilemma of collective action). "Potential pay-offs of organization are small for individual farmers and the chance of success is remote" (ib.:50). With regard to the gap between farmers and the (socialist) state and the enforcement of a modern work ethic, Hyden (1980) says:

"An enhanced contradiction between the peasantry and those who control the state is a pre-condition for development in Africa, capitalist or socialist. Even countries with a revolutionary ambition, like Mozambique, cannot escape this dilemma, particularly as long as the national economy suffers from poor management as a result of shortage of manpower and indiscipline among workers (ib.:203) [This text of Hyden is from 1980 when Frelimo was still pursuing a socialist policy] ... To expect self-discipline - the internalization of a modern work ethic - to develop more quickly under socialist forms of production is illusory in a society where pre-socialist forces still predominate ... The inevitable but unenviable task of socialist leaders [is] to subordinate other people to the demands of modern economic enterprise: to impose authority and discipline but at the same time find an ideological justification for their exercise of power" (ib.:223).

The formal 'hard' state and the ruling elites did not manage to impose a modern work ethic. Politicians' rhetoric on the importance of hard work got bogged down in their weak capacity to influence the population and to actually change behaviour. The apparent paradox of a simultaneously hard and soft (authoritarian and weak) state results from terminological ambiguity (see also chapter 4.1). An authoritarian or 'hard-handed' state is not necessarily effective in its attempts to impose behavioural change and thus cannot be called 'strong'. Autonomy in policy formulation is no guarantee for success in policy implementation (van Cranenburgh 1990:51).

11 Work Ethic and Mimetic Desire

The core issues in the work of the philosopher Thomas Hobbes are greed, envy and competition (in order to have more than others) (Achterhuis 1988:21). According to Hobbes happiness is a never ending movement, an incessant prolongation of desire. In his view desire is unlimited because we are entangled in a permanent comparison with others (ib.:34). The other person is continuously obstacle and reference material. We want to have or achieve something simply because others also want to have or achieve it. Between the subject and the object - that the subject wants to acquire - one always finds fellow man as obstacle and reference material; it is a triangular relation. Precisely because of this triangular relation almost everything in the universe of Hobbes becomes scarce. By definition there is never enough (ib.:24). Society is considered a kind of gigantic zero-sum-game, in which one person's gain is another person's loss. This triangular relation is the underlying principle of scarcity: scarcity has primarily to do with the relation between people.

The French philosopher René Girard speaks of mimesis or mimicry and this inclination to imitate is a human characteristic. Mimicry becomes dangerous, however, in the mimetic desire, in the unbounded desire as described by Hobbes: man preferably desires what fellow man desires. Hobbes characterizes 'the natural condition of man' as 'a war of all against all' (Achterhuis 1988:45,48). Why does not the collective mimetic struggle for objects lead to overt violence then? The answer is money: via money the equivalent of a desired object can be bought without having to fight with the other; the other is no longer an obstacle but just a model to be imitated. Money has thus a violence-controlling function. According to Adam Smith exchange (or the exchange-value) functions as a peace-making mechanism (ib.:56). Smith's 'invisible hand' is the constructive foundation of modern society.

However, scarcity appears continuously at higher and different levels via the unlimited process of mimetic desire. Or, in other words, man searches for happiness beyond a moving horizon (ib.:118). The typical discomfort in modern Western society is an unfulfilled and forever unfulfillable desire for something else - the persistent and restless desire, the eternal carrousel of the mimetic desire (ib.:145). The inescapable mimetic confrontation with fellow man makes (complete) liberation from desire illusory. Appeals to self-restraint and austerity lead at worst to impotent moralism, while at best they will be conceived as very unattractive options (ib.:108).

According to Otto Duintjer (1988c) we live in a 'structurally expansive society' in which the modern production system has become autonomous through the historically unique interwovenness of science, technology and industry. The system has become an end in itself and is merely directed to its own expansion. A structurally expansive society demands a modern work ethic and results into a very busy life characterized by a continuous lack of time. To step out of this rat race is not easy. It requires a mental (or spiritual) level of development in which status and societal recognition are no longer central, but higher values dominate. Maslow labelled it the phase of self-actualisation. For the time being I just want to say that liberation from the mimetic desire is possible via effective techniques for consciousness development.

Countries in sub-Saharan Africa are less egalitarian than Western societies. Large differences in economic and political power exist between men and women, old and young people, elites and lower classes, and city and countryside. This implies that the mimetic confrontation with fellow man is less than in Western countries. The self-evident inequality, the matter-of-course acceptance of a lower societal position and lower level of material welfare, the acceptance of one's lot and the sometimes indifferent attitude reduce mimetic confrontation. The restricted mimetic desire of many Africans may show up in an attitude of 'take it easy'.

The process of the unending mimetic desire in the West is linked to the Western work ethic. Without a modern work ethic the mimetic process cannot rise to such heights. After all, we can desire things which other persons have, yet we will have to work to earn the money to buy these goods and services. Work ethic and mimetic desire are thus inextricably intertwined. In sub-Saharan Africa the traditionalistic work ethic prevails, one works to live and generally speaking the mimetic desire functions at a lower level. One can accept the principle of the mimetic desire as a fact of life and even promote it, or one can attempt to fight or prevent it, but one cannot ignore it. That would be a denial of one of the largest contemporary problems (Achterhuis 1988:177). Instead of actively promoting the mimetic desire, as happens in Western consumption society, transcending this desire via techniques for consciousness development would, in my view, be more appropriate.

Mimesis plays also a role in foreign aid. Foreign aid by multi- and bilateral donors and NGOs can reinforce mimesis. The Western model that is imitated does not necessarily have evil intentions. The mimetic desire also works without evil intentions or hidden interests. Bad enough, also aid given with the best of intentions falls under the theory of mimetic desire (ib.:335). Aid given without any hidden motives does not automatically have positive effects (ib.:336). In addition to foreign aid, other factors have contributed to mimesis: Western colonisation and mission, training abroad, and television and other modern communication technology. Mimesis occurred long before the NGOs entered the stage, but their jargon, focussed on participation and local ownership, can effectively conceal mimesis. In sub-Saharan Africa fake-NGOs operate which are mainly established to get hold of donor funds by the smart use of up-to-date development jargon.

In Tanzania government is often depicted as the father (the model) who must help his children to grow up. Julius Nyerere was called *mwalimu* (teacher) and father of the nation. Politicians as well as rural people speak in such terms about higher authorities. On the part of the farmers this is on the one hand mere rhetoric to obtain as much as possible free government support; on the other hand the farmers know that they are largely independent of the same government within their economy of affection. Politicians and public servants, however, often speak naively about the necessity to 'educate' the population as if the millions of small farmers cannot take care of themselves. The fact that these farmers are more or less autonomous and largely outside the sphere of influence of government, does not seem to get across to these officials. Government at least does not explicitly recognize this as a problem.

African governments as well as donors have contributed to erosion of traditional social structures in the country by providing grants and loans (which are often identical concepts in sub-Saharan Africa). The positive aspect of the economy of affection (its function as safety net) is undermined, but the negative aspect (farmer independence) persists. For example: in the past crop failures were counteracted by community solidarity, but now government, donors and NGOs are often asked to provide (free) food aid.

Foreign aid can stimulate mimesis in which corrupt politicians and civil servants act as models. Although the mimetic desire in general is relatively low in sub-Saharan Africa, especially within local elites mimetic confrontation and desire can run high. The process of mimetic desire is clearly visible in the building of large, luxury houses by corrupt politicians and civil servants. The rule seems to be: the bigger, the better. The number of rooms in the house determines the status. These very expensive houses, built with stolen money, are very visible, so why would the rest of the population observe rules of law?

Experience teaches that the unbridled, unconscious (or subconscious) mimetic process increasingly leads to scarcity (of leisure time, pure air, clean water, mineral resources, peace of mind, etc.). One can attempt to guide mimesis in a positive direction by the conscious use of mimesis: the conscious choice of models without lapsing into the process of negative mimetic desire. The last process, however, is difficult to circumvent. Probably unconscious (and thus often negatively oriented) mimetic desire can only be fully transcended via techniques for consciousness development.

The continuing Westernization of the world via the process of (largely unconscious) mimesis is a fact of life. This mimesis impacts development cooperation between the West and sub-Saharan Africa. In Western consumption society the vicious circle of structurally expansive economic growth, initiated by the mimetic desire and an overdone work ethic, needs to be broken. Societies in sub-Saharan Africa, for their part, need to adopt a middle course between the overdone Northwest-European work ethic and their traditionalistic attitude towards work.

12 Mimetic Desire, Front Runner Model and Belief in the Technological Fix

The great majority of Dutch farmers are more or less automatically drawn into the maelstrom of continual modernization and scale-up. A small group of ecological farmers have demonstrated that some 'space for manoeuvre' to follow your own path is always available, in spite of great societal pressure to go along with the mainstream. Nevertheless, only very few individuals have the guts, endurance and strength to do this. In a structurally expansive society also agriculture is mainly concerned with its own expansion. Although Dutch front runner farms face many problems (one of them is their contribution to environmental pollution), these problems seem to accelerate their continuous expansion. The group of front runner farms becomes smaller and smaller: the ones that cannot compete anymore are pushed out. It is a true rat race (Van der Ploeg 1987:99).

The front runner model is underpinned by Cochrane's (1958) 'agricultural treadmill' in which front runners or early innovators capture wind-fall profits, while later adopters are forced to adopt the same new technology (or quit farming altogether) when productivity gains are passed on to agribusiness and consumers in the form of lower prices. The treadmill, the whiplash of competition, moves the individual farmers relentlessly on. The front runners get into a vicious circle of continuing growth and increasing debts. In the glutted markets a zero-sum-game develops: the costs of continuing growth are increasingly shifted on to other farmers. Fierce competition develops and once common interests start diverging (Van der Ploeg 1987:95-6). Since most farmers (and the research institutes, extension organizations, farmer unions, industry and government) have internalized the front runner model, it becomes a self-fulfilling prophecy. Farmers think (and are told) that continuing scientization is the only option to survive. In this way the front runner model is made reality, regardless of the consequences. The model as such does not have internal limits to in-cessant expansion; it lacks a normative framework and the model itself has become the dominant norm (ib.:99,108).

Technological innovation implies an in-time increasing pressure or co-ercion to apply it (Renkema 1986). When dairy farmers through technological innovation intensify their production, the increased milk supply lowers the price which in turn requires farm adjustments. A vicious circle of price changes and farm adjustments, in which causes and effects continuously interchange place, is the result. The two causes that keep the vicious circle going are technological innovation and diverging interests with regard to the most desirable volume of production - the individual producer and the group of dairy farmers as a whole hold differing interests (ib.). The vicious circle cannot be broken easily and the tendency is to look for solutions in 'more of the same'.

In spite of the irrationality of incessant production increases and the negative side-effects, the front runner model as such, until recently, was not questioned. One of the results is that overproduction and hunger occur simultaneously, as they are linked by a complex system of export subsi-dies, tariff walls, market liberalisation and globalisation. This description of the front runner model reveals a societal inescapability. Both the psy-chological principle of the mimetic desire (farmers do not want to be surpassed by other farmers) and the ensuing societal pressure to join the rat race find expression in the front runner model. This model requires also a modern work ethic. The internalization of the front runner model is linked to the internalization of a work ethic that relentlessly propagates hard work.

Transplanting the Western front runner model to sub-Saharan Africa (if, at all, effective competition in the world market is possible) would have disastrous consequences. It might push millions of resource-poor farmers out of agricultural production while no alternative employment opportunities are available. The current emphasis on global competition and decreasing public investments, as the best strategy to achieve global food security and sustainable agriculture, makes it very difficult for African smallholders to build up a livelihood. They are not able to compete with Western products, which after decades of public investments in agricultural education, extension and research, in land consolidation and farm reorganization, in agricultural subsidies, etcetera, have gained a nearly unapproachable position.

Is it possible for man to diminish or circumvent greed and envy, to collectively give up the mimetic struggle? We need to test Gandhi's famous saying that there is enough for everyone's need, but not for everyone's greed. Achterhuis (1988:341) says that this statement is correct, but also a half truth, an incomplete analysis, because the main cause of hunger is attributed to the greed of individual Western man, while the role of societal structures is ignored. The other extreme is to put all the blame on societal structures, on the intangible economic and political set-up of the world order. The two obvious remedies for the hunger problem that are often proposed are then to reduce the over-consumption of Western man (to limit Western needs) and/or to put pressure on governments and private companies to change policies and structures.

The front runner model has contributed to a European agricultural policy which harms farmers in less developed countries via export subsidies, income support for European farmers, import quota, etc. A runaway European agricultural policy, to a degree, shifts on to less developed countries the costs of continuing growth, the so-called externalities. The externalities (in fact internalities in a wider systems perspective) are passed on to third parties: to the Third World or other disadvantaged groups or the environment. If the mimetic desire is a psychological as well as societal mechanism, then fighting it demands changes in individual actors as well as collective structures. But inadequately performing structures, ultimately, are shaped by individuals with a largely unconscious (negatively oriented) mimetic desire which has gone astray. At the same time, however, individual behavioural change (by control of one's mimetic desire) is difficult to realize because of the pressure of the societal context to join the rat race.

The world food problem is embedded in issues of distribution of power and ultimately in the process of the mimetic desire. It is the invisible hand of Adam Smith which makes that individuals who all follow their own mimetic desire - every man for himself - nevertheless create societal welfare (Achterhuis 1988:57). Via the trickle-down-effect also the lower classes would benefit. While the 'invisible hand' undeniably advances the welfare of competing rivals and larger society, there is also an 'invisible foot' (Ophuls 1977:168). This invisible foot kicks third parties in the gutter (Achterhuis 1988:218). Very few people want to harm these third parties intentionally: personal moral intentions and societal consequences are not directly related. But modern Western society is characterized by a large tension between individual and society, between personal morals and collective policy (ib.:213).

The invisible hand and foot pass on externalities to third parties; in addition to the Third World and the environment, this can be lower social classes and women. The rural women in rain-fed farming systems on relatively poor soils in sub-Saharan Africa are in fact fourfold victims of the invisible hand and foot. Firstly they are women in a man-dominated society, secondly they live in the Third World, thirdly they must survive in relatively fragile ecosystems and fourthly they belong to the class of rural people. An example of the invisible foot is the subsidized export of Western agricultural products to sub-Saharan Africa, which pushes local farmers out of the market. Female farmers and their young children are often hit hardest by the invisible hand and foot. Within Europe especially the environment and agricultural animals are third parties which suffer the negative consequences of the invisible foot. The invisible hand and foot cannot operate without the modern work ethic.

One of the most troublesome issues in the development of sub-Saharan Africa is the ongoing destruction of potential capacities of young children by under- and malnourishment. Inadequate nutrition (in a quantitative and/or qualitative sense) of millions of young children keeps on eating away at their potential capacities. Prakash Shetty, a nutrition expert at FAO, says:

"It's an axiom of development to say that women are the linchpin of sustainable growth. The research on foetal undernutrition reinforces that message, because what hunger does to a foetus will shackle the adult to ill-health for life"[47].

The suboptimal development of a considerable part of the young children (in- and outside the womb) could be one of the most important causes of lagging development in sub-Saharan Africa. And this cannot be compensated by high quality nutrition and education at later age. The *prevention* of damage to potential capacity should be top priority. All investments at later age in curative interventions (such as improved nutrition, healthcare and education) are partly wasted money. The importance of human capital - not only its physiological aspect but also its psychological, social and spiritual facets - simply cannot be overrated.

Inadequate nutrition obviously also affects the quantity and quality of labour. Working hard on an empty stomach is not easy. According to Hans Eenhoorn, member of the United Nations Millennium Taskforce on Hunger, chronically underfed people are too hungry to work and too poor to eat[48]. In addition to the about 200 million chronically underfed people in Africa, many are affected by the phenomenon of 'hidden hunger'. Lack of vitamins and minerals slows down physical and mental development; the IQ lags behind for example by lack of iodine which affects one in three children in Africa. The intellectual capacity at birth will never material-ize[49].

The world food problem is not a technological problem. Agricultural experts and farmers do know how to produce sufficient food of high quality for all people on the planet. We have seen that one of the boosters of the vicious circle in the front runner model is the so-called 'autonomous' technology development. This technology development results in continuous productivity increases (per labour-day, unit of land and capital). The invisible hand in the modern economy is partly grounded in autonomous technology development, which results into a belief in a technological fix for all problems, including the hunger problem. This one-sided and sometimes destructive belief in a technological fix can be left behind when we realize that technology, ultimately, is socially constructed. It is always work of man.

Technology, which sometimes can degrade man and animal, is socially constructed and therefore can, in principle, be rectified or undone by man. But modern agricultural science has not been very successful yet in the realization of ecological and societal sustainability; and agricultural extension and education have not been very effective in changing behaviour. Fagan (1995) says similar things about medical science and health education:

"According to the U.S. Surgeon General, the majority of diseases is self-induced and as much as 80% of medical problems can be prevented through behavioural or lifestyle change (ib.:61) [With regard to education and behaviour modification, Fagan remarks:] The basic problem with the preventive approaches now in use is that they work on a level that is too superficial. Educational programs ... are not powerful enough to change the behaviour patterns and environmental conditions that cause disease. If external pressure is the primary influence in modifying behaviour, then the deeper problems that initially gave rise to that behaviour will manifest in some other way, causing other problems. The pressures that cause people to smoke often induce other harmful behaviours - overeating for example - if individuals are deprived, or deprive themselves, of tobacco (ib.:65) ...

For interventions to be successful, they need to work from a level much more fundamental than education or behavioural manipulation. The strategy of addressing risk factors one-by-one is a natural outgrowth of the objective, reductionistic scientific approach, upon which modern medicine relies (ib.:66) ... Health is not a function of the properties of isolated components of the physiology, but rather of the balanced, integrated functioning of the whole ... By attempting to deal with health piecemeal, medicine has been reduced to an unending exercise in correcting symptoms (ib.:73) ... [Medical] thinking has not been sufficiently comprehensive and coherent ... Physicians...have focused on progressively more isolated values of the physiology in their attempts to preserve and restore health. The move to dangerous and destructive genetic therapies is the logical and most extreme outgrowth of this trend (ib.:95) ...

Knowledge generated through the current scientific paradigm unavoidably creates side effects. This same paradigm creates a style of thinking in which society is willing to accept the damage caused by side effects as the unavoidable price that we must pay for 'progress'. In the final analysis, using this approach by itself will only perpetuate the problem" (ib.:17). [We must give up 'dreams of magic bullet, high-tech approaches' and enhance our capacity to make wiser, more far-sighted decisions] (ib.:99).

Ecological and societal sustainability do not go together with autonomous technology development, because this technology can produce unwanted side-effects. Yet science and technology, as societally constructed processes, can be collectively steered in a certain direction. The modern belief in the 'manageability of society' (a 'makable' society) is grounded in the Enlightenment (the Age of Reason). The optimistic idea that planning is an effective instrument is the modern form of the belief in reason. This belief in the manageability of extraordinarily complex processes cannot be rationally underpinned. As all beliefs, it does not have a need for underpinning (Achterhuis 1992:200).

The complex process of development in sub-Saharan Africa cannot be planned, really. Nobody has the overview and capacities to guide this multi-dimensional process in such a way that synergy among the manifold actors actually emerges. Which societal authority has the intellectual capability and the political power to realize the attunement of the many changes in technology and society that are required? The controversy in today's development debate between Jeffrey Sachs (2005) and William Easterly (2006) - between planners and searchers - demonstrates the glaring contrast between optimistic holistic planning and pessimistic piecemeal muddling on.

In chapter 4.7 we have seen that the development of modern technology was preceded and accompanied by the development of a modern work ethic. We also concluded that the modern work ethic is more than an individual mentality; it has a societal component. Both societal and psychological processes have played a role in the gradual development of the modern work ethic and technology. The starting point of all these processes, however, is the mimetic desire. The development of medical technology, for example, is often described as a kind of autonomous process, but basically it is determined by the desire to survive, the desire to live longer and longer, preferably longer than fellow-man (Achterhuis 1988:288). This desire could only flourish after in modern society the mimetic desire had thrown off its traditional religious and cultural shackles. Only when the mutual mimetic desire got free play, the technical control over nature became lucrative (ib.:235).

The unlimited mimetic desire is thus the starting point of autonomous technology development. Ultimately then, the mimetic desire is the engine of the economy. Only when the unrestrained mimetic desire is overcome (or, more accurately, transcended) autonomous technology development will end. In order to overcome the belief in the technological fix, we need to overcome the unlimited mimetic desire. Also less developed countries tend to a belief in the technological fix to solve their manifold problems. An example in sub-Saharan Africa is the (undue) emphasis on irrigated agriculture. Many politicians, civil employees and agricultural experts promote irrigation as the best way to solve the hunger problem.

The President of Tanzania, for example, spoke in January 2004 about a new irrigation project that would cover 230.292 hectares and produce 912.168 tons of food at the end of the year[50]. Firstly, the fact is that irrigated agriculture in sub-Saharan Africa will always be peanuts in comparison with rain-fed agriculture (in crop area, number of farmers and tons of food- and cash crops produced). Secondly, the statement of the President also points out that the policy makers seriously think to be able to plan and actually implement such a project - and all that with an amazingly high level of accuracy: the expected hectares and tons of food are very precisely defined. Taking into account that even in a rich, highly developed and well-organized country as The Netherlands, the implementation of large (infrastructural) projects usually gets pretty out of hand, how can Tanzania implement such projects according to plan? In chapter 6.6 Hyden correctly said: "To expect planning to be an important *economic* development tool in the context of the African economies is illusory". Yet African governments and international donors continue to waste a lot of time and money on economic planning.

When it is true that the positivist belief in the technological fix and in autonomous technology development can be overcome by 'rising above' the unlimited mimetic desire, then the question is *whether* and *how* the mimetic desire can be effectively transcended? This question will be dealt with in the next chapters.

13 Modes of Consciousness

The advance of a development-oriented work ethic in sub-Saharan Africa implies behavioural change. Changes in the behaviour of large numbers of people entail changes in the behaviour of many individual actors *and* changes in societal structures. Here the earlier mentioned actor-structure debate in the social sciences is relevant (chapter 4.7). The ongoing controversy on the primacy of actors *or* structures cannot be solved without focussing on the dynamic interaction between individual actors and collective structures. And this dynamic interaction, in turn, cannot be understood without introducing the concept 'collective consciousness'. In chapter 4.7 we have also seen that the work ethic is more than a mentality; it is as well grounded in societal structures. This implies that many issues simultaneously must be taken into account and mutually attuned. The change process is complicated and holistic by nature and therefore difficult to guide or steer. Also this process can be elucidated by the concept collective consciousness. Moreover, consciousness development offers opportunities to facilitate such complex processes.

In my view the concept 'consciousness development' is thus not only important to gain a proper theoretical understanding of the economic development process, but also to provide practical suggestions to accelerate development. Development encompasses scientific, technological, economic, political, socio-structural, cultural and psychological aspects, as we will see later on. The transformation of a traditionalistic work ethic into a modern one is guided by psychological, cultural and socio-structural processes, but is also affected by political, economic, technological and scientific factors. In the previous chapter we have seen that the mimetic desire is the engine of the economy. The unrestrained mimetic desire can result into an overdone work ethic: live to work. To avoid such a work ethic and to prevent the unwanted side-effects of autonomous technology development, we have to overcome the unlimited mimetic desire. We will see that the mimetic desire plays a role in behavioural change[51].

13.1 Rational-empirical consciousness

Most Dutch farmers have internalized the front runner model and thus make it a self-fulfilling prophecy (chapter 12). The majority of the farmers *identify* with this model and *comply* with its underlying logic, which however is no longer widely accepted by society at large. In Diagram 1 we see that the processes of *identification* and *compliance* are important mechanisms through which societal structures try to influence the behaviour of individuals (this Diagram will be further discussed in chapter 15). According to Duintjer (1983,1988b) the structurally expansive character of modern industrial society, including industrial agriculture, is rooted in the metaphysical starting point and background of this society (and its science). Also the prevalent ideas on development cooperation are subject to this underlying metaphysics.

Duintjer (1983) speaks of 'a shared metaphysical attitude towards reality'. Most Western philosophy is practised against the background of a certain kind of consciousness: the 'rational-empirical consciousness' (ib.:1988b). In this state of consciousness all experiencing and acting is accompanied and structured by discursive thinking, which rambles from one topic to another. Discursive thinking occurs at the level of the discursive consciousness, the part of consciousness which deals with knowledge that can be verbalized. Discursive thinking refers to an inner discourse of argumentative thinking. This continuous thinking - the non-stop talking to oneself, inner talk or internal dialogue - goes mainly unnoticed (ib.:60,99). The predominance of the mental mode 'thinking-being' is very subtle: it is difficult to become aware of its dominance because of the nothing-excluding universality at the object-side. Everything can come up as an object to think about: we can think about no matter what.

At the part of the subject, however, one-sidedness rules in the sense that we identify with the rational-empirical consciousness as if no other modes of consciousness are possible (ib.:121). The rational-empirical consciousness is then the presupposed and overarching (and therefore metaphysical) background of modern science and technology, and it has the tendency to spread to all sectors in society and all areas of life (ib.:8). However, the identification of the subject with the rational-empirical consciousness and its continuous expansion are unnecessary. The possibility of a consciousness in which inner talk calms down, in which inner silence goes together with alert attention, is indicated by Duintjer and others (ib.:100).

Diagram 1: Conceptual framework that links individual actors and societal structures, and consciousness and behaviour.

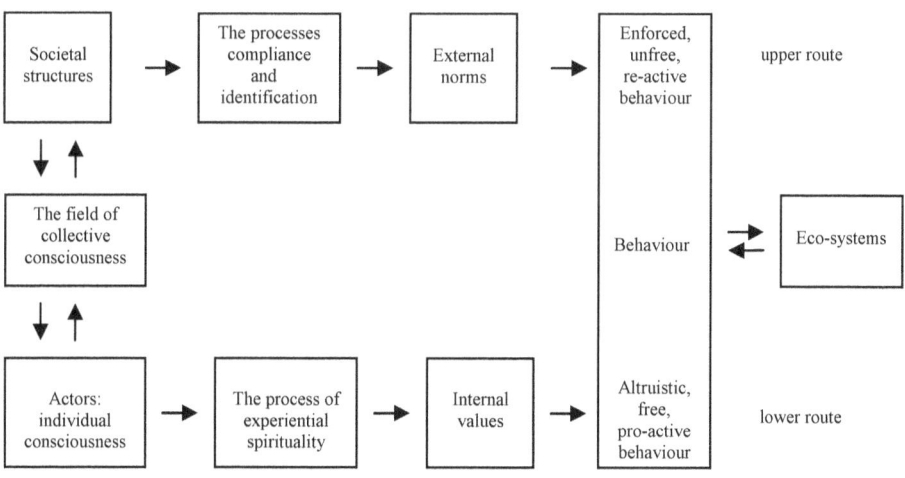

The dominant scientific paradigm in the theory and practice of foreign aid is the positivist paradigm, which is characterized by a belief in a technological fix. However, most people engaged in foreign aid (including

Western and non-Western scientists) do not realize that they are true believers in 'the cathedral of science' and that this non-awareness is due to
the continuous identification with the rational-empirical consciousness.
This identification and the belief in a technological fix are inextricably
linked.

13.2 Pure consciousness

The continuous identification with the rational-empirical consciousness is
a human choice; but a choice which most people make unconsciously or,
more accurately, subconsciously. There are other options, other modes of
consciousness. The fact that almost all people continuously identify with
the rational-empirical consciousness does not necessarily imply that it is
the only possible mode of consciousness or that it is the most desirable
one. Throughout the history of mankind numerous scientists, artists, philosophers, sages and common men in different cultures and ages have
referred to a deepest, most refined level of consciousness as a level of pure
consciousness, a consciousness-as-such without any *content* of consciousness, with only mental silence, without any thoughts, without inner talk.

Is it possible to deduce through logical thinking that a consciousness-
as-such must exist? Duintjer (1996) maintains that our conventional world
is an interpreted world: our perceptions, thoughts and actions are guided
and structured by *learned* frames of interpretation. These frames of interpretation are historically-situated cultural patterns. This is the
constructivist point of view: interpretation frames are learned, we ourselves construct them. The question which crops up then is: from where,
from which position can these frames be learned and entered, be put into
perspective and possibly be transcended? Do we perhaps participate in a
consciousness that precedes our cultural and personal consciousness?

Duintjer's affirmative answer is that this preceding consciousness is an all-encompassing, trans-discursive and trans-personal consciousness: the transcendental or pure consciousness (ib.). In my view straightforward, consistent and clear reasoning (which is the quintessence of science) stipulates the existence of 'something' which is beyond learned frames of interpretation.

The general assumption in modern Western society is that a state of consciousness without any interpretative activity of the mind is impossible. A state of pure consciousness, in which all thinking has been transcended, is deemed impossible, incomprehensible or even unthinkable. As a matter of fact, the state of pure consciousness *is* unthinkable: it can only be directly experienced by transcending all thinking. The 'problem' with the process of transcending is that it cannot be explained meaningfully to others; you just have to experience it, in the same way as you have to taste an apple in order to discern its specific taste, or to see a colour to appreciate its nuances. One can spend hours in explaining how an apple tastes, but without the actual experience of eating an apple it all remains superficial: the proof of the pudding is in the eating.

Tastes and colours are emergent properties. Capra (1996:38) gives the simple example of the taste of sugar. The emergent property 'taste of sugar' is lacking in the carbon-, hydrogen- and oxygen-atoms which constitute sugar. Even if we know how the constellation of atoms in sugar reacts with the atoms in our taste papals on our tongues, we still cannot explain what the taste of sugar is. You just have to experience it. The experience of pure consciousness is also an emergent property for which we can prepare ourselves through for example meditation techniques, but which is novel, emergent or different from experiences at other levels of consciousness. Descartes' dictum *cogito ergo sum* (I think therefore I am) implies that the only mode of 'being' is 'thinking-being'. It denies the possibility of a state of consciousness beyond all thinking - a state of just 'being'.

The step-by-step learning process to go beyond the continual identification with the rational-empirical consciousness can be labelled spirituality (Duintjer 1988b:140). Spirituality as an *experiential* path to deepen and broaden our consciousness - to 'let go' of this identification and to access the level of pure consciousness - is based on personal experience and practical self-investigation (ib.:1996). Spirituality is fundamentally different from belief in any authority; it is by definition no 'faith based on authority' as promoted by institutionalized religions. Theistic traditions, holy books and spiritual teachers can be helpful, but not with statements which we have to believe based on their authority. Rather they should provide practical methods that lead to personal experience of pure consciousness (ib.)[52].

Experiential spirituality implies transcending all thinking, but this does not imply that in all areas of life intellectual thinking must be abandoned. Rather it must be used with care, keeping in mind its inherent limitations. One of those limitations is that truly holistic thinking (the attempt to all-encompassing thinking) is not possible. I call that 'the illusion of intellectual holism' (van Eijk 1998:222). With the intellect alone, however much extended by computer power, we cannot solve complex problems. The present, single-minded emphasis on those factors in the development debate which are quantifiable and controllable is a symptom of such undue emphasis on the intellect. We simply have to accept the fact that development cannot be stage-managed. In addition to quantifiable scientific, technological and economic factors, other variables play a role which cannot be easily quantified and managed. The cultural and socio-structural factor 'work ethic' is one of them.

In Duintjer's view the identification with the rational-empirical consciousness goes hand in hand with rational control of nature (in modern science, technology and industrialization) *and* with rational control of our inner nature (in the civil morals of duty and work ethic for example) (ib.:1983). The modern work ethic - the inner compulsion to work which developed in a long-term process of disciplining to labour - goes hand in hand with the identification with the rational-empirical consciousness. In the Western world we must liberate ourselves from this identification, from the overwhelming predominance of the mode thinking-being, in order to be able to 'normalize' the often overdone work ethic. In sub-Saharan Africa a modern work ethic has not developed yet and full identification with the rational-empirical consciousness is still pending (as perhaps exemplified in the still common beliefs in witchcraft, magic, etc.).

The receptivity to gain access to the level of pure consciousness can be trained through for example meditation techniques. I want to define spirituality as the process in which one *systematically* trains the receptivity to gain *regular* access to pure consciousness. I emphasize purposively the importance of *systematic* training to gain *regular* experiences of pure consciousness, because methods and techniques for consciousness development which do not result in *regular* experiences of pure consciousness cannot be easily scientifically investigated. The scientific approach demands regular and repeatable experiences, in this case experiences of pure consciousness. The continual identification with the rational-empirical consciousness can be transcended by systematic practice of meditation techniques: inner talk makes place for inner silence (pure consciousness) by regularly transcending discursive thinking.

Deepak Chopra (1991:116) remarks: "Thinking your way out of thought is like trying to get out of quicksand by pulling yourself up by the hair". Fortunately there is more to the mind than thinking. We can transcend the thinking and experience the deeper reality of the 'silent witness'. Chopra gives the following analogy to clarify the position of this silent witness inside us.

"To project a movie requires a screen ... The images move and play on the screen; vivid emotions and high drama are enacted. Despite all that, the screen itself isn't engaged. It's not part of the movie ... The difference between the mind and a movie screen is that we do become engaged in the movie, because it's *our* life. The screen inside us becomes so soaked in compelling personal images that the sense of there being a screen - an unchanging, unaffected part of the mind - is lost ... If you strip all of these images away, something of 'me' is still left: the decision maker, the screen, the silent witness ... [The aim of meditation is] to systematically uncover the silent witness inside us, a possibility open to anyone at any time ... The process is like following a gossamer thread until you reach the spider that spun it. My thread may be very different from yours, because I have spun the web of inner reality according to my unique experiences" (ib.:107-10).

Koestler (1989:206) says:

"We must distinguish [between] *general states of consciousness* - degrees of wakefulness, fatigue, intoxication - and the degree of *awareness of a specific activity*. The first refers to 'being conscious', the second to 'being conscious *of* something'. The first corresponds to the overall lighting of the stage, the second to the beam concentrated on a particular actor".

Koestler (ib.:218) speaks of a state of "pure consciousness, without object or content other than consciousness itself". There must be a carrier (pure consciousness) and content of the carrier.

13.3 Modes of morality

Duintjer (1996) is of the opinion that a spiritual attitude to life is relevant to solving societal problems, because mutual co-operation and solidarity develop with less difficulty when the part of the consciousness that surpasses our person, group or culture is less clouded. This demands regular access to pure consciousness: the silent-witness-consciousness that under-lies all individual consciousnesses. Societally and ecologically sound behaviour would thus be facilitated. Morality which is grounded in authority is based on obedience to - and identification with - externally imposed norms. External societal structures, inhabited by persons who identify with the rational-empirical consciousness, apply moral pressure on individuals in order to force or convince them to implement behaviour which is deemed societally rational. This rational morality, resulting into external norms via the processes compliance and identification, needs to be supplemented with morality which is grounded in direct experience of pure consciousness. This last (internally inspired) morality results via the process of experiential spirituality into internal values (see Diagram 1). External norms and internal values apply simultaneously, but hitherto societal emphasis has been mainly on external norms.

Here the distinction between religion and spirituality is important. Religion can be institutionalized spirituality, but in many cases believers or worshippers do not have direct spiritual experiences. Experiential spirituality is religion in its original meaning, without religious institutions. Experiential spirituality has to do with the original meaning of religion, i.e., *religare, religio*: to reconnect. But reconnect to what? To the level of pure consciousness, to the silent witness inside us. Instead of religion it might be better to speak of 'church' or 'faith' in order to emphasize its institutionalized character and the inherent holding on to a belief based on authority. Experiential spirituality, on the other hand, is characterized by personal, direct experience of pure consciousness via techniques for consciousness development. It abhors any form of totalitarian behaviour.

Can we scientifically prove the existence of a level of pure consciousness? Positivist science, today's dominant scientific paradigm which is grounded in the continuous identification with the rational-empirical consciousness, cannot prove that pure consciousness exists. But positivist scientific research into the individual and collective *effects* of techniques for consciousness development generates indirect, circumstantial evidence for the existence of pure consciousness. Or, more accurately formulated, it generates statistically validated evidence that practice of such techniques results into societally sound behaviour at the individual and collective levels, which, presumably, is due to regular access to pure consciousness. This indirect, secondary evidence can be supplemented with primary (subjective) 'evidence': the personal, direct experience of pure consciousness via techniques for consciousness development. But it can also be supplemented with (intersubjective) verification by others in a community of peers: persons thus who are adequately trained in techniques for consciousness development.

The Transcendental Meditation (TM) technique is an example of a technique which provides systematic training in gaining regular access to pure consciousness. TM is only one meditation technique out of many, but it is probably one of the best researched techniques. The individual and societal effects of the TM technique have been thoroughly investigated. Extensive research, published in peer-reviewed scientific journals, confirms beneficial effects for individuals at the physiological and psychological level and favourable collective effects at societal level. For a bibliography of scientific studies on TM and some remarks about the quality of the research on TM I refer to the Annex at the end of this book. This Annex is based on the website of Dr. David Orme-Johnson, a psychologist who does not have a position in the TM movement now (although he formerly did), nor does he represent the TM organization. He is one of the principal researchers in the world on meditation and its effects, having over 100 publications, mostly in peer-reviewed journals. The Annex also provides the website address of Google Scholar Search on Transcendental Meditation (8700+ citations). Finally, I want to refer to my own Ph.D. thesis (van Eijk 1998:190-5), which also provides some information on scientific research on TM.

14 Synergistic Cooperation

Development is a multi-dimensional process which involves, in addition to economic growth, major changes in social structures and popular attitudes: comprehensive socio-cultural changes are needed. Moreover, full control of the development process is not possible: we can only facilitate it by creating the right conditions. Development is a process characterized by as many unanticipated as anticipated outcomes (Hyden 1980:260). A focus on only one societal subsystem is not sufficient in this partly predictable process. Only effective interplay among many actors can result into development. An important question is then how this effective interplay in the mix of actors (and the hopefully ensuing synergy) comes about? The actions (behaviours) of many actors in the development process need to be attuned so that potential synergies can be realized. One of the most crucial components of behaviour is how people work. The creation of a development-oriented work ethic is thus essential.

14.1   Holistic framework for multi-dimensional development

In the actual practice of planning and implementing development processes it is difficult to tackle problems of different nature (technical, socio-economic, political and cultural problems) and at different levels (for example, at district and regional level) simultaneously. A truly holistic approach is not easy to put into practice. This does not only apply to less developed countries but also to rich industrialised nations. But in countries without adequate infrastructure and without sufficient qualified manpower it is much more difficult. The integration of different factors and levels in the development process demands an appropriate conceptual framework.

In Diagram 2 I present such a framework with eight different categories of factors. The different categories in this holistic framework are interrelated: they can be distinguished but they cannot be separated in their effects. Although the categories are interrelated, they are not equally fundamental (Ransijn 1985).

Diagram 2: Holistic framework for the multi-dimensional development process. The eight categories of factors are interrelated, but the inner categories carry more weight.

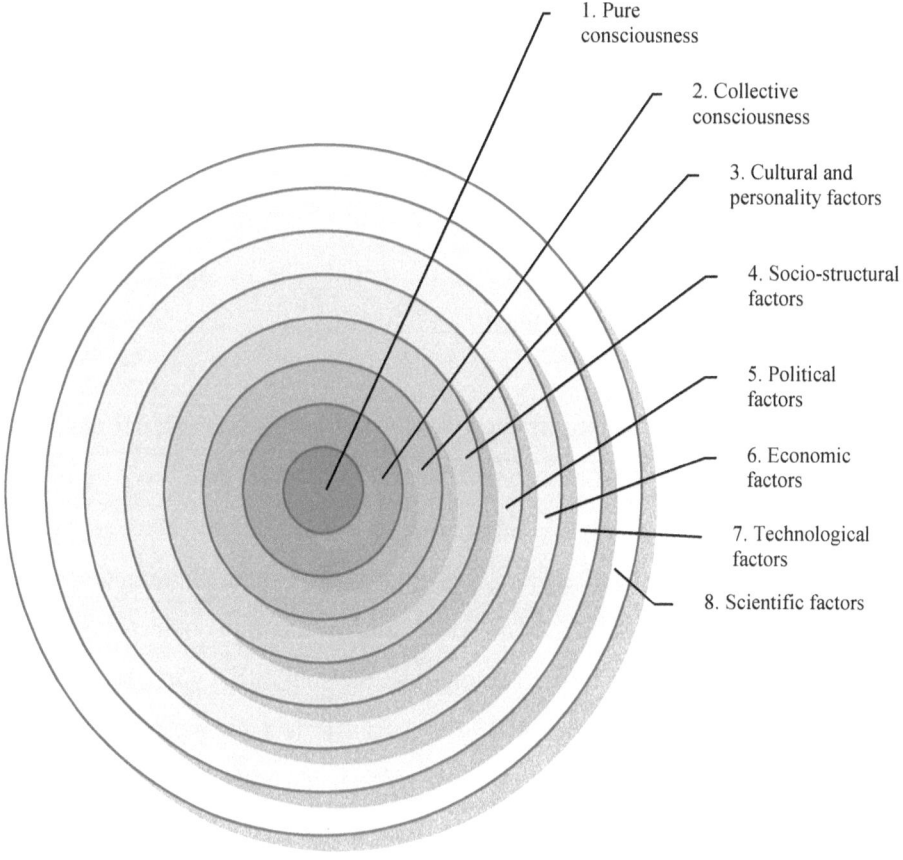

1. Pure consciousness

2. Collective consciousness

3. Cultural and personality factors

4. Socio-structural factors

5. Political factors

6. Economic factors

7. Technological factors

8. Scientific factors

Source: Ransijn 1985 (adapted by author)

In the interdependent totality of Diagram 2 the factors in the more inner categories (the consciousness factors) are the more independent variables, while the factors in the outer categories are the dependent variables. Moving from the outside to the inside in Diagram 2, from category eight to category one, the categories become more encompassing, more inclusive (ib.:46).

For example, the decision to use a certain technology is largely determined by economic factors. Economic factors, in turn, are strongly influenced by political factors. The main issue in today's politics is economics. Economic markets are political constructs (Chang 2008:175). Politics encompasses economics, but economics does not encompass politics. Political factors in turn are determined by socio-structural factors, and so on and so forth. Whereas feedback mechanisms between the different categories do occur, the more inner categories encompass the outer ones and are therefore more important and essential. The various categories are thus interrelated in a hierarchical order in which the inner categories carry more weight.

Diagram 2 is a holistic framework for the multi-dimensional development process. The holistic aspect (the whole is more than the sum of the parts) emerges because of the synergetic effects of the interactions between the parts. These effects are often elusive and unpredictable and sometimes unexplainable. A football team, for example, sometimes plays very well and then the whole is more than the sum of the parts, but another time performance is moderate and the team is just the sum of the parts. What causes the magic of holistic performance, how does effective and well-timed interaction come about, what causes the synergetic effect of interaction among players, what makes a group of eleven individuals an eleven-headed unit - a true team - rather than just an aggregate of eleven individuals? Successful sportsmen speak of 'the click of communality' or 'a group mind' (Sheldrake 1989:250).

With regard to the development process in sub-Saharan Africa the question is how the multiple stakeholders gain a holistic overview, how do they grasp the complex interdependencies at the especially high levels of integration, how do they gain a systems-perspective, a comprehensive view of the entire system, an inclusive or societal rationality? Experiences in development cooperation, but for example also with regard to environmental problems in the industrialised world, show that the use of the discursive intellect alone does not result into encompassing rationality. This is the earlier mentioned 'illusion of intellectual holism'.

Although the need for concerted action among the many actors in the development process is obvious, it is not so obvious how to create cohesion between the different categories in Diagram 2. And the higher the level of integration is, the more difficult it becomes to formulate and implement systematic and effective approaches to development. In my own field of specialization, Farming Systems Research and Development, it proved difficult to implement effective strategies at the level of single farms in sub-Saharan Africa. What about much higher levels of integration then? How to implement effective and efficient strategies at district, regional or national level? Also in highly developed countries such as The Netherlands higher levels of integration often surpass the abilities of policy makers and scientists. Even with the help of modern ICT these levels cannot be handled easily. The persistent problems in the Dutch agricultural sector show that a multidisciplinary, truly integrated approach has not materialized yet. The undesired side-effects of modern industrial agriculture (such as environmental pollution and large-scale killings when animal health problems occur) bear testimony to our inability to integrate ecological, technological, economic, political and ethical issues.

The various categories in Diagram 2 are to some extent autonomous, but at the same time they are part of larger wholes. In the development process the economic factor may often seem to be of overriding importance, but it is nevertheless part of the more encompassing political factor. The invisible hand and foot of the so-called 'independent' economy have been discussed before (chapter 12). And the so-called 'autonomous' technology development is a fabrication that can be undone by transcending the unlimited mimetic desire (chapter 12). The technological and economic categories are affected by the more inner categories.

All categories play a role in the multi-dimensional development process, but unfortunately hitherto mainly the outer categories receive attention: the categories 8, 7 and 6 (respectively scientific, technological and economic factors). Recently the categories 5 (political factors) and to a lesser degree 4 (socio-structural factors) receive more attention in the development debate: issues such as good governance and the development of an effective civil society have come up. A gradual tendency to take also the more inner categories into consideration can thus be discerned. The three most inner categories, however, play hardly a role in the debate. Category 3 (cultural and personality factors) is rarely discussed and the categories 2 and 1 (the consciousness factors) are completely ignored.

The work ethic - a mentality *and* a socio-structural reality - falls mainly under the categories 3 and 4, although also the other categories play a role in its development and upholding. I have elaborated on many aspects of the work ethic in the chapters 3 to 11. Diagram 2 puts all these aspects in a wider framework. The hierarchy of categories in Diagram 2 is a social construction for mainly analytical purposes. This hierarchical order is not absolute; rather it is a matter of categories being more or less encompassing. One can also use the metaphor of Russian puppets in which a puppet is enclosed by the next larger puppet. The various categories can be vertically distinguished but not radically separated in their effects, because they are interconnected. We will see that the attunement of the various categories can be enhanced by the underlying field of collective consciousness.

Culture is a pattern of thinking, feeling and acting. It is mental software. Hofstede (1994:5) defines culture as "the collective programming of the mind which distinguishes the members of one group or category of people from another". Culture is learned, not inherited. "It derives from one's social environment, not from one's genes" (ib.). One needs to make a distinction between culture and personality. While a culture is specific to a certain group of people and is learned, a personality is specific to an individual and partly learned, partly inherited. The inherited part of personality is due to an individual's unique set of genes, while 'learned' means here: "modified by the influence of collective programming (culture) *as well as* unique personal experiences" (ib.:6). In Diagram 2 cultural and personality factors constitute one category. It is a matter of discussion among social scientists where the border between culture and personality exactly lies (ib.:5).

Personality factors (part of category 3) are not considered in the development debate. Yet personality factors are often pivotal for interdisciplinary collaboration in multidisciplinary teams of development experts. Moreover, development workers with 'participatory' attitudes are required to promote active participation of the members of the target groups in foreign aid. But psychology as a discipline remains largely absent in development literature. Whereas the centrality of the human factor in the development process is beyond doubt, surprisingly enough little emphasis is placed on this key element. Most likely this is due to the fact that it is such a vague factor. The elusive character of behavioural change makes concrete action by development workers difficult. In the next subchapters the elusive character of the human factor will be clarified by the concept collective consciousness.

Also in agriculture (*agri-culture*) man and his culture are central. In the rural development process many interactions among numerous actors and their networks take place *and* interactions between these actors and nature - including effects which lie beyond the interface situation itself (Scoones & Thompson 1994). Human interventions in nature sometimes produce effects beyond the factual interface of actors and nature. The emergent character of many interactions (the whole is more than the sum of the parts) makes full human control of the development process illusory. This should also temper contemporary belief in the ability of the invisible hand to steer economic development. Nevertheless, the wish to enlarge our steering ability remains valid. If, however, we do not want to make simplistic judgements based on isolated, narrow-minded disciplinary analyses, but want to take into account the full range of interfaces and interactions, then we need a new paradigm of development. We need a paradigm that pays attention to the underlying base of all these interfaces and interactions.

In our quest for such a new paradigm we need to focus on a leverage mechanism with (preferably) broad impact. The concept collective consciousness is such an intervention mechanism with broad impact. The local actors and foreign change agents in the development process need a new conceptual framework that clarifies constraining *and* enabling factors *and* that is practically relevant. The Diagrams 1 and 2 can provide such a framework.

14.2   Collective consciousness

The *social structure* of a society can be defined as the pattern or web of social relationships, including all its economic, political, educational, religious and other substructures (Ransijn 1985:90). *Culture* is the pattern of norms, values, habits, ideas and goals that structure social behaviour and give meaning to life. Since culture forms social behaviour, with a web of social relationships as a result, one can speak of a 'socio-cultural structure'. The core of this socio-cultural structure is formed by a set of central ideas and values which are internalized in the collective consciousness of the members in a given society.

Social scientists as Sorokin and Durkheim say that society is something outside us and something inside us. Society has an objective aspect (a concrete social structure) and a subjective aspect (a collective consciousness) (ib.:91). Ransijn (ib.:47) defines the collective consciousness as "the totality of interacting human minds and the beliefs and sentiments held in common by the majority of a certain collectivity". The collective consciousness and the societal structure are the inner and outer side of the same socio-cultural reality. Visible societal structures are manifestations of invisible collective consciousness. One could say that societal structures are forms of 'crystallized' collective consciousness.

The central ideas and values, which are internalized in the collective consciousness, constitute the basis of all substructures in society. The technological, economic, political, social, cultural, educational and religious substructures are thus connected through this collective consciousness. All individuals, who inhabit these substructures and who together shape the collective consciousness, are connected through a field of collective consciousness. The collective consciousness is the integrating, inner structure of society. It is, so to speak, the internalized society. It is the integration of all more outer categories.

The collective consciousness is a crucial factor in processes of social change (ib.:52). It is a guiding or facilitating factor in the interactions between the various categories in Diagram 2. It is virtually impossible to change all interdependent substructures simultaneously. Integral or holistic change, however, implies exactly that: simultaneous change and mutual attunement of all substructures. Only the very factor that connects all substructures and their constituting individuals - the collective consciousness - can do this (ib.:53). If we can influence the underlying collective consciousness, holistic changes are possible.

The collective consciousness is an integral, holistic factor because it encompasses the categories 3 to 8 and is the more independent variable in the interdependent totality of categories in Diagram 2. The collective consciousness is the leading variable that integrates a society. It is the invisible hand that keeps things together. It has a kind of orchestrating quality; a statement which is supported by scientific research on the field effect of consciousness (see chapter 14.4 and the Annex at the end of this book).

Durkheim speaks of the 'social cement' without which no social groups can exist; it is the 'glue' which holds groups or organizations together (Grint 1998:127). The 'something' which holds a group together is today called 'social capital' or 'social cohesion' and civil society is supposed to create it. In my view this social cement, glue or capital refers to the collective consciousness. Social capital in the modern Western world has shrunk while in sub-Saharan Africa it is still relatively large within the economy of affection. But regression to earlier periods, in which the emancipation of the individual had not yet taken place, is neither possible nor desirable.

Röling (1988:66) distinguishes two sets of variables which influence human behaviour: structural variables (at societal level) and socio-psychological variables (at individual level). An agricultural example: the non-adoption of new agricultural technology can be blamed on structural variables (such as an ill-functioning input delivery service) or on individual characteristics of farmers (conservative or ignorant farmers) or on both. One could label these two extreme positions 'system blaming' and 'victim blaming'. Truth often may lie midway, but nevertheless it is important to realize that the 'building blocks' of any structure are individuals. The essence of the societal process is the individual (Fromm 1972). Progress is only possible when changes occur simultaneously in the economic and socio-political dimension (structural variables) and in the cultural dimension (socio-psychological variables). Progress limited to one dimension is destructive to progress in all dimensions (Fromm 1955). However, changes in structural variables are always made by (a collective

of) individuals. Societal changes are thus grounded in the (collective) behaviour of individuals.

Also Ransijn (1985:88) distinguishes two approaches to enlarge societal well-being: an individualistic approach which emphasizes 'betterment'
or development of individuals and a socio-structural approach which emphasizes upgrading of societal structures. The framework in Diagram 2
facilitates integration of individualistic-psychological and socio-structural
approaches. The collective consciousness integrates the individual and collective approaches in one single holistic approach (ib.). Since the
collective consciousness of societies (or other smaller groups) is grounded
in the individual levels of consciousness of its members, individuals have
direct impact on the collective consciousness of their society or group. The
quality of the collective consciousness of a group is a direct and accurate
reflection of the quality of the consciousness of its individual members
(Ransijn & Schulte 1982:271). A high quality collective consciousness
results into societally and ecologically sound behaviour (in the Annex
website addresses are given where scientific underpinning to this statement
can be found).

The collective consciousness, in turn, influences individual levels of
consciousness and thus the general functioning of individuals. This dynamic interaction - the principle of reciprocity which links individual and
collective consciousness - plays an important role in the field effect of
consciousness. Since societal structures are crystallized collective consciousness, changes in collective consciousness result into adaptations of
these structures. Transformation of consciousness results into changes in
societal structures from within (Ransijn 1983). Given that the collective
consciousness encompasses the more outer categories in Diagram 2, transformation of (individual and collective) consciousness is an inherently
holistic approach. The orchestrating quality of collective consciousness
results into maximal changes with minimal effort.

In Western democratic consumption society, driven by an unlimited mimetic desire and overdone work ethic, the public opinion is an important factor. The public opinion is the totality of opinions, ideas and thoughts - thus *contents* of consciousness - that characterize a certain society. The collective consciousness, on the other hand, is more fundamental or in-depth and encompasses also the internalized basic values of a society. The collective consciousness encompasses the public opinion, but the public opinion does not encompass the collective consciousness. The public opinion can force politicians to take action. The public opinion is part and parcel of the collective consciousness and since politicians, willy-nilly, are a mirror of the collective consciousness of their grassroots support, they 'automatically' take action when (especially negative) publicity 'tells' them to do so. While the public opinion is formed by mainly the discursive intellect, and thus remains rather superficial, the quality and coherence of the collective consciousness are determined by the levels of consciousness of its constituting members.

14.3   Social engineering

The various aspects of individual performance (perceptions, attitudes and behaviours) are linked by the individual consciousness since all these aspects are influenced by the mode of functioning of the nervous system (Ransijn & Schulte 1982:270). We all know that when we are tired, alert or over-excited, this influences our thoughts and actions considerably. Individual consciousness is the totality that arises from the collective activity of the various parts of the nervous system (ib.). The quality of individual consciousness determines the quality of individual thought and behaviour. And the quality of individual consciousness is a function of the degree of access to pure consciousness, which, in turn, is a function of the condition of the nervous system - of the purity of the nervous system. When the nervous system is free of impurities - when it is not contaminated with any stress - then one has free access to pure consciousness. Tuning in to pure consciousness can be done through, for example, meditation techniques. These techniques help to transcend the continuous 'inner talk' and to re-lease deep-seated stresses. If one regularly practises techniques for consciousness development the nervous system releases more and more deep-seated stresses and becomes increasingly pure. Scientific research indicates that persons with stress-free nervous systems perform better: their behaviour tends to be societally and ecologically sound (see the An-nex for scientific references).

Different levels of consciousness, different levels of refinement of con-sciousness, different qualities of consciousness: all these terms are linked to different levels of purity of the nervous system, different levels of being stress-free. In the same way that individuals can reduce their personal stress levels, societies can reduce their collective stress levels. This reduc-tion of collective societal stress is crucial to any development process. Societal stress is often caused by conflicting interests between individuals or groups of stakeholders and society at large. Comprehensive societal ra-tionality entails a convergence of individual and public interests. The reconciliation of these diverging interests is facilitated by a coherent col-lective consciousness of high quality; a collective consciousness in which noses point in the same direction and which is not contaminated with stress.

Such consciousness facilitates the cultivation of societally and ecologi-cally appropriate behaviour. I use the word 'to facilitate' to indicate that techniques for consciousness development are only one component in the total of measures needed to realize such behaviour. But it is certainly an important and hitherto neglected component. For example: with regard to environmental pollution or common property resource management we can decide, at last, that collective action can no longer be postponed as otherwise human existence will be endangered. In that case collaboration is the consequence of choosing the lesser of two evils. People realize that collective agency and concerted action are the only way to solve their common problem. But this is an *aposteriori* or re-active willingness to act. It is externally motivated behaviour.

Rational (externally motivated) morality is based on negotiated agreement among numerous stakeholders: the Dutch 'polder model'. This polder model should be complemented with internally motivated morality, morality which results into *apriori* or pro-active willingness to act. Techniques for consciousness development promote such internally motivated morality. I believe that both negotiated agreement (resulting into externally motivated morality) and experiential spirituality (resulting into internally motivated morality) play a role in the development of sustainable societies. To my mind it is prudent to bet on both horses (on both the upper and lower route in Diagram 1). Experiential spirituality does not automatically result into effective action in the domain of existence; experiential spirituality alone does not guarantee societally and ecologically sound behaviour. Relevant knowledge and practical skills are also necessary. Experiential spirituality, however, guides the application of such knowledge and skills in societally and ecologically appropriate directions.

In modern society the gap between cerebral-intellectual and emotional-moral-spiritual development results into technology which can get out of control (Ransijn & Schulte 1982:343). The problem however is not located in our technology, but in us. There is not an excess of technology, but a lack of consciousness: "this guiding factor leaves much to be desired" (Ransijn 1985:49). The root cause of the problem is human inability. Beets (1990:295) says that the socio-cultural dimensions of development are often more important than the technical ones. But project interventions that aim to change socio-cultural conditions are not formulated in foreign aid. Although such interventions should constitute the core of projects, they are at best attached to projects as a kind of after-thoughts. Beets calls the process of changing socio-cultural conditions 'social engineering' (ib.:338). This is an emotionally charged term, but nevertheless development of personality (part of category 3 in Diagram 2) is a *conditio sine qua non* for sustainable development.

The process of experiential spirituality gradually leads to highly developed individuals, who listen to their own internal values and who go through life without (unconscious) mimesis. They are not the plaything of external circumstances but follow their own path. Their need for externally imposed morality gradually diminishes. Social engineering, however, only becomes possible when effective and efficient techniques for consciousness development are available and people voluntarily use them. Experiential spirituality, by definition, cannot be enforced.

Individual actors and collective structures function best when their interfaces are embedded in a coherent collective consciousness of high quality, so that their interplay is effective and efficient. In this context Chambers (1997:220) distinguishes three interrelated dimensions in change processes: *institutional* change referring to partnership between institutions and sharing of information and experiences; *professional* change of working methods; and *personal* change of behaviour and attitudes. In his view personal change is primary: behaviour and attitudes are the key to change processes (ib.:210,215). He says:

"Behaviour and attitudes, what sort of people we are, how we relate to one another are so universally significant that their neglect [in the literature on development] is bizarre (ib.:208) ... The personal dimension is a bizarre blind spot in development (ib.:231) ... Given this primacy of the personal, psychological studies of 'uppers' [highly placed change agents] have been oddly absent from development studies ... Perhaps the most neglected aspect of development is the personal psychology of what powerful professionals believe and do ... Personal change is a minefield, the subject of much evangelism, mythology, popular writing, and psychological and managerial lore. It is value-laden" (ib.:232).

Chambers (ib.:188,209) argues that especially uppers have to change; professionals must relinquish power to 'lowers' (subordinated groups). Uppers need to disempower themselves and empower lowers. It is not just a matter of putting *the last first*, to place subordinated groups in the forefront via participatory methods - which ultimately is only altruism. But it is also necessary to put *the first last* which entails disempowerment of professionals (ib.:211). When power is no longer seen as a commodity, selfish behaviour (which is based on a zero-sum orientation in which one's gain is another's loss) can transform into altruistic or generous behaviour (based on a positive-sum orientation in which all gain) (ib.:234). Disempowerment is often a positive sum, but unfortunately most professionals do not realize this. They psychologically need the solid structures of their own realities, they are entrapped in their self- and socially constructed prisons (ib.:235).

I would say that most professionals are imprisoned in the continuous identification with the rational-empirical consciousness and are not even aware of the possibility of other modes of being. Instead of emphasizing (dis)empowerment of certain groups, the collective consciousness deserves more attention. When only uppers change, there is no guarantee that also lowers will change (partly because the number of facilitating uppers is always much lower than the number of disadvantaged lowers). Chambers' compassionate and sympathetic line of reasoning seems to be based on the assumption that a relatively small group of powerful professionals can frustrate development. I do not believe that this small group has so much impact (neither positive nor negative).

Moreover, the dilemma of empowerment (or the paradox of participatory, non-directive strategies) is that there is always a thin line between emancipation and manipulation (Long & Villareal 1994). Facilitation and empowerment are also forms of social engineering. The undoubtedly good intentions of most facilitators cannot prevent that some participatory strategies end up in manipulation. In my view techniques for consciousness development can diminish this risk, since experiential spirituality is by definition participatory, non-directive and emancipatory. It is true self-empowerment.

14.4 Field-effect of consciousness

Techniques for consciousness development can be subjected to scientific scrutiny. One can argue that the (individual and collective) effects of techniques for consciousness development are mere wishful thinking, self-deception or random coincidence. But one can also accept a more scientific point of view and actually investigate these effects with systematic research, even if we do not understand exactly how they come about and even if causality and directionality are not easy to interpret. In addition to the individual physiological and psychological effects, brain wave patterns, etcetera, also the field effect of consciousness can be scientifically investigated. Extensive research on the TM technique makes a wide-ranging field effect plausible.

This research shows that the TM technique does not only affect the practitioners themselves, but also persons in their (immediate and distant) surroundings. Especially when groups of meditators practise together advanced TM techniques, an influence of harmony, coherence and orderliness is radiated. The quality of societal life is determined by the coherence and quality of the collective consciousness. We can use the analogy of a magnet to clarify the field character of collective consciousness: the abstract, immaterial collective consciousness works as a magnetic field. A magnet covered by a sheet of paper is invisible and its magnetic field cannot be seen until small particles of iron are sprinkled on the paper, which then automatically are organized in coherent patterns. In the same vein the field effect of a coherent collective consciousness becomes visible in the coherent behaviour of numerous individual actors.

Radio, television and radar work by sending waves through an un-bounded, infinite, invisible and all-pervading electromagnetic field. Although these waves are invisible, they do have effects. The concept of a field is not only a guiding image but also an invisible reality. "As the basic mechanism of nature, invisible, immaterial waves move through invisible, immaterial fields ... Consciousness, too, is an infinite, invisible field - with waves that radiate throughout society" (Oates 1990:24,25). Scientific re-search on the TM technique indicates holistic and measurable effects. The result is improved quality of societal life - as expressed in reduced crime, violence, accidents and illness, and in better economic conditions and so-ciological indicators. Evidence to support this claim has been published in leading, peer-reviewed scientific journals as the *Journal of Mind and Be-haviour* and *Journal of Conflict Resolution* (see also the Annex).

The field effect of consciousness is holistic in nature and thus numer-ous indicators of the quality of life are simultaneously affected. In a similar way as an electromagnetic field mediates effects-at-a-distance, the field of collective consciousness mediates inter-human effects-at-a-distance. The field of collective consciousness is the medium for these non-local, inter-human effects; it acts as a kind of go-between. Mediation of behavioural change by verbal and non-verbal communication in direct social interactions - as commonly practised by social scientists, extension-ists, parents and others - needs to be supplemented with mediation of behavioural change-at-a-distance through consciousness. Conventional approaches to behavioural change (the upper route in Diagram 1) need to be supplemented with new approaches based on techniques for conscious-ness development (the lower route in Diagram 1).

Scientists can investigate the field effects of consciousness, they can map these effects in the 'objective' manifest world, but they cannot prove the existence of the field of collective consciousness as such. Although scientific research on the field effect provides only indirect evidence for the existence of the consciousness field, the reproducibility and predictability of this effect are so persuasive that it certainly warrants more attention from scientists. The theory of the field effect of consciousness results into predictions which can be tested and is thus scientific. Gerding (1996) says that the 'objective' aspect of reality in positivist science refers to the objective character of an inter-subjective world, a world which we call objective because we share it. This shared world is created or constructed by a shared mind: the collective consciousness. When this collective consciousness changes, our shared world also changes (perception and knowledge are structured in consciousness) and the results of research on the field effect of consciousness might become more acceptable. Changes in collective consciousness cause changes in scientific paradigms.

A coherent and high quality collective consciousness results into a harmonic atmosphere, which facilitates the emergence of high quality collective agency and synergistic cooperation. The field effect of consciousness facilitates the emergence of societally and ecologically appropriate behaviour. Personal behavioural change is a minefield and the subject of much psychological and managerial babble, as Chambers correctly argued, but a pro-active attempt to large-scale behavioural change (in other words, social engineering) is facilitated by effective use of the field effect of consciousness. The multi-facets of sustainable development comprise ecological responsibility, technical feasibility, economic viability, ethical defensibility, social desirability and aesthetic acceptability (Bawden 1995). To this long list I add consciousness-mediated manageability, because the field effect of consciousness facilitates the management and coordination of these multiple aspects of sustainable development. Synchronized cultivation of synergy in the mix of factors in Diagram 2 is facilitated.

Sustainability is the *emergent* property of numerous interactions among many stakeholders (and their societal structures) and interactions between these stakeholders and natural ecosystems. Sustainability is thus not 'makable'. It is the negotiated outcome of the collective action of many stakeholders, but it has an often puzzling facet. The problematic (lack of) development in sub-Saharan Africa in the past decades has shown that there are no positivist-oriented quick-fix solutions based on modern technology nor constructivist-oriented quick-fix solutions based on fashionable key words as participation, democratization, good governance and ownership. Similarly there is also no transcendentalist-oriented quick-fix solution based on consciousness-mediated manageability. Consciousness development is not an overnight solution: it takes time and relevant knowledge and skills grounded in the natural and social sciences remain indispensable in the search for sustainable development. But the 'good vibrations' of a coherent and high quality collective consciousness influence both the goal of development and the means to reach that goal.

Covey (1990:270) distinguishes three levels of communication which are related to different levels of trust and cooperation among people (Diagram 3). Low-trust situations are characterized by defensive, protective and often legalistic use of language: the communication results into win/lose or lose/lose situations. In the middle position the dominant mode of verbal interaction is respectful communication. Says Covey (ib.:271):

"This is the level where fairly mature people interact. They have respect for each other, but they want to avoid the possibility of ugly confrontations, so they communicate politely but not empathically. They might understand each other intellectually, but they really don't deeply look at the paradigms and assumptions underlying their own positions and become open to new possibilities ... In interdependent situations compromise is the position usually taken. Compromise means that 1 + 1 = 1½. Both give and take. The communication ... is honest and genuine and respectful. But it isn't creative or synergistic. It produces a low form of Win/Win".

Diagram 3: Three different levels of communication in relation to levels of trust and cooperation (Covey 1990:270)

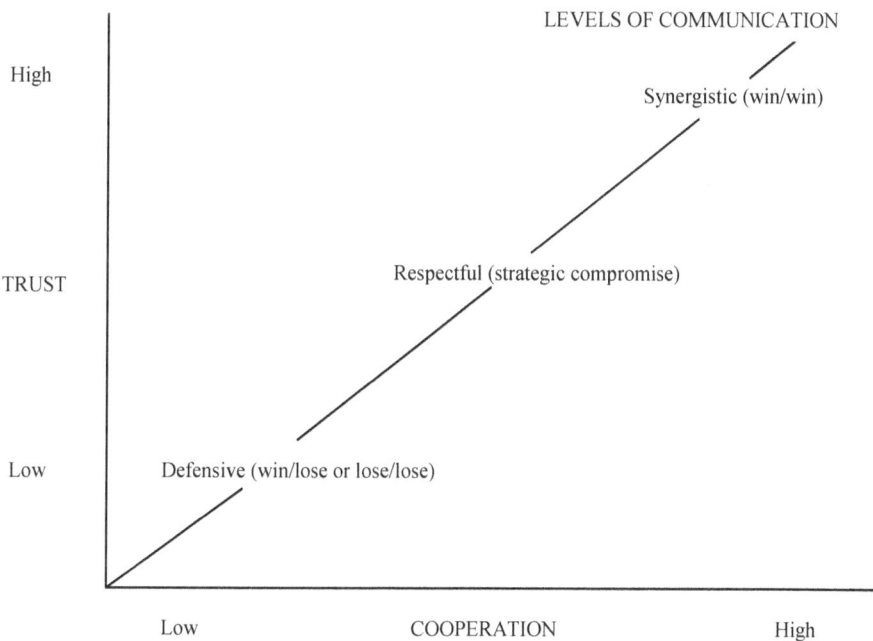

High-trust situations, finally, are characterized by synergistic communication resulting into win/win positions: synergy means that 1 + 1 = >2. 'Mini-cultures' develop in which new possibilities emerge (the whole is more than the sum of the parts).

My work experience in sub-Saharan Africa indicates that conditions in which synergies emerge cannot be easily created. The relation between citizens and state, for example, is characterized by low levels of trust and cooperation and defensive communication. And the communication between Western donor agencies and African recipient governments is at best respectful, more often however defensive. Also the relationship between employers and employees in sub-Saharan Africa is defensive. The traditionalistic work ethic is characterized by low levels of trust and cooperation and defensive communication, resulting into low labour productivity and thus low salaries. Higher salaries alone will not automatically result into higher labour productivity. The underlying reason is an incoherent collective consciousness full of mutual distrust. Rampant corruption and excessive bureaucracy are other symptoms of an incoherent and low quality collective consciousness.

Covey's description of the middle position, in which respectful communication and strategic compromise dominate, is the rule in The Netherlands: the Dutch polder model. The process to reach strategic compromises is time-consuming and does not really result into synergistic win/win situations. Nevertheless, the polder model does demonstrate moderate levels of societal trust and cooperation. Since the polder model took centuries to build up, it should not be too easily discarded. As long as the specific conditions in which synergistic win/win situations emerge are not accurately specified and cannot be effectively created, the polder model remains useful.

The financial crisis in 2008/2009 is a clear example of how lack of trust can slow down economic development. Inherently unstable financial markets got extremely volatile in 2008 due to distrust and fear. Suddenly and quickly a vicious circle of dropping share prices and rising societal distrust developed. In order to break this vicious circle, governments had to intervene with capital injections to reduce distrust and fear in the collective mood. The initial distrust which drove the vicious circle was caused by the irresponsible behaviour of high ranked bank staff, which in turn was caused by greed and envy, or, ultimately, by unrestrained mimetic desire. High quality individual consciousness (limiting the largely unconscious mimetic desire) and coherent and high quality collective consciousness (defusing societal distrust, fear and stress) could have prevented the vicious circle.

We have seen before that full control of the development process is not possible; we can only facilitate it by creating the right conditions for synergistic win/win situations. A coherent and high quality collective consciousness is the single most important condition. It generates a high level of societal trust and effective and efficient cooperation among many actors. Engel (1995:45) argues that innovation processes are mostly self-guiding in nature, they have dynamics of their own, many things 'just happen'. In that case it would be advisable to pay more attention to the self-regulative capability of groups of stakeholders. "The potential for synergy is to be taken not so much as an inherent property of a [group of stakeholders] but as a property which may emerge when certain conditions prevail. For example, when relevant actors *decide* to work together as if they were one 'system' " (ib.:37). Synergy emerges when the actors want - and are able - to create 'a group consciousness, an atmosphere of cordiality, an enthusiasm, a momentum' (ib.:237). These terms used by Engel refer to the field effect of group consciousness.

The actors in a group can orchestrate synergy, create synergistic performance and enliven their self-regulative capability, when their group consciousness is coherent. Positive-sum synergistic cooperation is not a transaction (giving and taking resulting into compromises) but a transformation. The key to inter-personal synergy is intra-personal synergy (Covey 1990:274). Integrated personal development - synergy within us - is necessary. We need to transcend the continual identification with the rational-empirical consciousness, so that we do not only use our intellect but make our body-intellect-spirit coordination optimal. Our ability to solve problems develops then 'from within' - as scientific research indicates.

15 Individual Actors, Societal Structures and Behavioural Change

In chapter 4.7 I concluded that a work ethic is more than an individual mentality; it is also rooted in a certain societal material reality. Actors *and* structures play a role. The materialization of a development-oriented work ethic in sub-Saharan Africa implies personal behavioural change *and* structural change. In chapter 4.7 I also referred to the actor-structure debate which should focus on the dynamic interaction between actors and structures. This dynamic interaction is a continuing circularity of cause and effect: a true 'chicken-and-egg' situation. Nevertheless, I argued that primacy rests with actors rather than structures. The discussion of Diagram 1 (already presented in chapter 13) which follows now will clarify this argumentation.

15.1 Re-active and pro-active behavioural change

The upper route of Diagram 1 depicts how societal structures (households, schools, churches, labour unions, police, advertisement agencies, etc.) try to influence the behaviour of people. The two main mechanisms in this route are the processes of compliance and identification (see also the chapters 13.1 and 13.3). Law enforcement by the police makes that people comply with certain rules. Parents can enforce certain behaviour by demanding obedience from their children. People can be motivated to work hard by payment of high salaries. Teenagers perform certain behaviour because of the identification with their peer group. Monetary rewards, punishments and social approval or disapproval are examples of external pressures which can enforce behaviour. Another example is power and countervailing power.

When for example resource-poor farmers in sub-Saharan Africa would have been organized in politically and financially strong farmer unions, then agricultural researchers would have to comply with the wishes and needs of this specific client group and perform research work which is relevant to these farmers (a form of appropriate behaviour). In other words, when these farmers would have gained enough countervailing power to demand for relevant research, then the upper route in Diagram 1 would apply. However, the mechanisms of the upper route fail when countervailing power of farmers is virtually absent, the monetary rewards of researchers very low, the intervention power of research and extension organizations minimal and the external pressure of (financing) donor agencies only temporary. Resource-poor farmers remain then dependent on the altruism of scientists to be responsive to their needs; they remain dependent on the voluntary willingness of researchers to do relevant research. In this case client-oriented research will remain exceptional. How can we move beyond the voluntarism or altruism of scientists to be responsive to resource-poor farmers? What about the lower route, the altruistic route?

Van Woerkum (1990) makes a distinction between voluntary and non-voluntary (compulsory) behaviour and between externally and internally motivated voluntary behaviour. An example of compulsory behaviour is behaviour enforced by laws and regulations: people are coerced into compliance. An example of externally motivated voluntary behaviour is behaviour enforced by group pressure. And an example of internally motivated voluntary behaviour is behaviour realized by extension via the influencing of reasoned opinions. Röling (1988:44), on the other hand, makes only a distinction between non-voluntary and voluntary behaviour. The two determinants of non-voluntary behaviour are compliance and identification: compliance with rules and regulations enforced by a system of surveillance and incentives, and identification with others by mechanisms of social control. Changes in voluntary behaviour can only be induced by communicative interventions, such as advertising, PR, political propaganda, publicity and extension, but not by compliance and identification (ib.).

According to Röling (ib.:43) extension is not a very powerful instrument, but it is the only instrument available to influence voluntary behaviour, i.e., behaviour that is enacted in the absence of surveillance and incentive structures. And Leeuwis (1993:64) says that this kind of extension starts from "a rather reactive and passive view of human behaviour". Human action is conceptualized as "a rather passive (if not externally determined), mechanical, rational, and individual process" (ib.:65). Says Leeuwis:

"As soon as one starts to look at actors as having agency (that is, the capacity to make a difference), Van Woerkum's and Röling's distinction between voluntary and non-voluntary behaviour becomes rather vague and gradual. Both power and constraints play a role in all human (inter)action, but are at the same time enabling, and leave a certain space for manoeuvre" (ib.:64).

I agree with Leeuwis that the distinction between voluntary and non-voluntary behaviour is vague and gradual. In Van Woerkum's vision extension is an instrument to influence *internally motivated* voluntary behaviour, while for Röling it is an instrument to influence voluntary behaviour (not specified whether internally or externally motivated). In my view, extension and other communicative interventions are part of the upper route in Diagram 1 because they all induce re-active behaviour. People re-act to externally provided information. Some people internalize this information (to some extent) and change their behaviour accordingly; others do not internalize it and do not change their behaviour. Only when *externally provided* information is fully internalized, *internally motivated* behavioural change is the outcome. But the process of internalization is a kind of black box: we do not know exactly how externally provided information (input) is transformed into internally motivated behaviour (output). And that is the reason communicative interventions, especially extension methodologies, are relatively ineffective and difficult to improve. I rather speak of re-active and pro-active behaviour. Re-active behaviour is to some extent unfree, because the processes compliance and identification are based on externally imposed norms which 'enforce' some behaviour. Pro-active behaviour, on the other hand, does not need the processes compliance and identification.

In the earlier example of the resource-poor farmers in sub-Saharan Africa many agricultural researchers in the region do irrelevant research, mainly due to farmers' lack of countervailing power, limited intervention power of research organizations and low salaries. At the same time, however, one will always encounter some researchers who do an excellent job. While low salaries understandably result in low motivation, and lack of countervailing and intervention power into poor client orientation (the upper route in Diagram 1), some individuals apparently are internally motivated to perform well in spite of lousy external conditions. It seems that they (also) follow the lower route. Leeuwis' observation that there is always a certain space for manoeuvre, which at least some people do use, corresponds with my working experience in sub-Saharan Africa. In any remote village in Africa one will always find some farmers who consistently perform better than their colleagues under similar ecological and socio-economic conditions. They have agency or the competence to make a difference; they perform pro-active behaviour because they also follow the lower route, in my view.

In Diagram 1 the upper and lower routes together determine behaviour. I distinguish between the two routes for mere analytical purposes, but in daily practice they cannot be separated. We are not (continually) conscious of learning processes and behavioural changes; we do not know to which extent our behaviour is the outcome of the upper and/or lower routes. Often we just do things. Still it is useful to develop models such as Diagram 1 for analytical purposes. The diagram is an attempt to design an ideal-typical model, but in daily practice both routes apply simultaneously. In extension science, however, the emphasis is single-mindedly on the upper route while the lower route is completely ignored.

When enough actors maintain or regain their agency, dramatic changes in societal structures can be the result. An example is the fall of the Berlin Wall in 1989 and the ensuing (mostly non-violent) structural changes in Eastern Europe. In my view these unexpected and remarkable changes were the consequence of a more coherent and higher quality collective consciousness. The interaction between individual actors and societal structures takes place via the field of collective consciousness. In the actor-structure debate the emphasis should not be on actors *or* structures but on the *interaction* between actors and structures. Societal changes are mostly both actor-driven and system-imposed, but the interaction between the two tends to be ignored. In the terminology of William Easterly and Jeffrey Sachs one could argue that both searchers (actor-driven, bottom-up approach) and planners (system-imposed, top-down approach) matter. But both Easterly and Sachs tend to focus on their own favourite change agent and forget to discuss the all-important interaction between searchers and planners, between bottom-up and top-down approaches.

In the upper route the emphasis is on re-active behavioural change. People respond to the ideas and actions of other people, to external information, to external objects, to peer pressure, etc. The processes compliance and identification are linked to the unrestrained mimetic desire. People comply and identify with ideas and objects held by other people because they want to be the same as others. The strong and unlimited process of mimesis operates mostly unconscious or subconscious: most people are not aware of the process, let alone of its huge impact on their behaviour. The mimetic desire results into re-active behaviour.

In the lower route, on the other hand, the emphasis is on pro-active behavioural change. Here people do not re-act to ideas and actions of others, but follow their own path. Their mimetic desire has been transcended and overcome by techniques for consciousness development. Schwartz (1977) developed a theory on altruism in which personal standards evoke feelings of moral obligations that result in altruistic behaviour. Altruistic behaviour is an expression of internal values without interference of networks of social and material reinforcements. Altruistic behaviour is not the result of externally imposed norms: it is the outcome of listening to one's internal values. The process in the lower route is 'spontaneous' in the sense that it functions without interference of the rational-empirical consciousness. It does not take place at the level of the discursive consciousness but at more refined levels of consciousness, which arise in the process of experiential spirituality.

While in the upper route external norms play a role, the lower route is characterized by internal values. Speaking about *external* norms and *internal* values is confusing, since in common parlance norms and values are always bracketed together. Moreover, values are always internal. Still I prefer to make a distinction between external norms and internal values in order to be better able to elucidate the difference between the upper and lower routes in Diagram 1, mind you an ideal-typical model. In the chapters 13.3 and 14.3 I have distinguished between externally and internally motivated morality. Externally imposed norms (grounded, for instance, in the authority of a church) and internally imposed values (grounded in experiential spirituality) are linked to the upper and lower routes respectively. Instead of speaking of internally 'imposed' values it would be better to use the words internally 'inspired' or 'motivated' in order to emphasize the pro-active or free nature of the lower route.

15.2 Personal and institutional change

The difference between re-active and pro-active behaviour is also under-lined by the eco-philosopher Zweers (1995:18). He stresses that the *interaction* between structures and actors is fundamental. In his view the question whether primacy lies with structures or actors is a chicken-and-egg problem. Nevertheless, he emphasizes that changes in basic attitudes or fundamental values are necessary. But norms and values do not operate in a social vacuum: societal institutions are needed in order to make them effective at large scale (ib.). Zweers maintains that institutional changes are impossible without changes in individual actors: institutional changes must be inspired and supported by changes in basic values. Institutional change requires public support or a social basis.

Positive and negative sanctions are not sufficient to change people, says Zweers: convictions are necessary, deep convictions which are laid down in internal values. Convictions can be *aposteriori* or *apriori* (ib.:20). *Aposteriori* convictions are enforced in the course of events; they result into re-active willingness to act when one sees that things go wrong, when negative sanctions become too large. *Apriori* convictions, on the other hand, are not enforced by external developments but are deeply internalized convictions or internal values (ib.). They result into pro-active willingness to act. An *aposteriori*-willingness to act results into re-active behaviour (upper route) whilst an *apriori*-willingness to act results into pro-active behaviour (lower route).

Pretty & Chambers (1994) advocate a new agricultural professionalism and they remark:

"Personal behaviour and attitudes remain the great blind spot of agricultural research and extension. The quality and sensitivity of personal interactions are critical ... Methodologically, a major frontier for institutional change is how first to enable individuals to change, for personal change will often have to precede as well as accompany changes in the cultures of organizations".

Just as Zweers, Pretty & Chambers say that personal change has to precede and accompany institutional change.

A multitude of actors have to cooperate in the multi-dimensional process of agricultural development in order to make it effective. They include various categories of farmers, extensionists, on-station and on-farm researchers, facilitators, input-suppliers, private traders, credit organizations, marketing organizations, NGO staff, politicians, governmental planners and donor agencies. All these actors have to engage in a collective learning process which ultimately should lead to joint agency, to a capacity to act as a like-minded group. The ability to create collective agency is apparently insufficiently developed in sub-Saharan Africa (otherwise the problem of rural underdevelopment would not exist). The question is then under which specific conditions collective agency emerges. The same question applies to other sectors in society (health, education, etc.).

Social dilemmas, such as environmental degradation and sustainable development in general, require the emergence of collective agency. Social dilemmas are defined as conflicts between individual and collective interests "in which it is rational for people to make selfish choices although it were better for everybody if all made co-operative choices" (Röling et al. 1997). In order to learn to manage the negative collective effect of individual selfish choices (for example a polluted environment), facilitation of social learning to take collective action is required. Also with regard to labour input it is rational for people to make selfish choices (work less hard) although cooperative behaviour (work all hard in a synchronized manner) would be better.

It is evident that the contrasting (sometimes conflicting) goals and interests and contending worldviews of all the actors in the development process cannot always be mended. The aim of most stakeholders, including facilitators, is to maximize their own interests in the negotiation process (Leeuwis 1993:41).

"Implicit to [participatory approaches] is the rather optimistic and naive assumption that the 'collective learning process' takes place in a very open and eventually harmonic atmosphere (ib.:40) ... It seems highly unrealistic that an 'independent' facilitator (or anyone else) could in practice create an 'ideal speech situation', and/or convince actors to set aside their personal or institutional interests ... In all, communicative rationality emerges as a highly utopian notion ... Too many participatory procedures have - in practice - turned out to be ritual facades in which very little real opportunities existed to influence the course of events. Thus, at best [...] extension agents [may] create *effective* higher quality collective agency in some cases, but in many contexts [they] may not" (ib.:98).

Differing interests and differential access to resources (including knowledge) are unavoidable, especially in social settings with a wide array of actors. When actors with too widely diverging goals, interests and convictions are included in the negotiations, then efforts to develop collective agency may have counter-productive consequences. The danger is that with a wide array of actors the negotiated consensus amounts to strategically maintained lip-service only (ib.:383). When the consensus is not based on a truly dialectic debate, the result is at best a strategic compromise (the middle position in Diagram 3 in chapter 14.4; characterized by respectful communication and only moderate levels of trust and cooperation).

In sub-Saharan Africa the traditional 'palaver' is a kind of dialectic debate which aims at negotiated consensus. Such palavers, however, are not very effective in today's rapidly changing society (increasing individualization, dwindling authority of village elders, more frequent intergenerational conflicts). My work experience confirms that 'strategically maintained lip-service' is a common phenomenon in meetings with re-searchers, extensionists and other actors in the rural development process. The often hierarchic relationships in research and extension organizations do not contribute to 'ideal speech situations' and low salaries do promote 'lip-service'.

When the formation of collective agency requires "the participation of outsiders to help create momentum", as Huijsman & Budelman (1996) argue, then large numbers of skilled facilitators, who are a rare breed in themselves, are needed. I think that it will be difficult to engage large groups of resource-poor farmers in participatory processes. Especially in sub-Saharan Africa this might be difficult because of low population densities, large distances, inadequate infrastructure and a hitherto non-participative culture of formal education and training. Many outsider-facilitators are thus needed to promote sustainable development in the vast spaces of sub-Saharan Africa.

It is evident that the quality of participatory approaches depends heavily on the quality of facilitators: communication professionals with both research and facilitation skills are needed (Engel 1995:252-53). For technical scientists the simultaneous role of technical expert and facilitator is difficult (Hamilton 1995:157). According to Engel (1995:269) intuition, knowledge, ability and context go hand in hand to produce an effective innovation networker. A large part of what successful networkers do is 'playing around' (ib.:270). These references to intuition and playing around indicate in my view that the ability to facilitate the emergence of collective agency is an 'art': it is not a skill that can be acquired outright. The aim of facilitators is "to develop a shared sense of direction among all the relevant actors" and to foster group synergy, but "the art of fostering group synergy is delicate" (Campbell 1996). Moreover, the role of facilitators as 'bureaucracy busters' (Carr 1994) is value-laden and political, and requires a fine understanding of power.

"Being a successful facilitator often means being able to bring about changes in attitudes, processes and organizational cultures within the employing institution" (Campbell 1996).

Zweers, Pretty & Chambers and Campbell all say that personal change has to precede and accompany institutional change. At the end of the day, this implies that primacy lies with personal change rather than structural change, with actors rather than structures. The simple reason is that the building blocks of societal structures are individuals.

The all-important dynamic *interaction* between actors and structures is clarified in Diagram 1 with the concept collective consciousness. Conventional approaches to behavioural change emphasize the upper route: they assign a big role to societal structures. These collective structures are thought capable of changing individual behaviour. I, on the other hand, want to emphasize the lower route to behavioural change. Individual actors can engage in pro-active behaviour - without too much interference of societal structures - when they take on techniques for consciousness development.

In the current debate on foreign aid, participatory methodologies (aiming at ownership and collective agency via multi-stakeholder processes) and institutional capacity building (aiming at good governance and effective civil society) play important roles. But one can wonder where the numerous high quality facilitators, who are needed, will come from? In my view conventional training programmes cannot generate the quantity and quality of facilitators needed. Moreover, even skilled and effective facilitators face two crucial issues: 'the art of fostering group synergy is delicate' and the specific conditions which make collective agency emerge have not been adequately defined yet. I think that the analytical perspective presented in Diagram 1 provides clues to clarify these two issues.

The delicate character of fostering group synergy (creating collective agency) is due to the somehow intangible nature of the field of collective consciousness. Its subtle and elusive nature makes that the field of collective consciousness cannot be managed or controlled in the way natural and social science do things. A coherent and high quality collective consciousness can be purposefully 'constructed' and it does 'work' but it remains a kind of black box: how exactly the beneficial outcomes are generated remains unpredictable. The main specific condition which makes collective agency emerge is a coherent and high quality collective consciousness. More emphasis on the lower route will enhance personal and structural change in two ways: 1) practise of techniques for consciousness development will increase the number of competent facilitators (who will demonstrate more altruistic and pro-active behaviour) and 2) all the persons engaged in this process of experiential spirituality will enhance the coherence and quality of the collective consciousness and thus improve the performance of societal structures.

Leeuwis said above that it is very unlikely that 'independent' facilitators can create an 'open and harmonic atmosphere'. I think that the lower route can increase the number of truly 'independent' (altruistic) facilitators and indeed can facilitate 'open and harmonic atmospheres'. Leeuwis also speaks of the 'optimistic, naive and highly utopian' assumption of 'ideal speech situations' which are supposed to underlie participatory approaches. As long as the concept of the field of collective consciousness remains absent in these approaches, I think that his qualifications 'naive and highly utopian' are valid. With inclusion of techniques for consciousness development, however, ideal speech situations and open and harmonic atmospheres can be much easier created. The lower route is probably the best facilitator of an 'open and harmonic atmosphere' (or, in my terminology, a high quality and coherent collective consciousness).

15.3   Free and unfree work ethic

The lower route is probably also the best facilitator of a free work ethic. In the introduction to each of the chapters 13-15 I have indicated the link between work ethic and the content of those chapters. Work ethic and consciousness development are related topics. After all, a change in work ethic implies behavioural change which, in turn, is facilitated by consciousness development. The concept collective consciousness is the missing link in the actor-structure debate: it is the interface or medium through which interaction between actors and structures takes place. Since collective consciousness is the invisible foundation of all interfaces and interactions, a high quality and coherent collective consciousness facilitates individual and collective behavioural change, also in the field of labour.

Examples of 'external' pressures which can foster individual and collective behavioural change are: government policies, market forces, subsidies, environmental degradation, countervailing power, extension interventions, peer group pressure, externally imposed morality, etc. The label 'external' is a bit unfortunate since such pressures first must be 'internalized' before they can have consequences (Leeuwis 1993:398). Let's take the simple example of anti-smoking campaigns. It would be interesting to know why some persons internalize anti-smoking information and subsequently stop smoking, while others - despite numerous extension campaigns - continue to smoke. In addition to the mechanisms identification (peer group pressure) and compliance (authorities such as doctors, teachers and parents tell people what to do and what not), other processes might play a role.

Although learning the TM technique entails no prescriptions for a specific life style, scientific research shows that people who start meditating spontaneously reduce the use of cigarettes, alcohol and drugs (see the Annex). Health-supportive behaviour develops, as it were, from 'within' - spontaneously, without any external pressure. The danger of 'we-know-best-for-you social engineering' always looms large, but experiential spirituality cannot be forced. Wilber (1985:291) says: "There are only *participants* in emancipation. You can only force slavery; you cannot force a person to be free". Similarly, a work ethic can be enforced by compliance and identification (the upper route), but also the lower route can play a role. In the latter case a free, pro-active work ethic develops which is not enforced by external pressures.

Roos Vonk, professor of social psychology at the Radboud University in Nijmegen in The Netherlands, thinks that the conventional distinction between externally and internally motivated behaviour is problematic. The common idea is that much behaviour is initially externally driven. Children do certain things simply because they must: their behaviour is externally enforced by parents and others. Adults have gradually internalized these externally imposed norms. More important than the distinction between externally and internally motivated, says Roos, is the fact that internally motivated behaviour, which people perform because they like it, is not by definition good behaviour[53]. Behaviour which feels pleasant can also be very compulsive, for instance smoking. Not all internally motivated behaviour is holy. Compulsive behaviour, just as externally motivated behaviour, is not 'free'. The distinction between free and unfree behaviour - *I want* as opposed to *I must* - is more interesting than the distinction between externally and internally motivated behaviour. When work ethics are externally imposed - for example, people feel that they must earn more money than their neighbours or that they must prove themselves in relation to others - then burn-outs are more common. Not because they work so hard, but because their heart is not in it and they build up aversion towards their work. Here the unlimited mimetic desire rules again: people want and must something because of others.

Not all internally motivated behaviour is free and autonomous, and some things which people do for the benefit of others *are* precisely that: free and autonomous[54]. In the latter case we speak of altruistic behaviour. In my view the starting point of internally motivated, compulsive behaviour, such as excessive smoking and drinking, is external. Most young people start smoking and drinking via peer pressure, they want to belong to a group, and only few will really like the taste of the first cigarettes or beers. The mechanism of identification in the upper route is the starting point and then it gradually becomes an automatic habit (with physical and mental addiction as possible result). Excessive smoking and drinking are unfree behaviours based on an 'I must' notion.

In a similar way compulsive (unfree) labour, due to an internalized overdone work ethic, is not autonomous. It is based on a re-active 'I must work' notion, since it is enforced by a lengthy process of disciplining to labour. It is not based on a pro-active 'I want to work' notion. The modern work ethic was developed via the mechanisms compliance and identification in the upper route and got deeply internalized in the long run. Nevertheless, it is not 'free' behaviour, although most people will not even be aware of this fact since the work ethic has become a kind of automatism. A truly free work ethic, based on an autonomous 'I want to work' notion, develops via the lower route. It is a vocation, not just an occupation. In chapter 3.3 Erich Fromm spoke of the inner compulsion to work as a desperate attempt to escape fear. This unfree work ethic can only be transformed into a free work ethic when fear and uncertainty are dissolved in a process of experiential spirituality.

Beder (2001) argues that the modern work ethic has become pathological and dysfunctional. Although Beder in the following quote does not speak of an 'unfree work ethic', the citation clearly describes the externally imposed character of the modern work ethic.

"The compulsion to work has clearly become pathological in modern industrial societies. Millions of people are working long hours, devoting their lives to making or doing things that will not enrich their lives or make them happier but will add to the garbage and pollution that the earth is finding difficult to accommodate … Unless the work/consume treadmill is overcome there is little hope for the planet. The work ethic, and the corresponding respect accorded to those who accumulate wealth, are socially constructed but rapidly becoming dysfunctional for social and environmental welfare.

Much has been written about the role of Protestant preachers in the rise of the work ethic but the continued reinforcement of a secular work ethic owes much to literature, particularly self-help books and children's literature of the nineteenth century, which promoted work as a route to success and a sign of good character. In the centuries following the Protestant reformation the emphasis on work as a religious calling was gradually superseded by a materialistic quest for social mobility and material success. This success-oriented work ethic encouraged ambition, hard work, self-reliance, and self-discipline and held out the promise that such effort would be materially rewarded.

Through example and reiteration, the myth that any man, no matter what his origins, could become rich if he tried hard enough became firmly established. The self-made man owed his advancement to habits of industry, sobriety, moderation, self-discipline, and avoidance of debt. In early America the middle classes controlled 'the major institutions of social influence' (the schools, churches, factories, political offices and publishing companies) and used them to propagate work values. Their children learned the value of hard work from their parents and this was reinforced by school teachers, classroom readers and popular books …

There were enough oft-repeated stories of individuals moving from poverty to wealth to keep alive, at least in the minds of the well-to-do, the idea that hard work could lead from rags-to-riches, despite this not being the case for the vast majority of people who were born in poverty and died in poverty after a life time of hard work. In this way the affluent were able to feel comfortable about poverty in their midst, blaming it on individual weakness rather than societal failings. In Britain, as in America, the myth of the self-made man persisted in children's literature into the twentieth century …

Although not everyone subscribes to the work ethic today, the myth of the self-made man remains a myth in most English speaking countries, even though the disparities between rich and poor are widening and it is becoming more and more difficult for the poor to become rich through talent, effort and opportunities. Despite the dysfunctionality of the work ethic it continues to be promoted and praised, accepted and acquiesced to. It is one of the least challenged aspects of industrial culture. Yet it is based on myths and fallacies which provide legitimacy for gross social inequalities. If we are to protect the planet and our social health we need to find new ways of judging and valuing each other which are not work- and income dependent".

Apparently an only externally imposed work ethic can get seriously distorted and needs some kind of modification by the lower (internal) route. Nevertheless, an important lesson for sub-Saharan Africa is that the middle classes propagated the modern work ethic via 'the major institutions of social influence'. Unfortunately, middle classes have hardly emerged in sub-Saharan Africa. Another issue is that the development of different work ethics and different gender relations needs to start at early age.

I am aware of the fact that emphasizing the lower route can be interpreted as an attempt to social engineering. Imperfect knowledge on the many factors that influence (especially collective) behavioural change is unavoidable; to think otherwise constitutes the illusion of intellectual holism. Nonetheless, scientific research indicates that facilitation of collective behavioural change via consciousness development is possible. Collective agency and concerted action can be effectively promoted. This is important, especially in relation to ecological sustainability. The interaction between eco-systems and human actors is depicted in Diagram 1. Multi-facetted sustainability demands ecologically and societally sound behaviour (chapter 14.4).

With regard to the distinction between free and unfree behaviour and the related distinction between internal values and external norms, I want to emphasize here once more that Diagram 1 is an ideal-typical model (see also chapter 15.1). Both the upper and lower routes apply simultaneously and thus the effects of external norms and internal values on behaviours cannot be separated, but norms and values can be distinguished for analytical purposes. According to Hofstede (1994:8-9) values are "broad tendencies to prefer certain states of affairs over others" and norms are "the standards for values that exist within a group or category of people". The work ethic can be seen as internal value and external norm. When the value is 'to work hard' then the norm is for example 'eight hours per day'. The norm is a kind of statistical variable which indicates the choices actually made by the majority of the people[55].

Young children follow the external norms set by their parents via the mechanisms compliance and identification in the upper route. These external norms become gradually a kind of automatic habit, but unfortunately positive *and* negative norms of parents (and other role models) are copied. Children follow parents' good *and* bad behaviour. The re-active behaviour in the upper route can be positively or negatively oriented. The pro-active behaviour in the lower route, however, tends to be altruistic and positively oriented, and the degree of altruism depends on the level of consciousness. Actors with a low level of consciousness will follow predominantly the upper route, while actors with a high level of consciousness will follow mainly the lower route.

Research on TM shows a wide range of practical benefits for all areas of life - physiological, psychological, sociological and ecological. Some of the more important benefits in the context of this book are (see Annex for website addresses with scientific references):

- Improved problem-solving ability;
- Increased inner-directedness: greater independence and self-supportiveness;

- Increased field independence, indicating broader comprehension and improved ability to focus attention;
- Greater ability to assign correct priorities;
- Increased morale, facilitative leadership, and increased influence in decision-making.

These characteristics of improved performance all point to more pro-active, free behaviour. As long as *only* the upper route is followed, the starting point of children's positive behaviour must be parental (and other persons') positive behaviour. One of the societal sub-structures in Diagram 1 is the family or household unit. Via the upper route this societal sub-structure can enforce positive behaviour, but the starting point is always some individuals who first themselves must perform positive behaviour. Thus primacy rests with actors. Van Spengler correctly argues that 'transfer' of norms and values is impossible[56]. Values cannot be transferred to somebody else, but must be individually developed in a process of personal growth. And *information* contained in norms (behavioural rules) can be transferred, but does not mean anything until it is internalised into personal *knowledge*, which subsequently still has to be transformed into actual changes in individual *behaviour*. The difference between word and deed is indeed crucial.

In a continuum of societies with differing levels of consciousness development, one extreme position is a society with no attention for consciousness development at all: the enforcement of (preferably democratically agreed upon) external norms is then the best option (the upper route is dominant). The other extreme position is an 'ideal' society in which consciousness development is absolutely central: positive internal values will then spontaneously emerge (the lower route is dominant). The 'realistic' middle position is a society with only moderate attention for consciousness development: a combination of enforcement of external norms (resulting into re-active behaviour) and spontaneous development of internal values (resulting into pro-active behaviour) is then the best option. In today's society, which is characterized by a rising level of individualization, the processes of social control and peer pressure in the upper route are increasingly weakened. This enhances the need to pay more attention to the lower route.

16 Work Ethic: Social and Cultural Capital

The modern work ethic was initially developed in North-Western Europe in a long-term process of disciplining to labour. This complex process (expounded in the chapters 3 to 11) mainly evolved in the upper route of Diagram 1. A work ethic should be effective (development-oriented), efficient (high labour productivity) and life-supporting (avoiding environmental degradation and human breakdown). It should support wealth and well-being: the goal is material, social, mental and spiritual welfare. Truly sustainable societies in both industrialized and non-industrialized countries would be characterized by this work ethic. The expansion of the life-supporting work ethic requires more attention for the lower route.

Unfortunately, the values and norms with regard to work cannot be changed at will. Béteille (2002) says:

"By any standard, the conditions of work in less-developed and transitional economies are often appalling. There is bonded labour, exploitation of women and abuse of children. Such conditions are a challenge to the conscience of right-minded people the world over. But they are different not only from the conditions that now prevail in the advanced industrial societies, but also from those that generally prevailed in stable agrarian communities before the advent of industrial capitalism. The social organization of work, whether in relatively stable agrarian communities or in rapidly changing industrial societies, is governed by a variety of factors: technology, size and density of population, social morphology, economic policy, legal rules, and religious and cultural traditions … The various elements act upon one another, and no single one among them, whether technology or religion, may be said to have a decisive or determining influence on all the others. New technology does bring about changes in the conditions of work, but so do new laws; and it would be futile to try to make a radical change in those conditions by altering any one element without considering all the others.

The value assigned to work and the norms for the regulation of work are not the same everywhere or at all times. 'Value' here refers to culturally prescribed ends, and 'norms' refer to regulatory rules. There is no society without its own culturally prescribed ends and none without its own regulatory rules, although values and norms as defined above are neither invariant nor immutable ... Norms and values change over time, but they do not change at the will and pleasure of well-intentioned individuals or even of benevolent organizations. Major social changes are in large part the unintended consequence of the actions of innumerable individuals and other social agents".

Béteille underlines here eloquently the role of innumerable actors and societal structures in social change, the unpredictable nature of social change and the need for a holistic approach. But the question how to handle all these crucial issues remains unanswered. I think that the Diagrams 1 and 2 are helpful at this point.

The systematic disciplining to labour in North-Western Europe was enforced by a mix of interrelated processes. The current work ethic in sub-Saharan Africa is also determined by a complex of (partly interrelated) factors. These factors include: geographical and climatological condition; length and intensity of exposure to colonization and mission; degree of penetration of money economy and wage labour; economy of affection and traditional communal land; level of mimetic desire; absence of an industrial revolution; degree of internalization of modern work ethic in postcolonial period via enforcement by religious, educational and governmental organizations; development cooperation; corruption; gender; and ethnic-cultural factors (chapter 8.2).

These are all external factors except the mimetic desire and the ethnic-cultural factors. But even the ethnic-cultural characteristics of certain population groups and the mimetic desire could be considered 'external' in the sense that they are externally imposed via social enculturation and social control. The work ethic as internal value, resulting into pro-active behaviour, deserves more attention if we want to develop sustainable societies.

With regard to African countries Van der Veen (2004:356) argues that, despite the lasting importance of the international environment, external factors cannot have been the overriding cause of the lack of development since independence. The Malian historian Tidiane Diakité wrote a book titled '*L'Afrique et l'aide. Ou comment s'en sortir?*': 'Africa and foreign aid. How do we get rid of it?' His main conclusion is that Africa should stand up and rescue itself. Van der Veen (2004:356-7) says:

"Compare an arbitrarily selected pair of countries, one in Africa and one in Asia: Zambia and South Korea, for instance. When the Zambians became independent in 1964, they were on average twice as wealthy as the South Koreans. By the turn of the century, the South Koreans were, on average, a full twenty-seven times as rich as the Zambians ... It would be absurd to attribute such huge differences to the international economic environment, which was essentially the same for all these countries".

With regard to foreign aid, Van der Veen (ib.:357) remarks that extra money for Africa would not have made any difference, since the domestic circumstances were such that it would not have been put to use profitably.

"A case in point is Nigeria, which for decades had several billion US dollars a year of 'extra' income from oil ... The billions of extra dollars did nothing at all to raise ordinary people's living standards. When Nigeria became independent in 1960, about twenty-five per cent of the population was below the poverty line. By 2000 this figure had risen to around seventy per cent.

In an attempt to provide more palatable reasons for Africa's failure - factors that Africans 'could do nothing about' - people often mention the borders that were drawn rather arbitrarily by colonial rulers ... However, such problems cannot seriously be put forward as obstacles to statehood. Other parts of the world have shown that nationhood and development are perfectly possible even in geographical units whose borders are the result of historical contingency.

Sometimes other geographical or environmental circumstances are cited, such as the fact that a country is landlocked or that it is not easy for people to live in a hot, humid climate. Yet numerous examples prove that this is of little relevance to a country's ability to modernise. If such theories were true, landlocked nations such as Switzerland and Austria or ones with extremely harsh climates, such as the Scandinavian countries, would be doomed to remain poor, whereas in fact they are the wealthiest countries in Europe.

The example of China shows to what extent domestic circumstances - especially the interaction between politics and culture - can determine a country's chances of modernisation. People in the West had long felt that the Chinese should be capable of becoming prosperous, given some of their more striking cultural characteristics such as industriousness, inquisitiveness, organisation, motivation and an emphasis on education. Chinese people living outside China showed the world what these virtues could achieve. In China itself, however, people could not take advantage of them, for the country's socio-political system was still pre-modern, still geared to maintaining the status quo … It was only in the 1980s, when the state … relaxed its grip on the economy and allowed free markets to develop, that the real Chinese revolution took place. These reforms fell on fertile soil … and economic growth is now taking place at an astonishing rate. The idea that this might be due to the international economic environment or to China's geographical location or climate is baseless. The main contributing factors have been internal ones, both political and cultural" (Van der Veen 2004:357-8).

Economic policy can achieve little when political and cultural factors are inadequate. Moreover, these factors cannot be influenced by donors: money is of little relevance here (chapter 10.3). Van der Veen refers to the work of Gunnar Myrdal (1968) who already in the 1960s spoke about the weak state in many developing countries.

"[Myrdal asserted] that the chief characteristic of a weak state was its lack of control over the public. People could easily evade the law. It was everyone for himself, and the overall impact in terms of development was minimal. Strong states, he claimed, had to 'capture' or discipline their citizens; in short, influence their behaviour. Myrdal thereby linked the state and politics with culture, something almost no-one has attempted since. 'Culture' had become almost sacred and untouchable. On the assumption that many roads led to Rome (i.e. to prosperity), hardly anyone noticed that certain cultural characteristics of developing countries were obstacles to progress. Even after 2000, culture still appeared sacrosanct. States were supposed to maintain law and order, provide services, 'facilitate' and do any number of things, but at no time did anyone say that they were supposed to influence their people's behaviour, i.e. their culture. The only exception to this was perhaps the fight against corruption. Even in the fight against AIDS, attempts to influence people's behaviour were effectively taboo" (Van der Veen 2004:320).

It is evident that a strong state alone is not sufficient to bring about economic development. The former communist states of the Eastern Bloc were 'strong', i.e. had an effective administration, but nonetheless poor policies led to economic failure. Both good governance and good policies are needed. The disciplining of citizens - or the attempt to influence their behaviour - by an effective state can be an important tool for development, but always in combination with good policies and linked to consciousness development. Strong states with good policies (i.e. policies which are sustainable and life-supporting) operate hitherto only via the upper route. More attention for the lower route would facilitate a more effective and efficient administration via a coherent and high quality collective consciousness and it would guide the goals of policies in sustainable and life-supporting directions.

We have seen in the chapters 9 and 10 that the strong economy of affection and the weak formal state in sub-Saharan Africa are not conducive to high levels of wealth and well-being. The weak formal state is central in

Van der Veen's book. The fact that the cultural characteristic 'work ethic' is mentioned only twice (and only casually) in his otherwise excellent book, indicates that for him this specific aspect of culture is not crucial in the debate on development (as in nearly all literature on development for that matter). The weak formal state has not been able to enforce a modern work ethic.

In my view our limited ability to influence cultural characteristics has led to the nearly religious, untouchable status of culture. It has simply been impossible to change cultural characteristics quickly; cultural and behavioural change takes time, at least decades if not a century. Societies and cultures are not static and change all the time, but effective and efficient methods to bring about cultural changes have not been available. This is probably also one of the reasons why the work ethic has been ignored in the debate on development. Category 2 (collective consciousness) encompasses category 3 (cultural and personality factors) in Diagram 2 and thus carries more weight. We have to focus on this leverage mechanism with broad impact (chapter 14.1). More attention for the lower route in Diagram 1 can speed up the process of cultural and behavioural change.

In addition to differences in natural resources - a matter of good or bad luck - culture and institutions can explain differences in national development. A combination of factors is at work in Diagram 2, including geographical and cultural factors. Both geographical generalizations (on large spatial scales and over long times) and cultural differentiations (to explain the always existing variation on smaller spatial scales and over shorter times) are necessary (chapter 8.2). It is likely, however, that in the future cultural and personality factors will carry more weight than geographical and ecological factors, because of technological advance. Drawbacks in the field of natural resources can be circumvented by more sophisticated technologies.

In chapter 5.3 I argued that manual labour needs to be more positively valued in sub-Saharan Africa. The current distaste for manual labour among many (male) young people - the white collar mentality - is detrimental to progress, since agriculture must be the engine of economic growth, and agriculture for some time to come will involve manual labour and rural women are already overstretched. Especially the relatively weak work ethic of men, of whom many are partially idle due to unequal gender relations, needs to be tackled.

Kombrink and Klamer (2004) argue that effective work within organizations requires trust (social capital) and inspiration (cultural capital): cohesion and motivation are the result. Today's dominant economic school of thought, however, is characterized by the concept 'measuring-is-knowing-is-managing' which results into an 'economization' of (also non-profit) organizations: i.e. the advance of economic vocabulary and businesslike management styles. Social and cultural aspects hardly get attention.

"The fact that the concept 'trust' plays an essential role in economic development has been emphasized by, among others, the social scientist Francis Fukuyama (1995) in his book of the same name *Trust*. Trust reduces the costs of transactions. Regions and countries with a high level of trust - the *high-trust societies* in his terminology - are thus more economically successful than countries without mutual trust - the *low-trust societies*. This is Fukuyama's economic interpretation of what sociologists have called 'social capital': i.e. the ability of people to voluntarily form groups or organisations and to co-operate for a common goal ...

Social capital is related to civil society: the societal midfield with all its intermediate organisations in between state and market ... Without this social web of organisations, society cannot adequately function ... [Social capital or trust shared] is a basic condition for effective co-operation and successful conclusion of business deals ... Co-operation within or between organisations - and thus productive work - is impossible without social capital ...

People who informally talk build up social capital, not so much in meetings but in casual and unstructured discussions ... Moreover, social capital is shared by all stakeholders in organisations and is not the property of shareholders ... It takes time to build up social capital and the process is often exceptionally inefficient and unproductive by economic standards. Trust arrives on foot and leaves on horse. But organisations generally are as effective and swift as their social mechanisms permit" (Kombrink and Klamer 2004).

In short, social capital makes organizations work. Both literally and figuratively we are then *in good company* (Cohen and Prusak 2001). A lack of social and cultural capital irrevocably manifests itself in lack of financial capital in the long run (Kombrink and Klamer 2004). Social and cultural capital constitutes the goodwill of organizations (Korver, Witteveen and Achterhuis 2004). The financial crisis of 2008/2009 clearly demonstrates the importance of trust, social capital and collective consciousness.

If Fukuyama's observation that high-trust societies are more economically successful than low-trust societies is correct, then the dire economic situation in sub-Saharan Africa must be (at least partially) the consequence of a low level of mutual trust among its citizens (see also Covey's Diagram 3 in chapter 14.4). Although this is in line with much of my work experience in the region, the general (unfortunately erroneous) romantic picture that many Westerners have of sub-Saharan Africa is exactly the opposite: African societies would be characterized by a high level of mutual trust and cooperation.

The work ethic obviously is part of cultural capital, but since it is also societally constructed (it is more than a mentality) it is as well social capital. A productive work ethic results into economic capital. Ultimately the economic, social, cultural and political capital comes together in 'human capital'. This human capital is the engine of not only businesses, but of all organizations and thus society as a whole. The business world and the government as well as the intermediate civil society are kept going by and through individual people. The quality of these individual actors and their joint co-operation are central. The value of human capital is determined by education, on-the-job training, work experience, knowledge, skills, commitment and work ethic, but particularly by the level of the underlying individual consciousness. This last factor could be labelled spiritual capital.

Hitherto foreign aid has been mainly focussed on generating economic capital; although at present social and political capital also start to get some attention. The fixation on economic capital will probably continue for some time, because it is not clear yet how political, social and cultural capital can be quickly built up (and measured). In Diagram 2 in chapter 14.1 the inner category of spiritual capital carries most weight and thus should receive more attention. The lower route in Diagram 1 builds up spiritual capital and thus facilitates the development of high quality human capital. Hofstede (1994:169) says: "Culture in the form of certain dominant values is a necessary but not a sufficient condition for economic growth". The work ethic is part and parcel of culture, but an effective, efficient and life-supporting work ethic does not operate in a societal vacuum (see Diagram 2).

Richard Douthwaite (1999:340) says in his book *The Growth Illu$ion*:

"Just because we have agreed that we have to work with capitalism because it is the only functioning economic system in the world does not mean we have to accept it warts and all. Indeed the whole point of enabling the political and moral-cultural systems to act independently of the economic one is so that they can transform their current master. Changing the scale on which capitalism operates is just one of several major modifications the other parts of the troika have to make. Or rather we do, because we make them up".

And Fareed Zakaria (2003:256) says on the last page of his book *The Future of Freedom*:

"Perhaps most difficult of all, it requires that those with immense power in our societies embrace their responsibilities, lead, and set standards that are not only legal, but moral. Without this inner stuffing, democracy will become an empty shell".

The current financial crisis shows that the political and especially the moral-cultural systems have failed. But we as individual actors make up the economic, political and moral-cultural systems; we make up all societal structures in fact, so only we can modify them - by modifying ourselves. The 'inner stuffing' of these human systems needs to be transformed. Personal development is thus a prerequisite for sustainable and democratic development in sub-Saharan Africa and elsewhere.

17 Another Voice: Culture as *Outcome* rather than *Cause* of Economic Development

In the previous chapter I remarked that the work ethic is part of cultural and social capital. In chapter 14.1 I indicated that cultural factors carry more weight than economic factors in the multi-dimensional development process represented in Diagram 2. In this chapter I discuss the highly original and provocative book *Bad Samaritans* written by Ha-Joon Chang (2008), professor at the Faculty of Economics and Politics at the University of Cambridge. Chang argues that the neo-liberal policies of the past two and a half decades have failed in developing countries, simply because they were wrong. These policies did not fail "because they have been overwhelmed by local anti-developmental factors, like corruption or 'wrong' culture" as the neo-liberals tend to reason today (Chang 2008:161). Chang refers to David Landes, who was extensively quoted in the chapters 7.1 and 7.2, as the leader in the renaissance of culturalist theories (ib.:187). He also characterizes Samuel Huntington (*The Clash of Civilizations*) and Francis Fukuyama (*Trust*) as cultural theorists, who say that pro-developmental forms of behaviour (like hard work, thrift, investment, education, organization, and discipline) are determined by culture and thus largely fixed. I discuss Chang's work here because his view on the relationship between work ethic and economic development seems to contradict my views.

17.1 Laziness

Chang says that it is very difficult to define cultures precisely and to determine whether they are inherently good or bad for economic development (ib.). The most frequently cited 'cultural' trait of people in poor countries is laziness. In this context Chang remarks that only a century ago Westerners considered for example the Japanese 'lazy' while to-day they see them as hardworking and loyal 'worker ants' (ib.:184). Before Japan's economic 'miracle', Westerners used to blame Confucian-ism for its underdevelopment and after its fast economic development the so-called unique form of Confucianism in Japan was held responsible. But broad categories, like 'Confucian', are simply "too crude to be analytically meaningful and […] even a country is too big a cultural unit to generalize about" (ib.:189). Chang maintains that cultures can result into 'positive' and 'negative' behavioural traits. He says:

"So which is an accurate portrait of Confucianism? A culture that values 'thrift, investment, hard work, education, organization, and discipline', as Huntington put it in relation to South Korea, or a culture that disparages practical pursuits, dis-courages entrepreneurship and retards the rule of law? Both are right, except that the first singles out only those elements that are good for economic development and the second only the bad. In fact, creating a one-sided view of Confucianism does not even have to involve selecting different elements. The same cultural ele-ment can be interpreted as having positive or negative implications, depending on the result you seek. The best example is loyalty […] Some people think that the emphasis on loyalty is what makes the Japanese variety of Confucianism more suited to economic development than other varieties. Other people judge the em-phasis on loyalty to be exactly what is wrong with Confucianism, since it stifles independent thinking and thus innovation" (ib.:191-2).

Chang says that in addition to the common prejudices against (especially poor) foreigners (i.e., cultural stereotyping), there is also an element of genuine 'misinterpretation' due to "the fact that rich countries are very differently organized to poor countries". With regard to laziness he re-marks:

"People from rich countries routinely believe that poor countries are poor because their people are lazy. But many people in poor countries actually work long hours in backbreaking conditions. What makes them *appear* lazy is often their lack of an 'industrial' sense of time. When you work with basic tools or simple machinery, you don't have to keep time strictly. If you are working in an automated factory, it's essential. People from rich countries often interpret this difference in sense of time as laziness. Of course, it was not *all* prejudice or misinterpretation [...] Early-20th-century Japanese *were*, on average, not as organized, rational, disciplined, etc. as the citizens of the successful countries of the time or, for that matter, as people are in today's [Japan]. It *is* true that there are a lot more people 'lazing around' in poor countries. But is it because those people culturally prefer lounging about to working hard? Usually not. It is mainly because poor countries have a lot of people who are unemployed or underemployed [...] This is the result of economic conditions rather than culture. The fact that immigrants from poor countries with 'lazy' cultures work much harder than the locals when they move to rich countries proves the point" (ib.:194-5).

In chapter 4.5 (*Underutilization of labour*) the authors Hyden, Collinson and Koponen illustrated that the traditionalistic work ethic in sub-Saharan Africa cannot be equated with laziness. Collinson referred specifically to the apparent paradox of 'excessive leisure preference in a situation of dire poverty' and the resulting misinterpretation of the African smallholder character. With regard to differences in sense of time between sub-Saharan Africa and especially North-Western Europe, I refer to chapter 6.2 in which Mumford said that the mechanical clock is the key instrument to understand the modern technological era. Chang's remark about hardworking immigrants surfaced earlier in chapter 7.2: it is the combination of hardworking people and facilitating government initiatives (good governments creating enabling conditions) that makes 'economic miracles' possible.

Chang (ib.:196) remarks that apparently unchangeable 'cultural' traits can be transformed quite quickly by changes in economic conditions. He cites an American missionary in early-20th-century Japan, who observed that 'the Japanese give the double impression of being industrious and diligent on the one hand and, on the other, of being lazy and utterly indifferent to the passage of time'. Workers in the new factories looked very industrious, while under-employed farmers and carpenters looked 'lazy'. In addition to an 'industrious' work ethic, also an 'industrial' sense of time can be developed very quickly with economic development, says Chang.

"My country Korea offers an interesting example in this regard. Twenty, maybe even 15, years ago, we used to have the expression, 'Korean time'. It described the widespread practice whereby people could be an hour or two late for an appointment and not even feel sorry about it. Nowadays, with the pace of life far more organized and faster, such behaviour has almost disappeared, and with it the expression itself [...] Culture is the *result*, as well as the cause, of economic development. It would be far more accurate to say that countries become 'hardworking' and 'disciplined' (and acquire other 'good' cultural traits) because of economic development, rather than the other way around" (ib.:196-7).

According to Chang the transformation of a traditionalistic into a modern work ethic can take place within a few decades and he refers to early-20th-century Japan, Germany and South-Korea to support his case. Could this happen in sub-Saharan Africa? An important question here is whether the general level of development in these countries at the beginning of the 20th century was more or less equal to the level of development in today's sub-Saharan Africa (a difference in time of more than a century)? This would include elements like the maturity of the nation-state, effectiveness of government, level of institutional development (civil society actors like labour unions and farmer organisations), presence of middle class, quantity and quality of physical infrastructure, level of education, percentage of population active in agriculture (chapter 4.1), and possibilities to absorb ex-farmers into alternative employment opportunities. All these factors have impact on the above transformation process. Especially with regard to the maturity of the nation-state and the related effectiveness of government (including its ability to discipline people) countries in today's sub-Saharan Africa might be worse off than early-20th-century Germany. The same might apply with regard to, for example, physical infrastructure. The other two countries mentioned by Chang, Japan and South-Korea, are homogeneous societies (and thus strong nation-states). Since the number of factors with possible impact on the development of a modern work ethic is large, it will always be difficult to compare different countries in different time periods.

The double impression of industrious labourers in new factories and lazy (underemployed) farmers, to which Chang refers, is probably characteristic of societies in a phase of early industrialization. However, the role of violence in the enforcement of the new work ethic (chapter 3.1) is not mentioned by Chang. Haveman talks about unskilled labourers in The Netherlands in the period immediately after the Second World War: they were considered 'shiftless and irresponsible' by the middle-class (chapter 3.1). Haveman argues that these habits are normal responses to the physical, social and economic environment of underprivileged workers. In chapter 4.7 I concluded that the work ethic is more than a mentality. Chang would probably agree. With regard to a modern 'industrial' sense of time, I can say that the expression 'Swahili time' applies until today in Eastern Africa.

Mumford said in chapter 6.2 that the mechanical clock is the key instrument to understand the modern technological era, because the very notion of labour productivity is a by-product of the clock. The advent of the mechanical clock in Europe started from the fourteenth century onwards, but it remained a Western monopoly for some three hundred years.

The high level of economic development in today's Western world might be (at least partially) due to this early penetration of the mechanical clock in all sectors of society. Without this all-pervading diffusion of the clock, the concept 'time is money' would be meaningless. In today's (rural and urban) sub-Saharan Africa the situation is still quite different. How quickly a modern sense of time and work ethic (and thus high labour productivity) can develop in sub-Saharan Africa, is difficult to predict, because of the numerous factors involved.

Here above Haveman indicated that still in the 1940s unskilled labourers in The Netherlands were considered lazy. Although in Europe remnants of the traditionalistic work ethic survived until into the twentieth century, by and large a modern work ethic had been established at the end of the nineteenth century (chapter 3.1). The British Industrial Revolution ran about a century, from 1770 to 1870, but it was well and long prepared, technologically as well as institutionally and culturally (chapter 7.1). Steam engine development, for example, took two hundred years, and it took Britain centuries to get good government. Especially mechanization gave rise to the disciplined organization of work under supervision in the factory system (chapter 7.1). Although the development of a modern work ethic in Britain, and later on in continental North-Western Europe, took at least one century, it is in theory possible that this process might go faster in sub-Saharan Africa. Mechanization, modern technology and the management of factory-systems are now well-known concepts, but can this knowledge easily be applied in sub-Saharan Africa?

The many differences between countries in *today's* sub-Saharan Africa and countries in North-Western Europe of (let's say) *one century ago* are crucial in understanding the present huge gap in economic development. As indicated above, especially differences with regard to the maturity of the nation-state (chapter 4.1), the effectiveness of government (chapters 10.1, 10.2 and 10.4), the strength of civil society (chapter 10.3), and the quality of the technological base (chapters 7.3 and 8.1) are important. Whether processes of institutional and political change can be effectively enhanced by foreign donors remains to be seen. In general, processes of institution-building and political change are slow, but sometimes unexpected and quick changes do occur (for example, the fall of the Berlin Wall in 1989 and the subsequent demise of the Soviet Union). Perhaps the transformation of the traditionalistic work ethic in sub-Saharan Africa can take place within a few decades *after* economic development has been kick-started, as Chang argues, but then first various obstacles need to be negotiated.

17.2   How to kick-start economic development?

In Chang's view, pro-developmental behavioural traits are not prerequisites for economic development, but rather follow from it. He argues that today's developing countries "can get development going through means other than a cultural revolution" (ib.:198). He recommends the following policy measures to kick-start economic development, other than cultural change through ideological persuasion[57]:

- A judicious mix of protection and open trade, constantly adjusted to changing needs and capabilities;
- Asymmetric protectionism, including more free use of the tools of infant industry promotion in order to develop advanced technological and managerial capabilities;
- More use of state-owned enterprises;
- With regard to intellectual property rights (patents, copyrights and trademarks): get the balance right between the interests of the (often foreign) IPR-holders and the rest of society (or the rest of the world);

- Pursue macroeconomic policies that allow for moderate inflation rates (up to 40%) and higher levels of government deficit spending than now permitted by donors.

Although today's neo-liberal free-trade free-market proponents do not want developing countries to use protectionist policies, all of the above policy measures have been used by today's rich countries in the past. These so-called 'Bad Samaritans' are saying: 'do as we say, not as we did' (ib.:16). They are 'kicking away the ladder' that they themselves have climbed to attain economic prosperity. Chang says: "The history of capitalism has been so totally re-written that many people in the rich world do not perceive the historical double standards involved in recommending free trade and free market to developing countries" (ib.).

In this context Chang strongly criticizes, and correctly so, the neo-liberal notion of the 'level playing field'. In his view a level playing field leads to *unfair* competition *when the players are unequal* (ib.:218). Global economic competition is, certainly today, a game of unequal players (how can, for example, Switzerland and Swaziland compete fairly?). It is only fair that we 'tilt the playing field' in favour of the weaker countries (ib.:219). Chang is in favour of *asymmetric protectionism* whereby today's rich countries allow developing countries "to use more freely the tools of infant industry promotion – such as tariff protection, subsidies and foreign investment regulation" (ib.:82). The economically less advanced countries should be allowed to protect and subsidise their producers (farmers and manufacturers) more vigorously until they have raised their technological and organizational capabilities to a level where they can compete with foreigners.

With regard to the practice of the 'Unholy Trinity' of the IMF, the World Bank and the WTO to block developing countries from using protectionist policies, Chang remarks: "It is actually quite curious how free-market economists who are so much in favour of choice and autonomy do not hesitate to oppose them when they are by developing countries" (ib.:219). Just as in most sports unequal players are not allowed to compete against each other (in sports we employ age groups, gender separation and weight classes to ensure fair competition), differential treatment for countries with differential capabilities and needs is simply fair (ib.:218-220). The notion of the level playing field has also been criticized in chapter 4.4.

Another important remark by Chang is:

"Once economic development gets going, it will change people's behaviour and *even the beliefs* underlying it (namely, culture) in ways that help economic development. A 'virtuous circle' between economic development and cultural values can be created" (ib.:198) (my italics).

In Chang's view economic development, to a large extent, creates the culture that it needs. But culture not only changes through changes in underlying economic conditions: it can also be transformed deliberately through ideological persuasion (ib.). Changes in attitudes through ideological persuasion, however, need to be *supported or accompanied* by real changes in policy measures that promote economic development and by institutional changes (for example, welfare schemes) that "can sustain the desired forms of behaviour over an extended period of time so that they turn into 'cultural' traits" (ib.:200). Thus, in Chang's view a mix of ideological persuasion, economic policy and institution building results into behavioural change that over time is 'internalized' into pro-developmental cultural values. His underlying assumption appears to be that when people perform certain pro-developmental behaviours over an extended period of time, they are more or less automatically internalized into pro-developmental cultural values. Chang also admits, realistically, that "*it is not an easy job to get this mix right*" (my italics) (ib.:201). But once you do, he says, "culture can be changed much more quickly than is normally assumed". It can change within a couple of decades.

In Chang's view, you *first* have to get economic development going, *then* people's behaviour will change, and *then* underlying cultural beliefs or values will follow suit[58]. The basic question becomes then how to kick-start economic development through a right mix of interventions? *Who* is going to 'orchestrate' this right mix of interventions? Who has the intellectual capacity and political power to do this? I will soon come back to this issue. Here I want to emphasize that the elements in Chang's mix (ideological persuasion, economic policy measures, and institution building) are all *external* instruments, which result into *re-active* behaviour (see chapter 15.3). The starting point is that one *first* needs some individuals (for example, parents and political leaders) who perform pro-developmental behaviour, *before* others can identify with them and copy their behaviour. If the process of behavioural change depends on only the upper route in Diagram 1, it might be difficult to create sufficient large numbers of such role-models, numbers big enough to generate large-scale impact. In my view, the process of consciousness development facilitates this upper route and adds the benefit of the lower route.

Since culture can be deliberately changed, says Chang, countries are not condemned to underdevelopment because of their culture. "But at the same time we must not forget that culture cannot be reinvented at will [...] The cultural 'reformer' still has to work with existing cultural attitudes and symbols" (ib.:201-2). Here Chang seems to suggest that cultural change is not *that* easy. In the same vein, at the end of his chapter on the relationship between economic development and culture, he says:

"[We need to] free our imagination both from the unwarranted pessimism of those who believe culture is destiny and from the naïve optimism of those who believe they can persuade people to think differently and bring about economic development that way" (ib.:202).

With regard to free trade and free capital markets, Chang remarks:

"Free trade demands that poor countries compete immediately with more advanced foreign producers, leading to the demise of [local] firms before they can acquire new capabilities [...] Investment in capacity-building can take quite a long time to bear fruit [...] It took Toyota more than 30 years of protection and subsidies to become competitive in the international car market, even at the lower end of it. It was a good 60 years before it became one of the world's top car makers [...] Free capital markets, with their pro-cyclical herd behaviour, make [such] long-term projects vulnerable [...] [Capability-building requires] sacrificing certain short-term gains [refusing to import higher-quality, lower-price foreign goods] for the sake of raising long-term productivity (and thus standards of living) – possibly for decades" (ib.:212-15).

Capability-building thus takes time, at least 3-5 decades. A serious bottleneck in sub-Saharan Africa is that it is unlikely, in the current power constellation, that the political and economic elites will ban the import of higher-quality, lower-price foreign goods. That would not be in their (short-term) interest. Moreover, cultures in sub-Saharan Africa tend to be characterized by a short-term orientation (Hofstede 1994:166). This implies that sacrificing short-term gains for the sake of raising long-term gains will not always be a priority.

An important question is whether developing countries should invest in higher capabilities in agriculture, manufacturing industry or services. Chang (2008:213-5) says:

"History has repeatedly shown that the single most important thing that distinguishes rich countries from poor ones is basically their higher capabilities in manufacturing, where productivity is generally higher, and, more importantly, where productivity tends to (although does not always) grow faster than in agriculture or services [...] Despite what the free trade economists recommend (concentrating on agriculture) or the prophets of post-industrial economy tout (developing services), manufacturing is the most important, though not the only, route to prosperity".

In this context it is significant that Chang shows that many developing countries pursued protectionist 'import substitution industrialization' in the mid-20th century and grew, on average, at double the rate that they are doing today under free trade (ib.:69). During the 1960s and the 1970s *per capita* income in the developing countries grew by 3.0% annually, which remains the best that they have ever recorded (ib.:27). This applies even to Africa, although its *per capita* income grew relatively slowly even in the 1960s and the 1970s (1-2% a year).

"But since the 1980s, the region has seen a *fall* in living standards. This record is a damning indictment of the neo-liberal orthodoxy, because most of the African economies have been practically run by the IMF and the World Bank over the past quarter of a century" (ib.:28).

The 'rapid, unplanned and blanket' trade liberalization had thus detrimental effects on sub-Saharan Africa. Nevertheless, the average annual economic growth in, for example, Tanzania in the recent period 2000-2005 was 5.8 percent (chapter 10.4). But, unfortunately, the largest part of the population (farmers) did not benefit from this growth, because it occurred in mining and tourism. The 2008/2009 worldwide financial and economic crisis, most likely, will lower these growth rates, because the prices of minerals decrease and Western consumers spend less. Chang remarks that labour productivity in manufacturing tends to grow faster than in agriculture. In Table 1 in chapter 1.1 we saw that labour productivity in agriculture in the period 1988-1998 increased with only 3% in sub-Saharan Africa, but with 123% in South Korea (Chang's native country). Apparently fast growth rates in agricultural labour productivity are, in principle, possible.

A crucial question is who has the intellectual capacity and political power to decide whether to invest in higher capabilities in agriculture, manufacturing industry or services? Who is going to orchestrate the right mix of interventions needed to kick-start economic development? As Chang (ib.:216) admits, most developing countries have few capable government officials. He remarks that, fortunately, you don't need 'first-best economists' to run good economic policy. But you do need some smart people, he says, who, I would add, should also be committed to pro-poor growth and who are able and willing to think out of the box. Deciding on the right mix for individual countries is difficult and complex, even for the 'first-best economists' of the IMF and World Bank (that's why they prefer blanket recommendations).

When the Western modernization process and front-runner model are uncritically copied in sub-Saharan Africa, it might result into unprecedented social-economic chaos (chapter 4.4). The labour resources that will be released from agriculture will be absorbed by which new industries or services? As Collier (2008:95) says in his book *The Bottom Billion*, many countries in sub-Saharan Africa face a high hurdle in "trying to break into diversified markets for exports because China, India, and the other successful developing countries have already done so". I have no idea on what kind of (new) labour-intensive manufacturing products sub-Saharan Africa should focus in order to raise its exports.

Apparently, some successful East-Asian countries have been lucky enough to have a minimal number of smart, relatively non-corrupt, innovative and charismatic leaders at the national level, who managed to kick-start economic development. I concluded in chapter 14.1 that the multi-dimensional process of development requires interventions in various, interdependent categories of factors (Diagram 2). The mix of interventions, proposed by Chang, contains ideological persuasion (category 3 and 5), economic policy measures (category 5 and 6), and institution building (category 4). In fact, simultaneous changes in all the categories 3-8 are needed. As I have indicated before, the *facilitation* of this multidimensional process (top-down planning and full control are illusory) can be upgraded through consciousness development. A 'virtuous circle' between the interdependent categories 3-8 in Diagram 2 can be created through upgrading the most basic category, i.e., the collective consciousness. The efforts of smart and charismatic leaders will be greatly enhanced when their interventions are supported by a coherent and high-quality collective consciousness. The quality of leaders (and their interventions) is always an unbiased reflection of the quality of the collective consciousness.

I realise that the introduction of the concept 'collective consciousness' and the methodology 'consciousness development' can create the impression of bringing in a kind of *deus ex machine*, an artificial stopgap, that, miraculously, will solve all the problems in the development process. However, consciousness development is not a quick-fix solution and the field effect of consciousness has been scientifically investigated (chapter 14.4). The reproducibility and predictability of the field effect are persuasive enough to warrant more attention from development practitioners.

17.3   The need for pro-active nonconformists

Chang (2008:74) shows convincingly in his book that, historically, trade liberalization has been the *outcome* rather than the *cause* of economic development. The rich countries of today did *gradually* liberalize their trade, but only when their producers had acquired sufficient capabilities to face foreign competition. "In the long run, free trade is a policy that is likely to condemn developing countries to specialize in sectors that offer low productivity growth and thus low growth in living standards" (ib.). Neoliberal orthodoxy forces developing countries to specialize in labour-intensive agriculture, while Chang argues that manufacturing industry is the best way to go. Initially, developing countries should focus on labour-intensive industry, but then as quickly as possible move on to capital- and knowledge-intensive industry through enhancement of their technological and organizational capabilities.

Hitherto the agricultural sector in sub-Saharan Africa has not been successful: productivity per man-day and per unit of land has remained low. In fact, in recent decades neither African governments nor international donors have paid much attention to agriculture. In spite of the rhetoric of African leaders on the importance of the agricultural sector to eradicate poverty, the African elites have always neglected the rural population. Moreover, African agricultural researchers and extensionists tend to focus on capital-intensive rather than labour-intensive agricultural technologies, because the last are often considered outdated. In my doctoral thesis I call this the 'modernization syndrome' (Van Eijk 1998:69). Since prospects for urban labour absorption hitherto are meagre, the focus ought to be on labour-intensive agriculture. Only when Chang's idea of kick-starting economic development through (labour-intensive) industrial manufacturing could be realised, millions of ex-farmers could find alternative employment in industry.

Since farmers in sub-Saharan Africa start from a very low level of labour- and land-productivity, quick increases in productivity are, in theory, possible. Investments in an enabling environment for agriculture (for example: rural infrastructure, price policy, credit, extension, and protectionism) would almost certainly result in fast productivity growth. At the same time, history shows that in today's rich countries agriculture has been a base for industrial development too (Koning in chapter 1.1). In chapter 7.1 Landes said that one can hardly exaggerate the contribution of agricultural improvement to Britain's Industrial Revolution.

Unfortunately, Chang says very little about agriculture; only in a foot-note at page 80 of his (otherwise excellent) book he mentions agriculture (in relation to poverty reduction, export earnings and state intervention).

"In the earlier stages of development, most people live on agriculture, so develop-ing agriculture is crucial in reducing poverty. Higher agricultural productivity also creates a pool of healthy and productive workers that can be used later for indus-trial development. In the early stages of development, agricultural products are also likely to account for a high share of exports, as the country may have little else to sell. Given the importance of export earnings for economic development that I discussed earlier, agricultural exports should be increased as much as possi-ble (although the scope may not be large). And, for this, greater opening of agricultural markets in the rich countries is helpful. But increased agricultural productivity and agricultural exports often require state intervention along the line of 'infant industry promotion'. Agricultural producers, especially the smaller ones, need government investment and support in infrastructure (especially irrigation for production and roads for exports), international marketing and R&D" (Chang 2008:80).

Chang remarks, correctly so, that the scope for agricultural exports may be small. Van der Veen (2004:214) says that in the past few decades even in the traditional export sectors (agricultural products and raw materials) Af-rica has been falling behind, relatively speaking. Apparently, Africa could not compete on the world market in terms of either price or quality. Its share of the world market for these products has been shrinking. In prac-tice, however, most trade in Europe is regional (chapter 1.1). Countries in sub-Saharan Africa too might, especially initially, focus on regional mar-kets, but then again most of them are producing the same kind of products.

Moreover, export of commodities produced by large numbers of small-holders can be difficult to manage, especially with low levels of farmer organization. An example of abuse of quality standards (with regard to aflatoxine) has been given in chapter 1.1.

I agree with Chang that state intervention along the line of 'infant industry promotion' is necessary to increase agricultural productivity and export. But the local elites in sub-Saharan Africa are not interested in state intervention in agriculture, and the countervailing power of the millions of small farmers is hitherto limited. They cannot enforce government invest-ment and support in agriculture[59]. Since reliance on the altruistic behaviour of local elites will be in vain, donor support to enhance the organizational capability and political power of farmers is necessary. However, changes in power constellations cannot be easily induced by outsiders.

Chang (2008:221) ends his book with a note of optimism when he ex-plains why he believes most Bad Samaritans can change their mind.

"What should give us real hope is that the majority of Bad Samaritans are neither greedy nor bigoted. Most of us, including myself, do bad things *not* because we derive great material benefit from them or strongly believe in them, but because they are the easiest thing to do. Many Bad Samaritans go along with wrong poli-cies for the simple reason that it's easier to be a conformist. Why go around looking for 'inconvenient truths' when you can just accept what most politicians and newspapers say? Why bother to find out what is really going on in poor coun-tries when you can easily blame it on corruption, laziness or the profligacy of their people? Why go out of your way to check up on your own country's history when the 'official' version suggests that it has always been the home of all virtues? - free trade, creativity, democracy, prudence, you name it".

In Chang's view, Bad Samaritans can change if they are given a more bal-anced view (as he tries to do in his book) and if they are willing to learn from earlier experiences. The specific experience he refers to is the period of protectionist 'import substitution industrialization' in the 1960s and 1970s, when developing countries were economically more successful than ever.

Chang argues that most Bad Samaritans are not bigoted or blinkered. In my view, however, many scientists are mentally imprisoned in the positivist scientific paradigm and quite some politicians in the neo-liberal political paradigm. According to Thomas Kuhn it is not easy to leave deeply engrained paradigms. Thus it is questionable whether the provision of a more balanced view and/or new information will easily change people's mind, and -more importantly- their actual behaviour (the difference between word and deed applies here). The easiest thing to do is, indeed, to stay within the confines of your conventional paradigm; in other words, to be a paradigmatic conformist. If most people are paradigmatic conformists, then learning from earlier experiences will only take place at small scale. History teaches that the impact of scientists (including historians) on politicians and policy makers is small. Perhaps most people have to experience certain things personally before change can take place, before they are willing and able to change their behaviour.

I agree with Chang that most people are conformists, simply because conformist behaviour takes the least energy and time. Conformist behaviour is also the hallmark of free marketeers who demonstrate pro-cyclical herd behaviour. How easy is it then to generate nonconformist behaviour? How can we get more 'rebels' who think independently and 'out of the box'? In chapter 15.3 we saw that techniques for consciousness development enhance inner-directedness, independence, problem-solving ability and pro-active behaviour. Conformists perform re-active behaviour, while nonconformists perform pro-active behaviour. And pro-active behaviour is what we need, if we want to kick-start economic development. Economic development demands pro-developmental forms of behaviour.

In Chang's view the conformist (and easiest) position with regard to the relationship between economic development and culture is: 'culture to a large extent determines economic development'. Economic development is determined by culture rather than the other way around ('culture → economic development' rather than 'economic development → culture'). In chapter 6.5 I referred to Norman Long who characterizes the relationship between economic development and socio-cultural factors (including religious disposition and work ethic) as correlation, not causality. Whether the relationship between cultural and economic change is based on two-directional causality (and whether the left- and right-pointing arrows carry equal weight) or is just simultaneous occurrence (correlation) is difficult to determine empirically, even on a case by case basis. Whether cultural or economic change is the unambiguous prime mover is difficult to say.

In chapter 4.7 Achterhuis argued that the distinction between changes in outer structures and changes in inner attitudes is artificial, because they affect one another and their effects on the multi-dimensional development process cannot be separated. A discussion on primacy would then be meaningless. Nevertheless, it is important to realise that all societal structures (civil society, state and market) are formed by the decisions and behaviour of individual actors. Personal change precedes and accompanies institutional change (chapter 15.2). With regard to the actor-structure debate, I would therefore say that primacy rests with actors. If Chang says that economic development, to a large extent, creates the culture it needs, then still some individual actors first have to kick-start economic development. These pro-active nonconformists are a rare breed. The number of pro-active citizens can be enhanced through techniques for consciousness development. In that sense, inner attitudinal change (personality factors in category 3 in Diagram 2) is primary. The exact border between culture and personality, however, is difficult to determine (chapter 14.1).

I would say that primacy rests with consciousness development, because this underlying factor speeds up processes of attitudinal, cultural and economic change (and changes in all other categories in Diagram 2). The normal process of learning by experience, that to a limited extent always takes place, can be supplemented with consciousness development. In order to allow developing countries to use the tools of protectionist 'infant industry promotion' in agriculture and manufacturing - tools that today's rich countries used themselves in the past (chapter 1.1) - a worldwide collective consciousness of high-quality and coherence is needed. This kind of altruistic behaviour of the rich countries will not emerge spontaneously, although in the long term they too will benefit economically from such policies.

18 Conclusion

18.1 Beyond treatment of symptoms

On the one hand, one can argue that underdevelopment in sub-Saharan Africa is largely due to the people themselves: a kind of 'victim blaming'. If only they would work harder, progress would come. The role of the prevailing work ethic has not been explicated yet in development literature. Although development experts and politicians consider the current work ethic often inadequate, it has at best been categorized under a vague heading as 'cultural constraints'. The (mostly implicit) leading motto is: it's your own fault. How to actually change work ethics is not topic of formal discussion or scientific investigation.

On the other hand, one can argue that underdevelopment in sub-Saharan Africa is mainly due to the international system. In this type of 'system blaming' the uneven global playing field in the area of technology, economics and politics is the decisive factor (in pre-colonial, colonial and post-colonial days). The leading motto is that only more international solidarity can eradicate underdevelopment. In between these two extreme positions of victim and system blaming, diverse combinations of local constraints and global relations can be distinguished on a sliding scale. These combinations determine the level of (under)development.

Truth, as usual, may lie midway (chapter 14.2). But we need to recognize that the uneven playing field is mainly dictated by the rich West. The behaviour of Western citizens, as consumers, producers and voters, determines the unequal relationships and thus (at least partially) Africa's underdevelopment. Ultimately, this is also a kind of victim blaming: it is the fault of Western citizens who are entrapped in a capitalist consumer society (whether or not they are fully aware of this identification with unrestrained consumption and unlimited mimetic desire is another question).

The over-consumption of Western man is seen as an important cause of underdevelopment elsewhere. Whatever way you look at it, primacy rests with actors, not structures. Also with regard to the work ethic, the fact is that individual actors will have to change it.

When we deal with complex problems, symptoms and causes get easily entangled. The result is often treatment of symptoms and disregard of underlying causes. Underdevelopment, poverty and hunger are symptoms. Although treatment of symptoms can be necessary and useful, treatment of underlying causes is more effective and efficient. The ultimate cause of the above mentioned symptoms is an underdeveloped individual and collective consciousness. The treatment of this ultimate cause aims to counteract these symptoms and, at least as important, to prevent new problems. Prevention is better than cure and also cheaper. In this book I have argued that the traditionalistic work ethic is an important underlying cause of the symptom 'underdevelopment' in sub-Saharan Africa. Furthermore I have argued that this problematic work ethic can be transformed via the upper and lower routes in Diagram 1. Reliance on the upper route alone will take time and the resulting enforced, re-active behaviour often implies treatment of symptoms. Supplementation via the lower route speeds up the process of behavioural change, deals with ultimate causes and results into more pro-active behaviour.

Quite some people argue that underdevelopment and hunger (a matter of unequal distribution of food) are political problems which require political solutions. Diagram 2, however, indicates that problems at certain levels can only be solved at deeper levels. Complex problems cannot be solved at the level where they emerged: the result is mere treatment of symptoms. For example: the attempt to solve the hunger problem with genetically modified crops implies treating a political problem with a technological solution (thus with a remedy of a more superficial, outer category). The attempt to solve the hunger problem via the free market implies treating a political problem with an economic solution (also a remedy of a more superficial category). The attempt to solve the hunger problem via campaigns to raise political awareness and promote political action implies treating a political problem with a political solution (a remedy of the same category).

This political solution has been extensively tried in the 1960s and 1970s and also in 2005 by the 'Make Poverty History' campaign. Politicians, however, simply reflect the level of collective consciousness of their grassroots support. Temporary public bursts of compassion and political awareness result into promises by politicians, which subsequently are not, or only partly, kept. The attempt to solve the hunger problem via a 'structural' approach implies treating a political problem with a socio-structural solution (this *is* a remedy of a more inner category). Such a structural approach, however, never really materialized. The reason is that structural transformation of the uneven global playing field is absolutely necessary, but demands changes in cultural and personality factors. Neither political awareness and action nor conventional social-psychological approaches have been able to generate such changes at large scale. These changes, most of all, require changes in levels of individual and collective consciousness. The most inner categories in Diagram 2 carry most weight.

The alleviation - but certainly the eradication - of hunger, poverty and underdevelopment demands a holistic, integrated perspective. *Eradication* implies dealing with *root* causes. The complex interactions between many variables and their inevitable feedback mechanisms can create a vicious circle of self-defeating causality. In order to break this cycle, simultaneous interventions in many areas are needed. These interventions can have intended and unintended effects, partly because we deal with numerous interrelated levels of social organisation. Interventions at one level can have unforeseen (sometimes harmful) effects at other levels. In order to go beyond treatment of symptoms, treatment of root causes is necessary. The

Diagrams 1 and 2 elucidate the root causes of underdevelopment and provide a holistic perspective.

At the end of the day, the collective consciousness determines how people use modern technology. The current large gap between science and conscience needs to be bridged. The application of modern science alone results in the illusion of intellectual holism. Landes (1999:512-3) says:

"We suffer from the asymmetry between our knowledge of nature and our knowledge of man, between outside awareness and self-ignorance … Note that my assumption of the ultimate advantage and beneficence of scientific knowledge and technological capability is today under sharp attack … The reasons for this reaction, often couched in preferences for *feeling* over *knowing*, range from disappointment at Paradise Unfound to fear and resentment by laymen of unknowable knowledge. Some of the anti's are millenarians: they look to an apocalyptic revolution to right wrongs and generalize happiness. Marxian Socialists and Communists, for all their lip service to science, fall in this category. Others are nostalgics, harking back to the mythic blessings of stateless, communal, primitive societies. The first group well illustrates the human limits of good intentions. The second is pissing into the wind. That is not where the world is going".

The gap between science and conscience, between outside awareness and inner awareness, can be bridged if we employ both routes in Diagram 1. Our knowledge of man can be enhanced if we pay more attention to the findings of the social sciences and to techniques for consciousness development. Good intentions are not sufficient in development cooperation and nostalgic yearning for earlier stages of human development is useless. A combination of modern science and effective techniques for consciousness development is needed. The addictive effect of foreign aid and its associated dependence-syndrome and loss of self-esteem can be circumvented by true self-reliance: reliance not only on outer local resources but also on man's inner self, on consciousness development.

I have referred before to the controversy between Jeffrey Sachs and William Easterly on the primacy of planners versus searchers (chapter 12). Although I incline more to the searchers' approach, I am also of the opinion that this approach of 'piecemeal muddling on' will not be very effective for the time being. This is so because the number of truly capable searchers is small and because synergistic effects through joint cooperation are difficult to realize in this individualistic approach. However, when we first search for man's inner self, we will get a bigger number of more *competent searchers or facilitators.*

18.2   Work on oneself

The process of disciplining to labour is influenced by a large number of actors and structures. I present here a list of recommendations that can generate a pro-developmental and pro-life work ethic, and a sustainable society, in sub-Saharan Africa. *The most important conclusion, however, is that the actual implementation of these recommendations will be facilitated by consciousness development.*

- Adequate nutrition for children (quantitatively and qualitatively) in the prenatal phase and in the first years of life is a prerequisite for the development of high quality human capital: i.e. people with adequate levels of intelligence and creativity and sufficient ability to work.
- The internalisation of a time discipline and the first disciplining to labour need to start at early age, especially via upbringing at home and primary education.
- High quality primary education (for boys and girls) with a nutritious meal provided at school is essential.

- Primary and secondary education must pay attention to change of gender relations, to nutrition, health and sexuality-education, to prevention of AIDS and promotion of a modern work ethic.

- In addition to parents and teachers, the following societal organizations must promote a modern work ethic: labour unions, employer organizations, political parties, churches, farmer organizations and other civil society entities. They need to set examples.

- The history of the process of disciplining to labour and civil society development in North-Western Europe can provide lessons learnt.

- Job promotion should be merit-based, not age-based (seniority) or gender-based.

- Pay adequate salaries (at least covering household expenditures and basic amenities) to well-performing and non-corrupt employees, linked to regular performance evaluation.

- Select hard working and incorruptible women for high ranked societal positions, also to serve as role models for youngsters.

- Proven incompetence, laziness or corruption should not result into transfer (relocation) but dismissal.

- Agriculture must be the engine of economic development, requiring that government creates an enabling environment for resource-poor farmers, which, in turn, requires that the farmers themselves appropriate countervailing power.

- Large investments in rural infrastructure (especially roads) are necessary.

The obvious question is: how do we generate sufficient individual motivation in society and sufficient political will at government level to implement these recommendations? Another question is: who will coordinate the attunement of the various actors, structures and the measures they take - in order to create synergistic effects? The development of individual motivation, collective political will and reciprocal attunement is facilitated by a coherent and high quality collective consciousness. The above mentioned recommendations can then easier be implemented.

Landes said in chapter 7.2 that, at bottom, no empowerment is as effective as self-empowerment. True self-reliance is self-empowerment by consciousness development. This form of self-empowerment requires that one 'works' on consciousness development. Only few development workers, policy makers, politicians and citizens take the time to reflect on their work experiences and even less persons spend time on consciousness development. Changes in individual ways of life are difficult to put into practice because of the large societal pressure to do the conventional thing.

Here the unlimited mimetic desire plays a role, which is an (externally motivated) attempt to identification with others, following the upper route in Diagram 1. The mimetic desire fuels a rat race based on 'more of the same'. In order to quit this race, that is aimed at ever more power and money, a deliberate decision is needed. Consciousness development can facilitate this step, because it promotes inner-directedness and greater independence of the opinion of others (chapter 15.3). This enhanced autonomy in the lower route goes together with more pro-active, free and altruistic behaviour - thus behaviour that also favours others. In principle all individuals can 'work on themselves' and build up a pro-developmental and pro-life work ethic.

Schumacher said in the *Introduction* of this book that our disappointment with the effectiveness of foreign aid has something to do with our materialist philosophy, which tends to overlook the most important preconditions of success. In his view the primary causes of poverty are immaterial: the material factors are entirely secondary, he says. We can produce 'economic miracles' when we focus our attention not on the tip of the iceberg, but on its invisible base - which is education, organisation and discipline. In Schumacher's view *people are the primary and ultimate source of any wealth whatsoever*. I fully agree with his analysis, but would add that the most important and fundamental part of the invisible base of the iceberg is the collective consciousness. The primacy of this invisible factor cannot be overrated. Development of individual, and thus collective, consciousness is essential.

Annex: About Research on the Transcendental Meditation Program.

(Source: website of David Orme-Johnson Ph.D:
http://www.truthabouttm.org/truth/Home/index.cfm)

David Orme-Johnson says:
"This website is not an official or unofficial TM organization web site. It is strictly an expression of my own understanding and personal experiences, stated as candidly and as clearly as I can. My qualifications for addressing these issues are that I am one of the principal researchers in the world on meditation and its effects, having over 100 publications, mostly in peer-reviewed journals ...

If you are interested in lists of research on the Transcendental Meditation technique, in studies comparing different meditation and relaxation techniques, or in questions such as whether the research is valid, whether the effects are due to self-selection or placebo, or are otherwise inconclusive, or whether the researchers on Transcendental Meditation are objective and committed to the scientific method, or whether outside reviews have discredited the research, ... in such issues as whether the TM technique has harmful effects or is a cult or religion, or whether enlightenment is just a metaphysical concept ... [then check this website].

Research on the Transcendental Meditation program has been published in 160 peer-reviewed scientific journals and edited books, including some of the leading journals in many fields ... Leading journals where TM research has been published include, but are not limited to, *Science, Scientific American, American Journal of Physiology, Clinical Neurophysiology, Hypertension, American Psychologist*, the *Journal of Personality and Social Psychology, Intelligence* (a multidisciplinary journal, widely considered the best in the field) and the *Journal of Conflict Resolution* (widely considered the best journal in the field). [All these journals are completely independent of the TM organization] ...

The research [on the Transcendental Meditation program] has been conducted at over 200 universities and research institutions in 34 countries. Doctoral dissertations on the Transcendental Meditation program have been carried out at 24 independent universities not affiliated with any of the TM organizations. Over the last 35 years the research has also been presented and discussed at numerous professional conferences ... Dr. Sidney Weinstein, Editor-in-Chief, International Journal of Neuroscience, says: "Over the past 10 years the editors and reviewers of the International Journal of Neuroscience have accepted several papers on Transcendental Meditation because they have met the rigorous standards of scientific publication. IJN is honoured to have two Nobel laureates on its editorial board, and has a distinguished group of scientists from leading universities on every continent who judge the scientific value of the papers submitted for consideration" ...

The Transcendental Meditation organization is not a cult and "thought reform" is not used in the Transcendental Meditation program ... Research on the Transcendental Meditation program shows that the effects it produces are the opposite to those found in people who allegedly get involved in cults. For example, a doctoral dissertation conducted at York University found that high school students became more autonomous, independent, and innovative through the Transcendental Meditation program, with increased ability to deal with abstract and complex situations. They also showed increases on creativity, general intelligence and self-esteem. Similarly, a doctoral dissertation at Harvard found that the Transcendental Meditation program increased autonomous thought in prisoners, and increased moral reasoning to levels that displays mature, independent judgement based on principles. This is highly significant, because cult following is allegedly based on the opposite - blind faith and rigid adherence to arbitrary rules and authority, which are characteristic of a lower level of moral reasoning measured by the psychological tests used in the study.

A wide variety of other research also demonstrates the growth of independent thinking in those who practice the Transcendental Meditation program. For example, well controlled studies have found that the Transcendental Meditation program increases field independence. Research has shown that field independent individuals are more independent in their thinking and are more resistant to peer-pressure to do anything that they feel is not right.

An essential feature of a cult is that it is a closed system of thought that does not submit itself to outside validation. The Transcendental Meditation organization is the opposite because it submits its theories to the rigors of scientific testing, encourages research by independent universities and research organizations (to date, 209 universities have conducted research on the Transcendental Meditation program), publishes in peer-reviewed journals, and participates actively in scientific conferences worldwide ...

The fact that the TM program has been derived from an ancient tradition in India and revived by a man revered there with a spiritual title [Maharishi Mahesh Yogi], of course should have no bearing on the validity of the use of the TM program. The TM program is not Hinduism, therefore, any more than Einstein's theory of relativity is Jewish, or Genetic theory, conceived of by Monk Gregor Mendel is considered to be Christian. The practice of the program involves no religious beliefs but is a mechanical and effortless technique for experiencing increasingly refined or restful levels of mental and physiological activity enjoyed by individuals of all religious (and non-religious) backgrounds ...

Transcendental [or pure] consciousness has been a metaphysical concept for centuries, because there was no practical technology for reliably producing it. With the availability of Maharishi's Transcendental Meditation program, taught worldwide in a standardized format, it has now been studied in many laboratories ... Many scholars have noted that experiences of transcendental consciousness are universal, found in all cultures, in both religious and secular settings. However, their interpretations vary according to their cultural context. Some philosophers and writers simply try to describe the experience without any interpretation. Others place the experience at the foundation of their philosophies, e.g., as the First Cause, the Good, the Self. Religious traditions describe it as union with God. Philosopher Dr. Ken Chandler has written books showing that the experience of transcendental consciousness is the foundation of all the great philosophical and religious traditions. It has taken quite a bit of scholarship to dig these experiences out of the writings of these great men and women. These experiences have remained overlooked and virtually forgotten in the modern materialistic world, in which the technologies for reliably having these experiences have been all but lost. These modern and historical experiences of transcendental consciousness, along with physiological research showing the distinctiveness of the state, demonstrate that it is not merely a metaphysical concept, but is a major state of consciousness …

[With regard to the field effect of collective consciousness, Orme-Johnson says:] In any event, none of the [earlier] theories relating to collective consciousness became mainstream pursuits in the social sciences because there was no way to operationally define the key components of the theories so that they could be empirically tested. Consequently, the paradigms of the social sciences have been dominated by the limited materialist worldview of classical Newtonian physics, which precludes the possibility of field effects of consciousness, and has focused the social sciences on direct behavioural interactions. Indeed, before the rise of materialism in the twentieth century, there were many mainstream thinkers in the West who spoke of an all-pervading field of consciousness (mind or spirit) at the basis of manifest world. In the context of history, the heterodox view is the materialist one that eliminates consciousness from the equation, not the view that there is an all-pervading consciousness. Twentieth century social scientists are in a minority of the historical view that there is a universal consciousness at the foundation of the world … However, the development of quantum mechanics has reopened the question of a more basic role of consciousness in natural law".

A Bibliography of Scientific Studies on TM:
   Physiological Studies
67 studies on Metabolic, Biochemical, and Cardiovascular Changes
41 studies on Electrophysiological and Electroencephalographical Changes
16 studies on Physiological Efficiency and Stability
26 studies on Motor and Perceptual Ability
49 studies on Overall Health
   Psychological Studies
49 studies on Intelligence, Learning, and Academic Performance
55 studies on Development of Personality
   Sociological Studies
44 studies on Rehabilitation
12 studies on Productivity and Quality of Life
41 studies on The Maharishi Effect
   Theoretical and Review Papers
24 studies on Physiology
25 studies on Psychology
17 studies on Sociology
28 studies on Other Academic Disciplines

All these studies can be found at:
http://www.mum.edu/tm_research/bibliography.html

Google Scholar Search on Transcendental Meditation (8700+ citations):
http://scholar.google.com/scholar?q=Transcendental+Meditation&ie=UTF-8&oe=UTF-8&hl=en&btnG=Search

Literature List

Achterhuis H. (1984). Arbeid, een eigenaardig medicijn [*Work, a peculiar medicine*]. Uitgeverij Ambo bv, Baarn, The Netherlands (4th print).

Achterhuis H. (1988). Het rijk van de schaarste. Van Thomas Hobbes tot Michel Foucault [*The realm of scarcity. From Thomas Hobbes to Michel Foucault*]. Uitgeverij Ambo bv, Baarn, The Netherlands (2nd print).

Achterhuis H. (1992) (Ed.) De maat van de techniek. Zes filosofen over techniek: Günther Anders, Jacques Ellul, Arnold Gehlen, Martin Heidegger, Hans Jonas en Lewis Mumford [*The measure of technology. Six philosophers on technology*]. Uitgeverij Ambo bv, Baarn, The Netherlands.

Adas M. (1989). Machines as the Measure of Men. Cornell University Press, Ithaca, London.

Allan W. (1965). The African Husbandman. Barnes and Noble Inc., New York.

Bawden R. (1995). On the systems dimension in FSR. Journal for Farming Systems Research-Extension, Vol.5, No.2: 1-18.

Beder S. (2001). The Promotion of a Secular Work Ethic. M/C: A Journal of Media and Culture 4(5), 2001.

Beets W.C. (1990). Raising and sustaining productivity of smallholder farming systems in the tropics. A handbook of sustainable agricultural development. AgBé Publishing, Alkmaar, Holland.

Benedict R. (1960). Patterns of Culture. Mentor, New York.

Béteille A. (2002). Work Practices and Norms: A Comparative and Historical Perspective. Discussion Paper Series No. 142, International Institute for Labour Studies, International Labour Organization, Geneva.

Campbell C.A. (1996). Land literacy in Australia: landcare and other new approaches to inquiry and learning for sustainability. In: Budelman A. (Ed.). Agricultural R&D at the crossroads. Merging systems research and social actor approaches. Royal Tropical Institute, Amsterdam. pp.169-84.

Capra F. (1996). Het levensweb. Levende organismen en systemen: verbluffend nieuw inzicht in de grote samenhang. Kosmos-Z&K Uitgevers, Utrecht. [Dutch translation of *The Web of Life*, Anchor Books, Doubleday, New York, 1996].

Carr A.J.L. (1994). Grass-roots and green tape: community-based environmental management in Australia. Ph D thesis. CRES, Australian National University, Canberra, Australia.

Chambers R. (1997). Whose reality counts? Putting the first last. Intermediate Technology Publications, London.

Chang H.-J. (2008). Bad Samaritans. The guilty secrets of rich nations and the threat to global prosperity. Random House Business Books, London.

Chopra D. (1991). Unconditional life. Mastering the forces that shape personal reality. Bantam Books, New York.

Cochrane W.W. (1958). Farm prices, myth and reality. University of Minnesota Press, Minneapolis.

Cohen D. and L. Prusak (2001). In Good Company: How Social Capital Makes Organizations Work. Harvard Business School Press, Boston, Massachusetts.

Collier P. (2008). The Bottom Billion. Why the poorest countries are failing and what can be done about it. Oxford University Press, New York.

Collinson M.P. (1972). Farm Management in Peasant Agriculture. A Handbook for Rural Development Planning in Africa. Praeger Publishers.

Collinson M.P. (1988). The development of African farming systems: some personal views. Agric. Admin. & Extension 29, 7-22.

Covey S.R. (1990). The seven habits of highly effective people: restoring the character ethic. A Fireside Book, Simon & Schuster, New York (First published in 1989).

Davis A. (1946). The motivation of the underprivileged workers. In: W.F. Whyte: Industry and Society, New York-London.

Diakité T. (2002). L'Afrique et l'aide. Ou comment s'en sortir? Publisher: L'Harmattan, Paris.

Diamond J. (1998). Guns, Germs and Steel. A short history of everybody for the last 13,000 years. Vintage, Random House, London.

Douthwaite R. (1999). The Growth Illu$ion. Green Books Ltd, Devon, UK [First published: 1992].

Duintjer O.D. (1983). 'Produceren' en andere wijzen van mens-zijn. Een kritisch onderzoek naar uitgangspunten bij Marx die liggen in het verlengde van de overheersende traditie [*'To produce' and other modes of 'to-be-human'. A critical investigation into Marx's points of departure which are in line with the dominant tradition*]. Tijdschrift voor Filosofie, Sept. 1983, p.421-458 [Philosophical Magazine, The Netherlands].

Duintjer O.D. (1988b). Hints voor een diagnose. Naar aanleiding van Kant. Over aard, grenzen en alternatieven van het rationeel-empirisch bewustzijn [*Hints for a diagnosis. With reference to Kant. On nature, boundaries and alternatives of the rational-empirical consciousness*]. Ambo, Baarn, The Netherlands.

Duintjer O.D. (1988c). Het belang van nieuwe spiritualiteit in een expansieve maatschappij [*The importance of new spirituality in an expansive society*]. In: Nagel B. (Ed.). Maken en breken. Over productie en spiritualiteit. Kok Agora, Kampen, The Netherlands.

Duintjer O. D. (1996). Opmerkingen over spiritualiteit - een optie voor humanisten? [*Remarks on spirituality - an option for humanists?*]. In: Weeda I. (Ed.) Spiritualiteit en wetenschap. Anthos, Amsterdam. pp. 270-78. [Also in: Rekenschap, jaargang 40, nr. 2, juni 1993, p. 69-73].

Easterly W. (2006). The white man's burden. Why the West's efforts to aid the rest have done so much ill and so little good. The Penguin Press, New York.

Eicher C.K. (1989). Sustainable institutions for African agricultural development. Working Paper No. 19. ISNAR, The Hague.

Elias N. (1939). Über den Prozess der Zivilisation, soziogenetische und psychogenetische Untersuchungen. 2 dln. Francke V., Bern/München.

Engel P.G.H. (1995). Facilitating innovation: an action-oriented approach and participatory methodology to improve innovative social practice in agriculture. Ph D dissertation, Wageningen Agricultural University, The Netherlands.

Fagan J. (1995). Genetic engineering: the hazards. Vedic engineering: the solutions. Maharishi International University Press, Fairfield, Iowa, USA.

Farrington J. and A.J. Bebbington (1993). From research to innovation: Getting the most from interaction with NGOs in FSRE. Journal for Farming Systems Research-Extension, Vol. 4, No. 1: 103-23.

Foucault M. (1975). Surveiller et punir. Paris.

Fromm E. (1955). The sane society. Rinehart & Co, New York.

Fromm E. (1972). De angst voor vrijheid. De vlucht in autoritairisme, destructivisme, conformisme. Bijleveld, Utrecht, The Netherlands (6th print) [Dutch translation of *Escape from freedom*, originally published in 1941 by Rinehart & Co, New York].

Fukuyama F. (1995). Trust: The Social Virtues and the Creation of Prosperity. The Free Press, New York.

Gerding J.L.F. (1996). Lichaam en geest in de parapsychologie [*Body and mind in parapsychology*]. In: M. Moerland (Ed.). De kool en de geit in de Nieuwe Tijd. Wetenschappelijke reflecties op New Age. Uitgeverij Jan van Arkel, Utrecht. p.190-204, The Netherlands.

Goody J. (1971). Technology, Tradition and the State in Africa. Cambridge University Press, New York.

Government of Tanzania (2002). Poverty and Human Development Report 2002. The Research and Analysis Working Group. Mkuki na Nyota Publishers, Dar es Salaam.

Gray J. (2003). Al Qaeda and what it means to be modern. Faber and Faber Limited.

Grint K. (1998). The sociology of work. An introduction. 2nd edition. Polity Press, Cambridge, UK [First published: 1991].

Hamilton N.A. (1995). Learning to learn with farmers. A case study of an adult learning extension project conducted in Queensland, Australia 1990-1995. Ph D thesis, Wageningen Agricultural University, The Netherlands.

Haveman J. (1952). De ongeschoolde arbeider. Een sociologische analyse. [*The unskilled labourer. A sociological analysis*]. Ph D thesis, Rijks-Universiteit Groningen, The Netherlands. Van Gorcum & Comp. N.V., Assen.

Heinemann E. and S.D. Biggs (1985). Farming Systems Research: an evolutionary approach to implementation. Journal of Agricultural Economics, XXXVI (1), 59-65.

Herskovits M. (1967). Man and his Works. The science of cultural anthropology. Knopf, New York.

Hofstede G. (1994). Cultures and Organizations. Software of the Mind. Intercultural Cooperation and its Importance for Survival. HarperCollinsBusiness, London [Originally published in 1991].

Huijsman A. and A. Budelman (1996). A crossroads for agricultural R&D: merging approaches on behalf of sustainable development. In: A. Budelman (Ed.). Agricultural R&D at the crossroads. Merging systems research and social actor approaches. Royal Tropical Institute, Amsterdam. pp. 9-17.

Hyden G. (1980). Beyond ujamaa in Tanzania. Underdevelopment and an uncaptured peasantry. Heinemann Educational Books Ltd, London.

Hyden G. (1983). No shortcuts to progress. African development management in perspective. Heinemann Educational Books Ltd, London.

Illich I. (1981). Shadow-Work. Boston/London.

Illich I. (1984). Man/Vrouw. Geslacht en sekse [*Gender* 1982]. Ambo, Baarn, The Netherlands.

Koestler A. (1989). The ghost in the machine. Arkana Books, London [First published by Hutchinson & Co in 1967].

Kombrink D. and A. Klamer (2004). Tijd voor sociaal en cultureel kapitaal [*Time for social and cultural capital*]. In: Witteveen, Korver en Achterhuis; 2004, p.226-239.

Koponen J. (1988). People and Production in Late Precolonial Tanzania. History and Structures. Finnish Historical Society, Studia Historica 28, Helsinki.

Koponen J. (1995). Development for Exploitation. German colonial policies in Mainland Tanzania, 1884-1914. Finnish Historical Society, Studia Historica 49/Lit Verlag, Studien zur Afrikanischen Geschichte 10, Helsinki/Hamburg.

Korver T., A. Witteveen and H. Achterhuis (2004). Bij de tijd - Woord vooraf [Concerning time - a preface]. In: Witteveen, Korver and Achterhuis; 2004, p.7-11.

Landes D.S. (1999). The Wealth and Poverty of Nations. Why some are so rich and some so poor. W.W. Norton & Company Ltd, New York.

Leeuwis C. (1993). Of computers, myths and modelling, the social construction of diversity, knowledge, information and communication technologies in Dutch horticulture and agricultural extension. Wageningen Studies in Sociology no. 36, Wageningen, The Netherlands.

Legum C. (1985). Africa's search for nationhood and stability. Journal of Contemporary African Studies (October), 21-45.

Long N. (1968). Social change and the individual: a study of the social and religious responses to innovation in a Zambian rural community. Manchester University Press, Manchester.

Long N. (1970). Rural entrepreneurship and religious commitment in Zambia. In: Internationalen Jahrbuch für Religionssoziologie, vol. VI, 1970, blz. 142-157.

Long N. (1977). An introduction to the sociology of rural development. Tavistock Publications, London.

Long N. and M. Villareal (1994). The interweaving of knowledge and power in development interfaces. In: Scoones I. & J. Thompson (Eds). Beyond farmer first. Rural people's knowledge, agricultural research and extension practice. Intermediate Technology Publications Ltd, London. pp. 41-52.

Mumford L. (1934). Technics and Civilizaton. Harcourt, Brace and World, Inc., New York.

Myrdal G. (1968). Asian drama. An inquiry into the poverty of nations. Pantheon, New York.

Nationale Advies Raad voor Ontwikkelingssamenwerking (NAR) (1989). Advies bestuurs- en managementcapaciteit in Sub Sahara Afrika. No. 95. Ministerie van Buitenlandse Zaken, 's-Gravenhage [NAR = National Advisory Council for Development Cooperation: Advice on governance- and management-capacity in Sub-Saharan Africa. Ministry of Foreign Affairs, The Hague].

Oates Jr. R.M. (1990). Creating heaven on earth. The mechanics of the impossible. Heaven on Earth Publications, Fairfield, IA, United States.

Ophuls W. (1977). Ecology and the politics of scarcity. Freeman, San Francisco.

Pretty J. and R. Chambers (1994). Towards a learning paradigm: new professionalism and institutions for a sustainable agriculture. In: Scoones I. & J. Thompson (Eds). Beyond farmer first. Intermediate Technology Publications Ltd, London. pp. 182-202.

Ransijn P. (1983). Bewustzijnsontwikkeling door TM: een rationele weg naar vrede en vervulling? [Consciousness development via TM: a rational path to peace and fulfilment?]. Civis Mundi 22, 183-89, The Netherlands.

Ransijn P. (1985). A rational way to peace and fulfilment. The unified field of consciousness in a sociological perspective. Soma Scientific Publisher, Lelystad, The Netherlands.

Ransijn P. and N. Schulte. (1982). Bewustzijn als bewapening. Vrede en ontwapening door groei van collectief bewustzijn [*Consciousness as armament. Peace and disarmament via growth of collective consciousness*]. MIU Nederland Pers, Laag Soeren, The Netherlands.

Renkema J.A. (1986). Het veehouderijbedrijf in ontwikkeling [*Cattle farm in development*]. Landbouwkundig Tijdschrift 98, nr.9, The Netherlands.

Röling N. (1988). Extension science. Information systems in agricultural development. Cambridge University Press, Cambridge.

Röling N. et al. (1997). Technical proposal FASOLEARN. Social learning for collective natural resource management: facilitation, institutions and policies. Proposal for the second phase of the environment and climate R&D programme (1997-1998) of the EU. Uppsala, Miles Keynes & Wageningen.

Sachs J.D. (2005). The end of poverty. How we can make it happen in our lifetime. Penguin Books.

Schumacher E.F. (1989). Small is beautiful. Economics as if people mattered. Reprint: Harper Perennial, New York (First published in 1973).

Schwartz S.H. (1977). Normative influence on altruism. In: L. Berkowitz (Ed.). Advances in experimental social psychology. McGraw Hill, New York.

Scoones I. and J. Thompson (1994). Knowledge, power and agriculture - towards a theoretical understanding. In: Scoones I. & J. Thompson (Eds). Beyond farmer first. Rural people's knowledge, agricultural research and extension practice. Intermediate Technology Publications Ltd, London. pp. 16-32.

Seur H. (1992). Sowing the good seed. The interweaving of agricultural change, gender relations and religion in Serenje District, Zambia. Ph D thesis, Agricultural University Wageningen, The Netherlands.

Sheldrake R. (1989). The presence of the past. Morphic resonance and the habits of nature. Vintage Books, New York.

Slicher van Bath B. (1977). De agrarische geschiedenis van West-Europa 500-1850 [*The agrarian history of Western Europe 500-1850*]. Aula-boeken 565, Uitgeverij Het Spectrum, Utrecht/Antwerpen [first published in 1960].

Van Cranenburgh O. (1990). The Widening Gyre. The Tanzanian One-Party State and Policy towards Rural Cooperatives. Ph D thesis, Rijksuniversiteit Leiden, The Netherlands.

Van den Ban A. (2002a). Poverty alleviation among farmers. The role of knowledge. In: Cees Leeuwis and Rhiannon Pyburn (Eds.). Wheelbarrows full of frogs. Social learning in rural resource management. Koninklijke Van Gorcum, The Netherlands.

Van den Ban A. (2002b). Increasing the Ability of Farmers to Compete in the Market. The Journal of Agricultural Education and Extension, 2002, vol. 8, 2.

Van der Ploeg J.D. (1987). De verwetenschappelijking van de landbouwbeoefening [*The scientization of agricultural practice*]. Mededelingen van de vakgroepen voor sociologie, 21. Agricultural University, Wageningen, The Netherlands.

Van der Veen R. (2004). What went wrong with Africa? A contemporary history. KIT Publishers, Amsterdam.

Van Eijk T. (1998). Farming Systems Research and Spirituality. An analysis of the foundations of professionalism in developing sustainable farming systems. Ph D thesis, Wageningen Agricultural University, The Netherlands. http://library.wur.nl/wda/dissertations/dis2546.pdf

Van Woerkum C.M.J. (1990). Het instrumentele nut van voorlichting in beleidsprocessen [*The instrumental use of extension in policy processes*]. In: Massacommunicatie, Jaargang 18, Nr 4, pp.263-278, The Netherlands.

Van Zanden J.L. and A. van Riel (2000). Nederland 1780-1914. Staat, Instituties en Economische Ontwikkeling [*The Netherlands 1780-1914. State, institutions and economic development*]. Uitgeverij Balans, The Netherlands.

Weber M. (1989). The protestant ethic and the spirit of capitalism. Unwin Hyman, London [first published in 1905: Die protestantische Ethik und der Geist des Kapitalismus].

Wesseling H.L. (2003). Europa's koloniale eeuw. De koloniale rijken in de negentiende eeuw, 1815-1919 [*Europe's colonial age. The colonial empires in the nineteenth century, 1815-1919*]. Bert Bakker, Amsterdam.

Wilber K. (Ed.). (1985). The holographic paradigm and other paradoxes. Exploring the leading edge of science. New Science Library, Shambhala Publications, Boston.

Witteveen A., T. Korver and H. Achterhuis (Ed.) (2004). Arbeid, tijd en flexibiliteit [*Labour, time and flexibility*]. Scriptum, Schiedam, The Netherlands.

World Bank (2001). World Development Report 2002. Building Institutions for Markets. Oxford University Press, New York.

Zakaria F. (2003). The Future of Freedom. Illiberal Democracy at Home and Abroad. W.W. Norton & Company, New York.

Zweers W. (1995). Participeren aan de natuur. Ontwerp voor een ecologisering van het wereldbeeld [*Participation in nature. Design of an ecological worldview*]. Uitgeverij Jan van Arkel, Utrecht, The Netherlands.

Endnotes

---

[1] One of the few authors who does say something about the work ethic is Beets (1990:307): "The desire for material goods does not always translate into an inclination for increased productivity: the need to work harder - in order to generate surplus production to increase income to be able to afford more material goods - is not always recognized".

[2] In my Ph D thesis on 'Farming Systems Research and Spirituality' I describe three different scientific paradigms with their ontological, epistemological and methodological premises: the positivist, constructivist and transcendentalist paradigm (Van Eijk 1998:124-127). This thesis can be downloaded at: http://library.wur.nl/wda/dissertations/dis2546.pdf

[3] In addition to formal, professional contacts with Africans also frequent informal contacts have shaped my point of view. I have a Tanzanian partner-in-life since 1991.

[4] World Bank (2005). World Development Report 2006 (Table 1: Key Indicators for Development).

[5] Paul Wolfowitz, President of the World Bank. 'Neo-optimism'. The World in 2006, The Economist, 2005.

[6] Joris Tielens. Report on the 75th International Conference on Agricultural Development, Wageningen University, The Netherlands, 20-11-2003. In: Wageningen Update, 4/2003.

[7] Interview with Otto Genee in: BZ, 02-04. Magazine for Employees of the Dutch Ministry of Foreign Affairs, The Hague, 6 February 2004.

[8] Niek Koning and Cees Veerman. Wageningsuniversiteitsblad (Wb) 2, 17 January 2002 (Wageningen University magazine), The Netherlands.

[9] Niek Koning in: LT Journaal, 20 december 2001 (Dutch Agricultural Magazine).

[10] Rosan Holak. Book review of Geraldine Bedell's Make Poverty History. NRC Handelsblad, 14 October 2005 (NRC Handelsblad is a Dutch newspaper).

[11] Chris van der Heijden in Vrij Nederland, 11 September 2004 (Vrij Nederland is a Dutch weekly magazine).

[12] These three IMF studies are: The dynamic implications of foreign aid and its variability; What undermines aid's impact on growth?; Aid and growth: what does the cross country evidence really show?

[13] Piet Emmer in NRC Handelsblad, 8/9 February 2003.

[14] Bourguignon as quoted by Reinoud Roscam Abbing in NRC Handelsblad, 25 February 2004.

[15] Koert Lindijer in an article about Sauri in NRC Handelsblad, 12 September 2005.

[16] Ibid.

[17] The five thousand inhabitants of Sauri received 100 dollars per person per year in aid since the start of the project in 2004. If the 300 million Africans living below the poverty line would receive 100 dollars per person per year, a total amount of 30 billion dollars per year would be required. Of course the rich countries can easily supply this money, but whether this will actually happen is another story.

[18] Interview with Per Pinstrup-Andersen in *Wagenings Universiteitsblad*, Wb 33, 15 November 2001 (Wageningen University Magazine).

[19] *NRC Handelsblad*, 12 March 2005 (Source: OECD).

[20] Richard Dowden in an interview in the program *Hard Talk*, BBC, 22 December 2005.

[21] http://www.developmentex.com/development_intelligence/news_and_analysis/briefing/ :30-09-2005.

[22] In: *Algemeen Dagblad*, 2 June 2001 (Algemeen Dagblad is a Dutch newspaper).

[23] Noreena Hertz in *NRC Handelsblad*, 2/3 July 2005.

[24] Noreena Hertz in *NRC Handelsblad*, 9/10 April 2005.

[25] Translation of article in the Los Angeles Times in *NRC Handelsblad*, 13 June 2005.

[26] Louise O. Fresco in *Vrij Nederland*, 15 October 2005.

[27] Nassoro W. Malocho. 'Speech by the Minister of the State President's Office'. Business Times, 11 June 1999, Dar es Salaam.

[28] Venance Konan in *NRC Handelsblad*, 22/23 May 2004.

[29] Ferdinand van Dam in *NRC Handelsblad*, 2/3 July 2005.

[30] Wouter van Dieren in *NRC Handelsblad*, 17 June 2005.

[31] Martin Wolf (2005). Why globalization works. Yale University Press, New Haven; Thomas L. Friedman (2006). The world is flat. Penguin Books, London; Jagdish Bhagwati (2007). In Defense of globalization. Oxford University Press.

[32] Hans Achterhuis in *Vrij Nederland*, 8 april 1989.

[33] In this chapter I discuss the work ethic in North-Western Europe. It is evident that within Europe differences in work ethic exist. Italians, for example, have a different view on work from Germans. And even within countries differences exist: in the small country of The Netherlands, for example, people in the Southern provinces have a different view on work from people in the Northern provinces (although these differences between the Catholic South and Protestant North tend to become smaller). Although differences in work ethic do exist, one cannot generalize. There will always be some individuals who have a different work ethic from the rest of their community. The exception proves the rule. If we say that sub-Saharan Africans, in general, have a different work ethic from North-West Europeans, it simply means that if we compare the work ethic of large groups of sub-Saharan Africans and North-West Europeans differences in work ethic will show up. Some sub-Saharan Africans, however, will work harder than the average North-West European and some North-West Europeans will work less hard than the average sub-Saharan African. Exceptions do exist.

[34] Olivier Roy in *NRC Handelsblad*, 8/9 May 2004.

[35] Niels Röling in Wageningen University Magazine, Wub, 35, 21-11-1996.

[36] Weber M. (1958). The protestant ethic and the spirit of capitalism. Charles Scribner's Sons, New York, p.62.

[37] The Standard Swahili-English Dictionary (Oxford University Press, Nairobi 1982) says: "A common salutation used by dependents to superiors, and young people to elders, formerly much used by slaves to masters. In full *nashika miguu yako*, I hold your feet, as a sign of respect, reverence, or of inferiority, submission, &c.".

[38] FAO, june 2002:
http://www.fao.org/worldfoodsummit/english/newsroom/focus/index.html
[39] Caspar Schweigman. 'The CEDRES/AGRISK Project on risk in food supply on the Mossi Plateau, Burkina Faso; Some Lessons'. Paper presented at the Conference on 'Development-related Research; the Role of The Netherlands', March 1989, Groningen, The Netherlands.
[40] Paul Scheffer in *NRC Handelsblad*, 23 May 2003.
[41] The Hutterites are a sect founded in 1529 by Jakob Hutter, kindred to the Mennonites and Amish.
[42] Martindale (1971:xx), as quoted by Long (1977:63).
[43] These data are based on the District Integrated Agricultural Survey 1998/99: Ministry of Agriculture and Food Security (MAFS) 2001:27. Dar es Salaam, Tanzania.
[44] Here Van der Veen mentions the word 'work ethic' for the second time in his book. It is earlier mentioned on page 78.
[45] Thallam Balaji in *NRC Handelsblad*, 10 February 2006.
[46] Mkapa in *NRC Handelsblad*, 29 September 2005.
[47] FAO 2002:
http://www.fao.org/worldfoodsummit/english/newsroom/focus/index.html
[48] Hans Eenhoorn in *NRC Handelsblad*, 20 August 2004.
[49] Dick Wittenberg in *NRC Handelsblad*, 1 December 2004.
[50] President Mkapa in *The Guardian*, January 1, 2004.
[51] The chapters 13-15 are largely based on my Ph.D. thesis: Farming Systems Research and Spirituality (van Eijk 1998).
[52] The Transcendental Meditation (TM) technique is an example of a true self-help technique that does not rely on a belief in whatsoever. I practise this technique since 1972.
[53] Roos Vonk, in *NRC Handelsblad*, 21/22 May 2005.
[54] Ibid.
[55] Possibly an arrow could run from the box with 'external norms' to the box with 'internal values' in Diagram 1. When children perform certain (positive) behaviour often enough by following the external norms set by their parents via the processes compliance and identification in the upper route, then this might ultimately result into deeply internalized values. In this way external norms could become internal values. See also endnote 58.
[56] Lukas Van Spengler, in *NRC Handelsblad*, 10 December 2003.
[57] These policy measures are explained in detail in the chapters 3 to 7 of his book *Bad Samaritans*.
[58] In Diagram 1 there is no feedback arrow from behavioural change to changes in norms and values. In Chang's argumentation, however, this feedback process is central. I discuss this feedback process in my Ph.D. thesis, but there I consider it unlikely that it occurs at large scale, because from the perspective of the attitude-behaviour models in social psychology it amounts to putting the cart (behaviour) before the horse (beliefs, attitudes, norms and values) (Van Eijk 1998:31,38,213). However, after reading Chang's book I am inclined to assign a greater role to this feedback process, in the sense that successful economic development can change

actual behaviour and then, in turn, underlying values. Nevertheless, the starting-up problem remains.

[59] I do not think that African governments should invest heavily in irrigation infrastructure. The overwhelming majority of the farmers in sub-Saharan Africa will continue to depend on rain-fed agriculture. The total acreage under irrigation and the total number of irrigating farmers will always remain small, simply because of the limited presence of water resources. Moreover, irrigation is expensive, labour-intensive and demands high-quality cooperation. Improvement of rain-fed agriculture is a better option (see also chapter 12).